Daily Planetary Guide

ISBN: 978-0-7387-1128-7. Astrological calculations compiled and programmed by Rique Pottenger based on the earlier work of Neil F. Michelsen.

Edited by Sharon Leah
Cover design by Lisa Novak
Interior design by Sharon Leah
Astrological proofreading by Jim Shawvan & Ana Ruiz
Cover photo © Photodisc Spacescapes

Llewellyn Worldwide Ltd.
2143 Wooddale Drive
Woodbury, MN 55125-2989
www.llewellyn.com

2010

SEPTEMBER	OCTOBER	NOVEMBER	DECEMBER
S M T W T F S	S M T W T F S	S M T W T F S	S M T W T F S
1 2 3 4	1	1 2 3 4 5 6	1 2 3 4
5 6 7 8 9 10 11	2 3 4 5 6 7 8	7 8 9 10 11 12 13	5 6 7 8 9 10 11
12 13 14 15 16 17 18	9 10 11 12 13 14 15	14 15 16 17 18 19 20	12 13 14 15 16 17 18
19 20 21 22 23 24 25	16 17 18 19 20 21 22	21 22 23 24 25 26 27	19 20 21 22 23 24 25
26 27 28 29 30 31	23 24 25 26 27 28 29	28 29 30	26 27 28 29 30 31
	30		

2011

JANUARY	FEBRUARY	MARCH	APRIL
S M T W T F S	S M T W T F S	S M T W T F S	S M T W T F S
1	1 2 3 4 5	1 2 3 4 5	1 2
2 3 4 5 6 7 8	6 7 8 9 10 11 12	6 7 8 9 10 11 12	3 4 5 6 7 8 9
9 10 11 12 13 14 15	13 14 15 16 17 18 19	13 14 15 16 17 18 19	10 11 12 13 14 15 16
16 17 18 19 20 21 22	20 21 22 23 24 25 26	20 21 22 23 24 25 26	17 18 19 20 21 22 23
23 24 25 26 27 28 29	27 28	27 28 29 30 31	24 25 26 27 28 29 30
30 31			

MAY	JUNE	JULY	AUGUST
S M T W T F S	S M T W T F S	S M T W T F S	S M T W T F S
1 2 3 4 5 6 7	1 2 3 4	1 2	1 2 3 4 5 6
8 9 10 11 12 13 14	5 6 7 8 9 10 11	3 4 5 6 7 8 9	7 8 9 10 11 12 13
15 16 17 18 19 20 21	12 13 14 15 16 17 18	10 11 12 13 14 15 16	14 15 16 17 18 19 20
22 23 24 25 26 27 28	19 20 21 22 23 24 25	17 18 19 20 21 22 23	21 22 23 24 25 26 27
29 30 31	26 27 28 29 30	24 25 26 27 28 29 30	28 29 30 31
		31	

SEPTEMBER	OCTOBER	NOVEMBER	DECEMBER
S M T W T F S	S M T W T F S	S M T W T F S	S M T W T F S
1 2 3	1	1 2 3 4 5	1 2 3
4 5 6 7 8 9 10	2 3 4 5 6 7 8	6 7 8 9 10 11 12	4 5 6 7 8 9 10
11 12 13 14 15 16 17	9 10 11 12 13 14 15	13 14 15 16 17 18 19	11 12 13 14 15 16 17
18 19 20 21 22 23 24	16 17 18 19 20 21 22	20 21 22 23 24 25 26	18 19 20 21 22 23 24
25 26 27 28 29 30	23 24 25 26 27 28 29	27 28 29 30	25 26 27 28 29 30 31
	30 31		

2012

JANUARY	FEBRUARY	MARCH	APRIL
S M T W T F S	S M T W T F S	S M T W T F S	S M T W T F S
1 2 3 4 5 6 7	1 2 3 4	1 2 3	1 2 3 4 5 6 7
8 9 10 11 12 13 14	5 6 7 8 9 10 11	4 5 6 7 8 9 10	8 9 10 11 12 13 14
15 16 17 18 19 20 21	12 13 14 15 16 17 18	11 12 13 14 15 16 17	15 16 17 18 19 20 21
22 23 24 25 26 27 28	19 20 21 22 23 24 25	18 19 20 21 22 23 24	22 23 24 25 26 27 28
29 30 31	26 27 28 29	25 26 27 28 29 30 31	29 30

MAY	JUNE	JULY	AUGUST
S M T W T F S	S M T W T F S	S M T W T F S	S M T W T F S
1 2 3 4 5	1 2	1 2 3 4 5 6 7	1 2 3 4
6 7 8 9 10 11 12	3 4 5 6 7 8 9	8 9 10 11 12 13 14	5 6 7 8 9 10 11
13 14 15 16 17 18 19	10 11 12 13 14 15 16	15 16 17 18 19 20 21	12 13 14 15 16 17 18
20 21 22 23 24 25 26	17 18 19 20 21 22 23	22 23 24 25 26 27 28	19 20 21 22 23 24 25
27 28 29 30 31	24 25 26 27 28 29 30	29 30 31	26 27 28 29 30 31

Table of Contents

Introduction to Astrology

by Kim Rogers-Gallagher

Your horoscope is calculated using the date and time you were born from the perspective of your birth location. From this information, a clock-like diagram emerges that shows where every planet was located at the moment you made your debut. Each chart is composed of the same elements, rearranged, so everyone has one of everything, but none are exactly alike. I think of planets, signs, houses, and aspects as the four astrological building blocks. Each block represents a different level of human existence.

The eight planets along with the Sun and Moon are actual physical bodies. They represent urges or needs we all have. Chiron also falls into this category. The twelve signs of the zodiac are sections of the sky, and each is 30 degrees. The signs describe the behavior a planet or house will use to express itself. The twelve houses in a chart tell us where our planets come to life. Each house represents different life concerns—values, communication, creativity, and so on—that we must live through as life and time progress.

Basically, aspects are angles. Some of the planets will be positioned an exact number of degrees apart, forming angles to one another. For example, 180 degrees is a circle divided by two and is called an opposition. A square is 90 degrees and divides the circle by four. A trine is 120 degrees and divides the circle by three, and so forth. Aspects show which planets will engage in constant dialogue with one another. The particular aspect that joins them describes the nature of their "conversation." Not all planets will aspect all other planets in the houses.

Planets: The First Building Block

Each planet acts like the director of a department in a corporation, and the corporation is, of course, you. For example, Mercury directs your Communications Department and Jupiter oversees your Abundance and Growth Department. When you have the need to communicate, you call on your Mercury; when it's time to risk or grow, you use your Jupiter. Let's meet each of the planets individually and take a look at which job duties fall under each planet's jurisdiction.

The Sun

☉ Every corporation needs an executive director who makes the final decisions. The Sun is your Executive Director. The Sun in your chart is your core, your true self. Although each of the planets in your chart is important in its own right, they all "take their orders," figuratively speaking, from the Sun.

Everyone's Sun has the same inner goal: to shine. The house your Sun is in shows where you really want to do good, where you want to be appreciated and loved. Your Sun is your inner supply of pride and confidence, your identity. The Sun is you at your creative best, enjoying life to the fullest.

The Sun shows the focus of the moment, where the world's attention will be directed on that particular day. In fact, in horary and electional astrology, the two branches that pertain most to timing and prediction, the Sun represents the day, the Moon the hour, and the Midheaven the moment. In the physical body, the Sun rules the heart, upper back, and circulatory system.

The Moon

☽ Speaking of the Moon, a good place to meet her and begin to understand her qualities is by the water on a clear night when she's full. Whether you're looking up at her or at that silvery patch she creates that shivers and dances on the water, take a deep breath and allow yourself to be still. She represents the soft interior of each of us that recalls memories, that fears and dreams.

She's a lovely lady who oversees the Department of Feelings; she's the bringer of "moods" (a great Moon word). Her house and placement in your chart reveal how your intuition works, what your emotional needs are, and how you want your needs met. She is the ultimate feminine energy, the part of you that points both to how you were nurtured and to how you will nurture others. In the body, the Moon has jurisdiction over the breasts, ovaries, and womb—all of which are necessary for creating and nurturing life. She also rules our body fluids, the internal ocean that keeps us alive.

Mercury

☿ Back when gods and goddesses were thought to be in charge of the affairs of humanity, Mercury shuttled messages between the gods and mortals. In today's world, he's the computer, the telephone, and the Internet. He's the internal computer that constantly feeds you data about the world. His position and house in your chart shows how you think and reason, and how you express yourself to others. You'll recognize him in your speech patterns, your handwriting, and in the way you walk, because moving through your environment means communicating with it. He operates through your five senses and your brain, and makes you conscious of opposites—light and dark, hot and cold, up and down. He's what you use when you have a conversation, exchange a glance or gesture, or interpret a symbol. Mercury represents the side of you living totally in the present.

If you ever tried to collect mercury after it escaped from a broken thermometer, you learned something about Mercury. Just as your Mercury never stops collecting data, those tiny beads you tried so hard to collect brought back a bit of everything they contacted—dog hair, crumbs, and grains of dirt. In the body, Mercury also acts as a messenger. He transmits messages through his function as the central nervous system that lets your eyes and hands collaborate, your eyes blink, and breathing continue.

Venus

♀ Venus spends her energy supplying you with your favorite people, places, and things. If you want chocolate, music, flannel sheets, or the coworker you've got a mad crush on, it's your Venus that tells you how to get it. Venus enjoys beauty and comfort. She shows how to attract what you love—especially people. When you're being charming, whether it's by using your manners or by adorning yourself, she's in charge of all behavior that is pleasing to others—social chit-chat, smiles, hugs, and kisses. Whenever you're pleased, satisfied, or content enough to purr, it's your Venus who made you feel that way. Since money is one of the ways that we draw the objects we love to us, she's also in charge of finances. Venus relates to your senses—sight, smell, taste, touch, and sound—the body's receptors. After all, it is the senses that tell us what feels good and what doesn't. She responds to your desire for beautiful surroundings, comfortable clothing, and fine art.

Mars

♂ Mars is in charge of your Self-Defense and Action Department. He's the warrior who fights back when you're attacked—your own personal SWAT team. Your Mars energy makes you brave, courageous, and daring. His placement in your chart describes how you act on your own behalf. He's concerned only with you, and he doesn't consider the size, strength, or abilities of whomever or whatever you're up against. He's the side of you that initiates all activity. He's also in charge of how you assert yourself and how you express anger.

"Hot under the collar," "seeing red," and "all fired up" are Mars words. He's what you use to be passionate, adventurous, and bold. But he can be violent, accident-prone, and cruel, too. Wherever he is in your chart, you find constant action. Mars pursues. He shows how you "do" things. He charges through situations. This "headstrong" planet corresponds to the head, the blood, and the muscles.

Jupiter

♃ Jupiter is called "the Greater Benefic," and he heads the Department of Abundance and Growth. He's the side of you that's positive, optimistic, and generous. He's where you keep your supply of laughter, enthusiasm, and high spirits. It's Jupiter's expansive, high-spirited energy that motivates you to travel, take classes, and meet new people. Wherever he is in your chart is a place where you'll have an extensive network of friends and associates—folks you can visit, count on, and learn from. Jupiter is the side of you that will probably cause you to experience the "grass-is-greener" syndrome. Your Jupiter is also what you're using when you find yourself being excessive and wasteful, overdoing, or blowing something out of proportion. Words like "too" and "always" are the property of Jupiter, as are "more" and "better." In general, this planet just loves to make things bigger. In the body, Jupiter corresponds with the liver, the organ that filters what you take in and rids your body of excess. Jupiter also handles physical growth.

Saturn

Saturn represents withholding and resistance to change. He heads the Boundaries and Rules Department. Locate Saturn in your chart to find out where you'll build walls to keep change out, where you may segregate yourself at times, where you'll be most likely to say "No." Your Saturn is the authority inside you, the spot where you may inhibit or stall yourself throughout life—most often because you fear failure and would rather not act at all than act inappropriately. This planet teaches you to respect your elders, follow the rules, and do things right the first time. Wherever Saturn is in your chart is a place where you'll feel respectful, serious, and conservative. Your Saturn placement is where you'll know that you should never embellish the facts and never act until you're absolutely sure you're ready. Here is where you won't expect something for nothing. Saturn is also where you're at your most disciplined, where you'll teach yourself the virtues of patience, endurance, and responsibility. Because this planet is so fond of boundaries, it's also the planet in charge of organization, structures, and guidelines. In the physical body, Saturn correlates with the bones and the skin, those structures that hold your body together.

Uranus

There's a spot in everyone's chart where independence is the order of the day, where rules are made specifically to be broken, and where personal freedom is the only way to go, regardless of the consequences. Here's where you'll surprise even yourself at the things you'll say and do. Meet Uranus, head of the Department of One Never Knows, the place in your chart where shocks, surprises, and sudden reversals are regular fare.

Your Uranus energy is what wakes you up to how confined you feel, breaks you out of the rut you're in, and sets you free. He's a computer wizard and involved in mass communications. Where he's strong in your chart, you will be strong, too. Here is where you'll have genius potential, where you'll be bold enough to ignore the old way to solve a problem and instead find a whole new way. Major scientific and technological breakthroughs like the space program and the Internet were inspired by Uranus. In the body, Uranus rules the lower part of the legs, including the calves and ankles, and it corules with Mercury the central nervous system.

Neptune

Next time you hear yourself sigh or feel yourself slip into a daydream, think of Neptune. This is the planet in charge of romance, nostalgia, and magic. Although her official title is head of the Department of Avoidance and Fantasy, she's also one of the most creative energies you own. Wherever she is in your chart is where you're psychic. It's also where you're capable of amazing compassion and sensitivity for beings and creatures less fortunate than yourself. It's where you'll be drawn into charity or volunteer work because you realize that we're all part of a bigger plan, that there are no boundaries between you and what's out there.

This combination of sensitivity and harsh reality doesn't always mix well. This may also be a place where you'll try to escape. Sleep, meditation, and prayer are the highest uses of her energies, but alcohol and drugs are also under her jurisdiction. Neptune's place in your chart is where you're equally capable of fooling all of the people all of the time, and of being fooled yourself. In the body, Neptune and the Moon corule fluids. Neptune also has a connection with poisons and viruses that invisibly infiltrate our bodies, and with the body's immune system, which is how we keep our barriers intact.

Pluto

Pluto is head of the Department of Death, Destruction, and Decay. He's in charge of things that have to happen, and he disposes of situations that have gone past the point of no return, where the only solution is to "let go." He also oversees sex, reincarnation, recycling, regeneration, and rejuvenation. Pluto's spot in your chart is a place where intense, inevitable circumstances will arrive to teach you about agony and ecstasy. Pluto's place in your chart is where you'll be in a state of turmoil or evolution, where there will be ongoing change. This is the side of you that realizes that, like it or not, life goes on after tremendous loss. It is the side of you that will reflect on your losses down the road and try to make sense of them. Most importantly, since Pluto rules life, death, and rebirth, here's where you'll understand the importance of process. You'll be amazingly strong where your Pluto is—he's a well of concentrated, transforming energy. In the body, Pluto is associated with the reproductive organs since here is where the invisible process of life and death begins. He is also in charge of puberty and sexual maturity. He corresponds with plutonium.

Signs: The Second Building Block

Every sign is built of three things: an element, a quality, and a polarity. Understanding each of these primary building blocks gives a head start toward understanding the signs themselves, so let's take a look at them.

The Polarities: Masculine and Feminine

The words "masculine" and "feminine" are often misunderstood or confused in the context of astrology. In astrology, masculine means that an energy is assertive, aggressive, and linear. Feminine means that an energy is receptive, magnetic, and circular. These terms should not be confused with male and female.

The Qualities: Cardinal, Fixed, and Mutable

Qualities show the way a sign's energy flows. The cardinal signs are energies that initiate change. Cardinal signs operate in sudden bursts of energy. The fixed signs are thorough and unstoppable. They're the energies that endure. They take projects to completion, tend to block change at all costs, and will keep at something regardless of whether or not it should be terminated. The mutable signs are versatile, flexible, and changeable. They can be scattered, fickle, and inconstant.

The Elements: Fire, Earth, Air, and Water

The fire signs correspond with the spirit and the spiritual aspects of life. They inspire action, attract attention, and love spontaneity. The earth signs are solid, practical, supportive, and as reliable as the earth under our feet. The earth signs are our physical envoys and are concerned with our tangible needs, such as food, shelter, work, and responsibilities. Air signs are all about the intellectual or mental sides of life. Like air itself, they are light and elusive. They love conversation, communication, and mingling. The water signs correspond to the emotional side of our natures. As changeable, subtle, and able to infiltrate as water itself, water signs gauge the mood in a room when they enter, and operate on what they sense from their environment.

Aries: Masculine, Cardinal, Fire

♈ Aries is ruled by Mars and is cardinal fire—red-hot, impulsive, and ready to go. Aries planets are not known for their patience, and they ignore obstacles, choosing instead to focus on the shortest distance between where they are and where they want to be. Planets in Aries are brave, impetuous, and direct. Aries planets are often very good at initiating projects. They are not, however, as eager to finish, so they will leave projects undone. Aries planets need physical outlets for their considerable Mars-powered energy— otherwise their need for action can turn to stress. Exercise, hard work, and competition are food for Aries energy.

Taurus: Feminine, Fixed, Earth

♉ Taurus, the fixed earth sign, has endless patience that turns your Taurus planet into a solid force to be reckoned with. Taurus folks never, ever quit. Their reputation for stubbornness is earned. They're responsible, reliable, honest as they come, practical, and endowed with a stick-to-it attitude other planets envy. They're not afraid to work hard. Since Taurus is ruled by Venus, it's not surprising to find that these people are sensual and luxury-loving, too. They love to be spoiled with thve best—good food, fine wine, or even a Renoir painting. They need peace and quiet like no other, and don't like their schedules to be disrupted. However, they may need a reminder that comfortable habits can become ruts.

Gemini: Masculine, Mutable, Air

♊ This sign is famous for its duality and love of new experiences, as well as for its role as communicator. Gemini is mutable air, which translates into changing your mind, so expect your Gemini planet to be entertaining and versatile. This sign knows a little bit about everything. Gemini planets usually display at least two distinct sides to their personalities; are changeable, even fickle at times; and are wonderfully curious. This sign is ruled by Mercury, so if what you're doing involves talking, writing, gesturing, or working with eye-hand coordination, your Gemini planet will love it. Mercury also rules short trips, so any planet in Gemini is an expert at how to make its way around the neighborhood in record time.

Cancer: Feminine, Cardinal, Water

♋ Cancer is cardinal water, so it's good at beginning things, like emotions and families. It's also the most privacy-oriented sign. Cancer types are emotionally vulnerable, sensitive, and easily hurt. They need safe "nests" to return to when the world gets to be too much. Cancer types say "I love you" by tending to your need for food, warmth, or a place to sleep. The problem is that they can become needy, dependent, or unable to function unless they feel someone or something needs them. Cancer rules the home and family. It's also in charge of emotions, so expect a Cancer to operate from his or her gut most of the time.

Leo: Masculine, Fixed, Fire

♌ Leo is fixed fire, and above all else he represents pride and ego. Sun-ruled Leo wants to shine and be noticed. Natural performers, people in this sign are into drama, and attract attention even when they don't necessarily want it. Occasionally your Leo friend may be touchy and "high maintenance." Still, they are generous to a fault. Leo appreciates attention and praise with lavish compliments, lovely gifts, and creative outings designed to amaze and delight. Leo's specialties are having fun, entertaining, and making big entrances and exits.

Virgo: Feminine, Mutable, Earth

♍ Virgo seems "picky" and "critical," but that may be too simplified. As a mutable earth sign, your Virgo planet delights in helping, and it's willing to adapt to any task. Having a keen eye for details may be another way to interpret a Virgo planet's automatic fault-finding ability. When Virgo's eye for detail combines with the ability to fix almost anything, you have a troubleshooter extraordinaire. This sign practices discrimination—analyzing, critiquing, and suggesting remedies to potential problems. This sign is also wonderful at lists, agendas, and schedules. Keep your Virgo planet happy by keeping it busy.

Libra: Masculine, Cardinal, Air

♎ Libra adores balance, harmony, and equal give and take—no easy task. A more charming sign would be difficult to find, though. Libra's cardinal airy nature wants to begin things and entertaining and socializing are high priorities. These expert people-pleasing Venus-ruled planets specialize in manners, courtesy, and small talk. Alone time may be shunned, and because they're gifted with the ability to pacify, they may sell out their own needs, or the truth, to buy peace and companionship. Seeing both sides of a situation, weighing the options, and keeping their inner balance by remaining honest may be Libra's hardest task.

Scorpio: Feminine, Fixed, Water

♏ Planets in this sign are detectives, excelling at the art of strategy. Your Scorpio planets sift through every situation for subtle clues, then they analyze clues to determine what's really going on. They're also gifted at sending subtle signals back to the environment, and at imperceptibly altering a situation by manipulating it with the right word or movement. Scorpio planets are constantly searching for intimacy. They seek intensity and may be crisis-oriented. They can be relentless, obsessive, and jealous. Remember, this is fixed water. Scorpios feel things deeply and forever. Give your Scorpio planets the opportunity to fire-walk, to experience life-and-death situations.

Sagittarius: Masculine, Mutable, Fire

♐ The enthusiasm of this mutable fire sign, ruled by Jupiter, spreads like a brush fire. These planets tend never to feel satisfied or content, and to always wonder if there's something even more wonderful over the next mountain. Your Sagittarius planets are bored by routine; they're freedom oriented, generous, and optimistic to a fault. They can be excessive and overindulgent. They adore outdoor activities, foreign places and foreign people, and they learn by first having the big picture explained. They're only too happy to preach, advertise, and philosophize. Sagittarius planets can be quite prophetic, and they absolutely believe in the power of laughter—embarrassing themselves at times to make someone laugh.

Capricorn: Feminine, Cardinal, Earth

♑ Your Capricorn planets, ruled by Saturn, have a tendency to build things, such as erecting structures and creating a career for you. It will start up an organization and turn it into the family business. These planets automatically know how to run it no matter what it is. They're authority figures. They exercise caution and discipline, set down rules, and live by them. Capricorn is the sign with the driest wit. Here's where your sense of propriety and tradition will be strong, where doing things the old-fashioned way and paying respect to the elders will be the only way to go. They want a return for the time they invest, and don't mind proving how valuable they are.

Aquarius: Masculine, Fixed, Air

♒ Aquarian planets present some unexpected contradictions because they are fixed air *and* unpredictable. This sign's ruler, Uranus, gets the credit for Aquarius's tumultuous ways. Aquarian energy facilitates invention and humanitarian conquests, to the amazement of the masses, and planets in this sign are into personal freedom like no other. They create their own rules, fight city hall whenever possible, and deliberately break tradition. They adore change. Abrupt reversals are their specialty, so others often perceive them as erratic, unstable, or unreliable energies. But, when

Aquarius energy activates, commitment to a cause or an intellectual ideal has a steadfastness like no other sign possesses.

Pisces: Feminine, Mutable, Water

♓ Mutable Pisces can't separate itself emotionally from whatever it's exposed to. While this is the source of Pisces' well-deserved reputation for compassion, it's also the source of your desire to escape reality. Planets in this sign feel everything—for better or worse—so they need time alone to unload and reassemble themselves. Exposure to others, especially in crowds, is exhausting to your Pisces planets. Here is where you may have a tendency to take in stray people and animals and where you'll need to watch for the possibility of being victimized or taken advantage of in some way. Pisces planets see the best in people or situations, and they can be disappointed when reality sets in. These planets are the romantics of the zodiac. Let them dream in healthy ways.

Houses: The Third Building Block

Houses are represented by twelve pie-shaped wedges in a horoscope chart. (See blank chart on page 187.) They're like rooms in a house, and each reflects the circumstances we create and encounter in a specific area of life. One room, the Sixth, relates to our daily routine and work, while the Eleventh relates to groups we may be affilliated with, for example. The sign—Aries, Taurus, etc.—on the cusp of each house tells us something about the nature of the room behind the door. Someone with Leo on the Sixth House cusp will create different routines and work habits than the person with Capricorn on that cusp. The sign influences the type of behavior you'll exhibit when those life circumstances turn up. Since the time of day you were born determines the sign on each of the houses, an accurate birth time will result in more accurate information from your chart.

There Are Twelve Houses

The First House

The First House shows the sign that was ascending over the horizon at the moment you were born. Let's think again of your chart as one big house and of the houses as "rooms." This house symbolizes your front door. The sign on this house cusp (also known as the Rising Sign or Ascendant) describes the way you dress, move, and adorn yourself, and the overall condition of your body. It relates to the first impression you make on people.

The Second House

This house shows how you handle the possessions you hold dear. That goes for the money, objects, and qualities you value in yourself and in others. This house also holds the side of you that takes care of what you have and what you buy for yourself, and the amount of money you earn. This house shows what you're willing to do for money, too. So this house is also a description of your self-esteem.

The Third House

This house corresponds to your neighborhood, including the bank, post office, and the gym where you work out. This is the side of you that performs routine tasks without much conscious thought. This house also refers to childhood and grammar school, and it shows our relationships with siblings, our communication style, and our attitude toward short trips.

The Fourth House

This house is the symbolic foundation brought from your child-hood home, your family, and the parent who nurtured you. Here is where you'll find the part of you that decorates and maintains your nest. It decides what home in the adult world will be like and how much privacy you'll need. This house deals with matters of real estate. Most importantly, this house contains the emotional warehouse of memories you operate from subconsciously.

The Fifth House

Here's the side of you that's reserved for play, that only comes out when work is done and it's time to party and be entertained. This is the charming, creative, delightful side of you, where your hobbies, interests, and playmates are found. If it gives you joy, it's described here. Your Fifth House shines when you are creative, and it allows you to see a bit of yourself in those creations—anything from your child's smile to a piece of art. Traditionally, this house also refers to speculation and gambling.

The Sixth House

This house is where you keep the side of you that decides how you like things to go along over the course of a day, the side of you that plans a schedule. Since it describes the duties you perform on a daily basis, it also refers to the nature of your work, your work environment, and how you take care of your health. It's how you function. Pets are also traditionally a Sixth House issue since we tend to them daily and incorporate them into our routine.

The Seventh House

Although it's traditionally known as the house of marriage, partnerships, and open enemies, this house really holds the side of you that only comes out when you're in the company of just one other person. This is the side of you that handles relating on a one-to-one basis. Whenever you use the word "my" to describe your relationship with another, it's this side of you talking.

The Eighth House

Here's the crisis expert side of you that emerges when it's time to handle extreme circumstances. This is the side of you that deals with agony and ecstasy, with sex, death, and all manner of mergers, financial and otherwise. This house also holds information on surgeries, psychotherapy, and the way we regenerate and rejuvenate after loss.

The Ninth House

This house holds the side of you that handles new experiences, foreign places, long-distance travel, and legal matters. Higher education, publishing, advertising, and forming opinions are handled here, as are issues involving the big picture such as politics, religion, and philosophy.

The Tenth House

This spot in your chart describes what the public knows about you. Your career, reputation, and social status are found here. This is the side of you that takes time to learn and become accomplished.

It describes the behavior you'll exhibit when you're in charge, and also the way you'll be in the presence of an authority figure. Most importantly, this house describes your vocation or life's work—whatever you consider your "calling."

The Eleventh House

Here's the team player in you, the side of you that helps you find your peer groups. This house shows the type of organizations you're drawn to join, the kind of folks you consider kindred spirits, and how you'll act in group situations. It also shows the causes and social activities you hold near and dear.

The Twelfth House

This is the side of you that only comes out when you're alone, or in the mood to retreat and regroup. Here's where the secret side of you lives, where secret affairs and dealings take place. Here, too, is where matters like hospital stays are handled. Most importantly, this is the room where you keep all traits and behaviors you were taught early on to stifle, avoid, or deny—especially in public. This side of you is very fond of fantasy, illusion, and pretend play.

Aspects and Transits:
The Fourth Building Block

Planets form angles to one another as they move through the heavens. If two planets are 90 degrees apart, they form a square. If they're 180 degrees apart, they're in opposition. Planets in aspect have twenty-four-hour communication going on. The particular angle that separates any two planets describes the nature of their conversation. Astrologers use seven angles most often, each of which produces a different type of relationship or "conversation" between the planets they join. Let's go over the meaning of each of the aspects.

Ptolemic Aspects

The Conjunction: (0–8 degrees)

♂ When you hear that two things are operating "in conjunction," it means they're operating together. This holds true with planets, as well. Two (or more) planets conjoined are a team, but some planets pair up more easily than others. Venus and the Moon work well together because both are feminine and receptive, but the Sun and Mars are both pretty feisty by nature, and may cause conflict. Planets in conjunction are usually sharing a house in your chart.

The Sextile: (60 degrees)

The sextile links planets in compatible elements. That is, planets in sextile are either in fire and air signs or earth and water signs. Since these pairs of elements get along well, the sextile encourages an active exchange between the two planets involved, so these two parts of you will be eager to work together.

The Square: (90 degrees)

A square aspect puts planets at cross-purposes. Friction develops between them and one will constantly challenge the other. You can see squares operating in someone who's fidgety or constantly restless. Although they're uncomfortable and even aggravating at times, your squares point to places where tremendous growth is possible.

The Trine: (120 degrees)

Trines are usually formed between planets of the same element, so they understand each other. They show an ease of communication not found in any of the other aspects, and they're traditionally thought of as "favorable." Of course, there is a downside to trines. Planets in this relationship are so comfortable that they can often get lazy and spoiled. (Sometimes they get so comfy they're boring.) Planets in trine show urges or needs that automatically support each other. The catch is that you've got to get them operating.

The Quincunx: (150 degrees)

This aspect joins two signs that don't share a quality, element, or gender, which makes it difficult for them to communicate with each other. It's frustrating. For that reason, this aspect has always been considered to require an adjustment in the way the two planets are used. Planets in quincunx can often feel pushed, forced, or obligated to perform. They seem to correspond to health issues.

The Opposition: (180 degrees)

When two planets oppose, they work against each other. For example, you may want to do something, and if you have two opposing planets, you may struggle with two very different approaches to getting the job done. If Mars and Neptune are opposing, you may struggle between getting a job done the quick, easy way or daydreaming about all the creative possibilities open to you. It's as if the two are standing across from one another with their arms folded, involved in a debate, neither willing to concede an inch. They can only break out of their standoff by first becoming aware of one another and then compromising. This aspect is the least difficult of the traditionally known "hard" aspects because planets "at odds" with one another can come to some sort of compromise.

Transits

While your horoscope (natal chart) reflects the exact position of planets at the time of your birth, the planets, as you know, move on. They are said to be "transiting." We interpret a transit as a planet in its "today" position making an aspect to a planet in your natal chart. Transiting planets represent incoming influences and events that your natal planets will be asked to handle. The nature of the transiting planet describes the types of situations that will arise, and the nature of your natal planet tells which "piece" of you you're working on at the moment. When a planet transits through a house or aspects a planet in your chart, you will have opportunities for personal growth and change. Every transit you experience adds knowledge to your personality.

Sun Transit

A Sun transit points to the places in your chart where you'll want special attention, pats on the back, and appreciation. Here's where you want to "shine." These are often times of public acclaim, when we're recognized, congratulated, or applauded for what we've done.

Of course, the ultimate Sun transit is our birthday, the day when we're all secretly sure that we should be treated like royalty.

Moon Transit

When the Moon touches one of the planets in our natal charts, we react from an emotional point of view. A Moon transit often corresponds to the highs and lows we feel that often last only a day or two. Our instincts are on high during a Moon transit and we're more liable to sense what's going on around us than to consciously know something.

Mercury Transit

Transiting Mercury creates activity in whatever area of life it visits. The subject is communication of all kinds, so conversation, letters, and quick errands take up our time now. Because of Mercury's love of duality, events will often occur in twos—as if Hermes the trickster were having some fun with us—and we're put in the position of having to do at least two things at once.

Venus Transit

Transiting Venus brings times when the universe gives us a small token of warmth or affection, or a well-deserved break. These are often sociable, friendly periods when we do more than our usual share of mingling and are more interested in good food and cushy conditions than anything resembling work. A Venus transit also shows a time when others will give us gifts. Since Venus rules money, this transit can show when we'll receive financial rewards.

Mars Transit

Mars transiting through a house can create high energy times. You're stronger and restless, or maybe you're cranky, angry, accident-prone, or violent. When Mars happens along, it's best to work or exercise hard to use up this considerable energy. Make yourself "too tired to be mad." These are super times to initiate projects that require a hard push of energy to begin.

Jupiter Transit

Under this transit, you're in the mood to travel, take a class, or learn something new about the concerns of any house or planet

Jupiter visits. We ponder the big questions. You grow under a Jupiter transit, sometimes even physically. Now is the time to take chances or risk a shot at the title. During a Jupiter transit, you're luckier, bolder, and a lot more likely to succeed. This transit provides opportunities. Be sure to take advantage of them.

Saturn Transit

When Saturn comes along, we see things as they truly are. These are not traditionally great times, but they are often times when your greatest rewards appear. When Saturn transits a house or planet, he checks to see if the structure is steady and will hold up. You are then tested, and if you pass, you receive a symbolic "certificate" of some kind—and sometimes a real one, like a diploma. We will always be tested, but if we fail, life can feel very difficult. Firming up our lives is Saturn's mission. This is a great time to tap into Saturn's willpower and self-discipline to stop doing something. It is not traditionally a good time to begin new ventures, though.

Uranus Transit

The last thing in the world you'd ever expect to happen is exactly what you can expect under a Uranus transit. This is the planet of last-minute plan changes, reversals, and shock effects. So if you're feeling "stuck" in your present circumstances, when a Uranus transit happens along, you won't be stuck for long. "Temporary people" often enter your life at these times, folks whose only purpose is to jolt you out of your present circumstances by appearing to provide exactly what you were sorely missing. That done, they disappear, leaving you with your life in a shambles. When these people arrive, enjoy them and allow them to break you out of your rut—just don't get comfortable.

Neptune Transit

A Neptune transit is a time when the universe asks only that you dream and nothing more. Your sensitivity heightens to the point that harsh sounds can actually make you wince. Our compassion deepens, and psychic moments are common. A Neptune transit inspires divine discontent. We sigh, wish, feel nostalgic, and don't see things clearly at all. At the end of the transit, you realize that everything about you is different, that the reality you were living at the beginning of the transit has been gradually eroded or erased right from under your feet, while you stood right there upon it.

Pluto Transit

A Pluto transit is often associated with obsession, regeneration, and inevitable change. Whatever has gone past the point of no return, whatever is broken beyond repair, will pass from your life now. As with a Saturn transit, this time is not known to be wonderful, but when circumstances peel away everything from us and we're forced to see ourselves as we truly are, we do learn just how strong we are. Power struggles often accompany Pluto's visit, but being empowered is the end result of a positive Pluto transit. The secret is to let go, accept the losses or changes, and make plans for the future.

Retrograde Planets

Retrograde literally means "backwards." Although none of the planets ever really throw their engines in reverse and move backward, all of them, except the Sun and Moon, appear to do so periodically, from our perspective here on Earth. What's happening is that we're moving either faster or slower than the planet that's retrograde, and since we have to look over our shoulder to see it, we refer to it as retrograde.

Mercury Retrograde: A Communication Breakdown

The way retrograde planets seem to affect our affairs varies from planet to planet. In Mercury's case, it means often looking back at Mercury-ruled things—communications, contracts, and so on. Keep in mind that Mercury correlates with Hermes, the original trickster, and you'll understand how cleverly disguised some of these errors can be. Communications become confused or are delayed. Letters are lost or sent to Auckland instead of Oakland. Or they end up under the car seat for three weeks. We sign a contract or agreement and find out later that we didn't have all the correct information, and what we signed was misleading in some way. We try repeatedly to reach someone via telephone but can never catch them in, or our communications devices themselves break down or garble information in some way. We feel as if our timing is off, so short trips often become more difficult. We leave the directions at home or write them down incorrectly. We're late for appointments due to circumstances beyond our control, or we completely forget about them.

Is there a constructive use for this time period? Yes. Astrologer Erin Sullivan has noted that the ratio of time Mercury spends moving retrograde (backward) and direct (forward) corresponds beautifully with the amount of time we humans spend awake and asleep—about a third of our lives. So this period seems to be a time to take stock of what's happened over the past three months and assimilate our experiences.

A good rule of thumb with Mercury retrograde is to try to confine activities to those that have "re" attached to the beginning of a word: reschedule, repair, return, rewrite, redecorate, restore, replace, renovate, or renew, for example.

Retrogrades of the Other Planets

With Venus retrograde every eighteen months for six weeks, relationships and money matters are delayed or muddled.

With Mars retrograde for eleven weeks, and then direct for twenty-two months, actions initiated are often rooted in confusion or end up at cross-purposes to our original intentions. Typically, under a Mars retrograde, the aggressor or initiator of a battle is defeated.

Jupiter retrogrades for four months and is direct for nine months. Saturn retrogrades for about the same amount of time. Each of the outer planets, Uranus, Neptune, and Pluto, stays retrograde for about six or seven months of every year. In general, remember that actions ruled by a particular planet quite often need to be repeated or done over when that planet is retrograde. Just make sure that whatever you're planning is something you don't mind doing twice.

Moon Void-of-Course

The Moon orbits Earth in about twenty-eight days, moving through each of the signs in about two days. As she passes through the 30 degrees of each sign, she visits with the planets in order by forming angles or aspects with them. Because she moves one degree in just two to two-and-a-half hours, her influence on each planet lasts only a few hours. As she approaches the late degrees of the sign she's passing through, she eventually forms what will be her final aspect to another planet before leaving the sign. From this point until she actually enters the new sign, she is referred to as void-of-course (v/c).

The Moon is the emotional tone of the day, carrying feelings of the sign she's "wearing" at the moment. She rules instincts. After she has contacted each of the planets, she symbolically "rests" before changing her costume, so her instincts are temporarily on hold. It's during this time that many people feel fuzzy, vague, or scattered. Plans or decisions do not pan out. Without the instinctual knowing the Moon provides as she touches each planet, we tend to be unrealistic or exercise poor judgment. The traditional definition of the void-of-course Moon is that "nothing will come of this," and it seems to be true. Actions initiated under a void-of-course Moon are often wasted, irrelevant, or incorrect—usually because information needed to make a sound decision is hidden or missing, or has been overlooked.

Now, although it's not a good time to initiate plans, routine tasks seem to go along just fine. However, this period is really ideal for what the Moon does best—reflection. It's at this time that we can assimilate what has occurred over the past few days. Use this time to meditate, ponder, and imagine. Let your conscious mind rest and allow yourself to feel.

On the lighter side, remember that there are other good uses for the void-of-course Moon. This is the time period when the universe seems to be most open to loopholes. It's a great time to make plans you don't want to fulfill or schedule things you don't want to do. In other words, like the song says, "To everything, there is a season." Even void-of-course Moons.

The Moon's Influence

As the Moon goes along her way, she magically appears and disappears, waxing to full from the barest sliver of a crescent just after she's new, then waning back to her invisible new phase again. The four quarters—the New Moon, the second quarter, the Full Moon, and the fourth quarter—correspond to the growth cycle of every living thing.

The Quarters

First Quarter

This phase begins when the Moon and the Sun are conjunct one another in the sky. At the beginning of the phase, the Moon is invisible, hidden by the brightness of the Sun as they travel together. The Moon is often said to be in her "dark phase" when she is just new. The New Moon can't actually be seen until 5 ½ to 12 hours after its birth. Toward the end of the first quarter phase, as the Moon pulls farther away from the Sun and begins to wax toward the second quarter stage, a delicate silver crescent appears. This time corresponds to all new beginnings; this is the best time to begin a project.

Second Quarter

The second quarter begins when the Moon has moved 90 degrees away from the Sun. At this point, the waxing Moon rises at about noon and sets at about midnight. It's at this time that she can be seen in the western sky during the early evening hours, growing in size from a crescent to her full beauty. This period corresponds to the development and growth of life, and with projects that are coming close to fruition.

Third Quarter

This phase begins with the Full Moon when the Sun and Moon are opposite one another in the sky. It's now that she can be seen rising in the east at sunset, a bit later each night as this phase progresses. This time corresponds to the culmination of plans and to maturity.

Fourth Quarter

This phase occurs when the Moon has moved 90 degrees past the full phase. She is decreasing in light, rises at midnight, and can be seen now in the eastern sky during the late evening hours. She doesn't reach the highest point in the sky until very early in the morning. This period corresponds to "disintegration"—a symbolic "drawing back" to reflect on what's been accomplished. It's now time to reorganize, clear the boards, and plan for the next New Moon stage.

The Moon Through the Signs

The signs indicate how we'll do things. Since the Moon rules the emotional tone of the day, it's good to know what type of mood she's in at any given moment. Well, here's a thumbnail sketch to help you navigate through every day by cooperating with the Moon no matter what sign she's in.

Aries

The Moon in Aries is bold, impulsive, and energetic. It's a period when we feel feisty and maybe a little argumentative. This is when even the meekest aren't afraid to take a stand to protect personal feelings. Since Aries is the first sign, it's a natural starting point for all kinds of projects, and a wonderful time to channel all that "me first" energy to initiate change and new beginnings. Just watch out for a tendency to be too impulsive and stress-oriented.

Taurus

The Moon in Taurus is the Lady at her most solid and sensual, feeling secure and well rooted. There's no need to stress or hurry—and definitely no need to change anything. We tend to resist change when the Moon is in this sign, especially change that's not of our own making. We'd rather sit still, have a wonderful dinner, and listen to good music. Appreciating the beauty of the Earth, watching a sunset, viewing some good art, or taking care of money and other resources are Taurus Moon activities.

Gemini

This mutable air sign moves around so quickly that when the Moon is here we're a bit more restless than usual, and may find that we're suddenly in the mood for conversation, puzzles, riddles, and word games. We want two—at least two—of everything. Now is a great time for letter writing, phone calls, or short trips. It's when you'll find the best shortcuts, and when you'll need to take them, too. Watch for a tendency to become a bit scattered under this fun, fickle Moon.

Cancer

The Moon in this cardinal water sign is at her most nurturing. Here the Moon's concerns turn to home, family, children, and mothers, and we respond by becoming more likely to express our emotions and to be sympathetic and understanding toward others. We often find ourselves in the mood to take care of someone, to cook for or cuddle our dear ones. During this time, feelings run high, so it's important to watch out for becoming oversensitive, dependent, or needy. In all, now is a great time to putter around the house, have family over, and tend to domestic concerns.

Leo

The Leo Moon loves drama, with a capital D. This theatrical sign has long been known for its big entrances, love of display, and need for attention. When the Moon is in this sign, we're all feeling a need to be recognized, applauded, and appreciated. Now, all that excitement, pride, and emotion can turn into melodrama in the blink of an eye, so it's best to be careful of overreacting or being excessively vain during this period. It's a great time to take in a show (or star in one), be romantic, or express your feelings for someone in regal style.

Virgo

The Moon is at her most discriminating and detail-oriented in Virgo, the sign most concerned with fixing and fussing. This Moon sign puts us in the mood to clean, scour, sort, troubleshoot, and help. Virgo, the most helpful of all the signs, is also more health conscious, work-oriented, and duty bound. Use this period to pay attention to your diet, hygiene, and daily schedules.

Libra

The Libra Moon is most oriented toward relationships and partnerships. Since Libra's job is to restore balance, however, you may find yourself in situations of emotional imbalance that require a delicate tap of the scales to set them right. In general, this is a social, polite, and friendly time, when others will be cooperative and agree more easily to compromise. A Libra Moon prompts us to make our surroundings beautiful, or to put ourselves in situations where beauty is all around us. This is a great time to decorate, shop for the home, or visit places of elegant beauty.

Scorpio

Scorpio is the most intense sign, and when the Moon is here, she feels everything to the nth degree—and needless to say, we do, too. Passion, joy, jealousy, betrayal, love, and desire can take center stage in our lives now, as our emotions deepen to the point of possible obsession. Be careful of a tendency to become secretive, suspicious, or to brood over an offense that was not intended. Now is a great time to investigate a mystery, do research, "dig"—both figuratively and literally—and allow ourselves to become intimate with someone.

Sagittarius

The Moon is at her most optimistic and willing to let go of things in Sagittarius. Jupiter, the planet of long-distance travel and education of the higher mind, makes this a great time to take off for adventure or attend a seminar on a topic you've always been interested in—say, philosophy or religion. This is the sign with the gift of prophecy and wisdom. When the Moon is in this sign, spend time outdoors, be spontaneous, and laugh much too loudly; just watch for a tendency toward excess, waste, and over-doing.

Capricorn

☽♑ The Moon is at her most organized, practical, and businesslike in Capricorn. She brings out the dutiful, cautious, and pessimistic side of us. Our goals for the future become all-important. Now is the time to tend to the family business, act responsibly, take charge of something, organize any part of our lives that's become scattered or disrupted, set down rules and guidelines, or patiently listen and learn. Watch for the possibility of acting too businesslike at the expense of others' emotions.

Aquarius

☽♒ The Aquarius Moon brings out the rebel in us. Use this time to break out of a rut, try something different, and make sure everyone sees us for the unique individuals we are. This sign is ruled by Uranus, so personal freedom and individuality are more important than anything now. Our schedules become topsy-turvy, and our causes become urgent. Watch for a tendency to become fanatical, act deliberately rebellious without a reason, or break tradition just for the sake of breaking it.

Pisces

☽♓ When the Moon slips into this sign, sleep, meditation, prayer, drugs, or alcohol is often what we crave to induce a trancelike state that will allow us to escape from the harshness of reality. Now is when we're most susceptible to emotional assaults of any kind, when we're feeling dreamy, nostalgic, wistful, or impressionable. Now is when we're at our most spiritual, when our boundaries are at their lowest, when we're compassionate, intuitive, and sensitive to those less fortunate. This is the time to attend a spiritual group or religious gathering.

2011 Eclipse Dates

Times are in Eastern Time and are rounded off to the nearest minute. The exact time of an eclipse generally differs from the exact time of a New or Full Moon. For solar eclipses, "greatest eclipse" represents the time (converted from Local Mean Time) of the Moon's maximum obscuration of the Sun as viewed from the Earth in right ascension. For lunar eclipses, the time shown is when the Moon reaches the centermost point of its journey through the shadow cast by the Earth passing between it and the Sun. Data is from *Astronomical Phenomena for the Year 2011*, prepared by the United States Naval Observatory and Her Majesty's Nautical Almanac Office (United Kingdom).

January 4

Solar Eclipse at 3:50 am EST — 13° ♑ 39'

June 1

Solar Eclipse at 5:16 pm EDT — 11° ♊ 03'

June 15

Lunar Eclipse at 4:12 pm EDT — 24° ♐ 22'

July 1

Lunar Eclipse at 4:38 pm EDT — 09° ♋ 12'

November 25

Solar Eclipse at 1:20 am EST — 02° ♐ 38'

December 10

Lunar Eclipse at 9:32 am EST — 18° ♊ 08'

2011 Retrograde Planets

Planet	Begin	Eastern	Pacific	End	Eastern	Pacific
Saturn	01/25/11		**10:10 pm**	06/12/11	11:51 pm	**8:51 pm**
	01/26/11	1:10 am				
Mercury	03/30/11	4:48 pm	**1:48 pm**	04/23/11	6:04 am	**3:04 am**
Pluto	04/09/11	4:50 am	**1:50 am**	09/16/11	2:24 pm	**11:24 am**
Neptune	06/03/11	3:27 am	**12:27 am**	11/09/11	1:54 pm	**10:54 am**
Uranus	07/09/11	8:35 pm	**5:35 pm**	12/09/11		**11:04 pm**
				12/10/11	2:04 am	
Mercury	08/02/11	11:50 pm	**8:50 pm**	08/26/11	6:03 pm	**3:03 pm**
Jupiter	08/30/11	5:17 am	**2:17 am**	12/25/11	5:08 pm	**2:08 pm**
Mercury	11/23/11		**11:19 pm**	12/13/11	8:43 pm	**5:43 pm**
	11/24/11	2:19 am				

Eastern Time in plain type, **Pacific Time in bold type**

2011 Planetary Phenomena

Information on Uranus and Neptune assumes the use of a telescope. Resource: *Astronomical Phenomena for the Year 2011*, prepared by the U.S. Naval Observatory and the Royal Greenwich Observatory. The dates are expressed in universal time and must be converted to your local mean time. See the World Map of Time Zones on page 189.

Planets in Morning and Evening

	Morning	Evening
Venus	01/01–07/11	09/23–12/31
Mars	04/17–12/31	
Jupiter		01/01–03/24
	04/21–10/29	10/29–12/31
Saturn	01/01–04/04	04/04–09/26
	10/31–12/31	

Mercury

Mercury can be seen low in the east before sunrise, or low in the west after sunset. It is visible in the mornings from these approximate dates: January 1 to February 13, April 18 to June 5, August 25 to September 19, and December 10 to 31. The planet is brighter at the end of each period. It is visible in the evenings from March 7 to April 2, June 20 to August 9, and October 12 to November 28.

Venus

Venus can be observed in the morning sky until the middle of July, when it becomes too close to the Sun for observation. It reappears in the evening sky during the second half of September, where it stays until the end of the year.

Mars

Mars is too close to the Sun for observation until mid-April, when it appears in the morning sky in Pisces. It is in conjunction with Mercury on April 19 and May 20, with Jupiter on May 1, and with Venus on May 11.

Jupiter

Jupiter can be seen in the evening sky in Pisces at the beginning of January. It becomes too close to the Sun for observation in late March and reappears in the morning during the second half of April. From early August, it can be seen more than half the night. It is opposing the Sun on October 29 when it is visible throughout the night.

Saturn

Saturn rises shortly after midnight at the beginning of the year in Libra and remains in this constellation throughout the year. It is at opposition to the Sun on April 4, when it can be seen throughout the night. From early July until late September, Saturn is visible only in the evening sky. It reappears in the morning sky in late October and remains in the morning sky the rest of the year.

Uranus

Uranus is visible in the evening sky from the beginning of the year until early March, when it becomes too close to the Sun for observation. It reappears the second week of April in the morning sky. Uranus is at opposition to the Sun on September 26. From late December it can be seen only in the evening sky.

Neptune

Neptune is visible in the evening sky during the first three weeks of January. In late January it becomes too close to the Sun for observation and reappears in the second week of March, when it is visible the morning sky. It is at opposition to the Sun on August 22, and from late November through the end of the year, it can be seen only in the evening sky.

Do not confuse: (1) Jupiter with Mercury from mid-March with Mars in early April to late May: Jupiter is the brighter object; (2) Mercury with Mars in the second half of April: Mars is the brighter object. (3) Venus with Mercury in late April to late May and mid-October to late November, with Jupiter in the first half of May, with Mars from mid-May to early June, and with Saturn in late September: Venus is the brighter object. (4) Mercury with Mars in mid-May: Mercury is the brighter object.

2011 Weekly Forecasts

by Pam Ciampi

Overview of 2011

This will be quite a year. With a series of major changes and upheavals ahead, both personal and global challenges are indicated. Four of the outer planets that affect worldwide shifts—Jupiter, Saturn, Uranus, and Pluto—will be traveling through cardinal signs. The cardinal signs of Aries, Libra, and Capricorn are action signs that accept challenges and make things happen, and you will see plenty of both. This year marks the first time Jupiter and Uranus have blended together in groundbreaking Aries since 1927, which was also a time of huge financial and social change. In Aries, Jupiter represents the drive toward expansion, while Uranus corresponds to reversals and turmoil. This is an indication of a big shift in the creation of a new world order. Another cardinal pattern emerges in the middle of the year when Uranus and Saturn in Aries get tangled with Pluto in Capricorn in an edgy configuration called a T-square. This pattern will be repeated several times in 2011, which points to a series of major showdowns between the old establishment (Saturn) and the new world order (Uranus) with the transformer (Pluto) placed squarely in the middle of this arrangement. This is a major indication that the transformations experienced this year will be worldwide. These outer planets will spend much of the year in challenging relationships. The inevitable changes that come will help prepare the way for the rare alignment of the solar system with the core of the Milky Way Galaxy that is expected in 2012, the last year of the Mayan calendar. Yes, the world will still exist after 2012,

---

Note: In the forecasts, when you read planet-planet (with a hyphen), the hyphen indicates that the planets are conjoined. When you read planet/planet (with a backslash), the backslash indicates that the planets are either opposed, square, sextile, quincunx, or trine to each other.

but it will be a different world. Knowing the celestial influences week-by-week in 2011 and working with them will help you be better prepared for the major shift that will be occurring in 2012.

January 3–9

A "lucky" carryover from last year—Jupiter linked to Uranus in Pisces—will kick off the year. Under this aspect, you could either experience an intense dislike of restrictions or a sudden and unexpected (Uranus) gain (Jupiter). The action peaks on Tuesday when the Capricorn New Moon coincides with a solar eclipse. Although this eclipse is not visible in the United States, the eclipse pattern indicates that Capricorns as well as Cancers will experience its impact in their lives. If your birthday falls on or within a day of the eclipse, or opposite it (July 4), this could be a benchmark year for you. The New Moon signals a good time to start something new but since this is also a New Moon eclipse, it is better to put off important events for a few days. The reason behind this advice is that the special alignment of a solar eclipse creates an intense field of energy that can cause a disturbance in new beginnings. In general, Capricorn energies affect a variety of different areas, including senior citizens, hard-to-reach places, and personal or professional boundaries. Also on Tuesday is the final get-together of Jupiter and Uranus in Pisces. Enjoy the unpredictable joy of this pairing because the next time they meet up will be in twelve years. You can count on Saturday to be a day when personal relationships take a leap away from very intense toward a more adventurous landscape. That's when Venus leaves emotional Scorpio to take a tour in exploratory and fun-loving Sagittarius for the next four weeks. Under these energies, the next month is prime time to plan an exciting vacation or an educational experience in a place far from home.

January 10–16

This week begins and ends with a buzz. It starts off with the Aries Moon in harmony with Venus and Mercury in Sagittarius, which is a sure sign of easy times filled with optimism and inspiration.

On Tuesday the pace slows a little when the Aries Moon opposes Saturn in a showdown, but any glitches will be only temporary because by Thursday the practical Taurus Moon moves to a harmonious wavelength with Pluto and promises a positive outcome to any project. Starting on Thursday, when Mercury enters Capricorn, if you keep your nose to the grindstone, you will have earned the right to be happy, wealthy, and wise for the next three weeks. With a harmonious trine between the Sun and Moon in earth signs, Friday evening is the perfect time to enjoy time with loved ones or longtime acquaintances. On Saturday, when Mars leaves conservative Capricorn and enters experimental Aquarius, you will feel your assertive energies shift gears. If you're ready to try something new and different, do it during the next six weeks. While Aquarius promises an exciting ride, it can also be an indication of an erratic and unpredictable energy that will keep you on your toes.

January 17–23

This week could feel like an emotional handful as you head toward its climax, the Cancer Full Moon, on Wednesday. In Cancer the light of this Full Moon is focused on women, families, the real estate market, and the general public. Among other things this Full Moon could be a sign that either the housing market is on the upswing, a woman is thrust into the headlines, or that you are personally consumed with emotion about a mother, sister, daughter, or wife. Following the Full Moon is always the right time of the month for closure and the next two weeks offer the best days to bring Cancer-related affairs to completion. This Full Moon is especially powerful if your birthday falls on January 19–20 or July 22–23, because it is in the same placement as the solar eclipse of July 2009. You could see matters that began then brought to a close. The day after the Full Moon, the Sun shifts away from dependable Capricorn to follow after Mars in progressive and unpredictable Aquarius. The focus for the next month is on Aquarian idealism that is embedded in the word *hope*. On Sunday Jupiter moves into Aries to make the first of its three sign changes this year. In 2011 Jupiter will spread good luck between the signs of Pisces, Aries, and Taurus. If you have an Aries birthday, you will have the pleasure of enjoying Jupiter's blessings in two parts. Your first lucky period was from June through September 2010; the second period starts on Sunday and lasts until next June. Lucky you!

January 24–30

If you are an Air sign (Gemini, Libra, or Aquarius) this is your week to express yourself. That's because assertive Mars has joined the Aquarius Sun with an assist from the Libra Moon. This emphasis in air signs focuses on ideas, theories, and inventions; it could indicate anything from the launch of a device that will take you to a new level of virtual reality, to a manned mission to Mars, to an uncontrollable social urge to contact everyone you know. There is a shadow lurking in the wings and it will show up on Wednesday when Saturn turns retrograde. Saturn retrograde indicates a six-month period of general slowdown; it is not a favorable time to start anything new. Retrograde Saturn's gift to you is time in which you can reorganize the skeletons in your closet. This includes unresolved issues that involve commitments, time or money management, and setting boundaries. On a lighter note, if you are looking for ways to infuse your love relationship with some exciting sparks, Saturday night is your date night. That's when the feminine charms of the Moon join up with Venus, the goddess of love, in adventuresome Sagittarius.

January 31–February 6

The big day of this week is Thursday. That's when the Aquarius New Moon ushers in the Chinese New Year. Because the Chinese zodiac is based on a lunar calendar, the Chinese New Year occurs on a different day each year, but it always coincides with the Aquarius New Moon. According to Chinese astrology, 2011 is the Year of the Rabbit. The rabbit rules the fourth sign of the Chinese zodiac and is considered to be a lucky omen. Because Aquarius is an impersonal sign that prefers the head to the heart, you can use this

New Moon to experiment with new ideas and have fun relating to strangers. Communications take on a lighter note the day after the New Moon, when Mercury leaves dutiful Capricorn and joins the Sun in idealistic Aquarius for the next three weeks. Under this airy influence, all forms of communication and networking could burn up the airwaves. On Saturday Venus also makes a sign change that could downshift your love life into a more serious gear. That's the day Venus leaves Sagittarius and enters commitment-loving Capricorn. With Venus in this mode for the next four weeks you might want to start shopping for the ring.

February 7–13

This week starts off with a bang as newly minted Jupiter in Aries meets up with the waxing Aries Moon on Monday. This fiery duo is a signal that now could be the right time to start something big. When Venus, the planet that rules love and money, bumps into Pluto in the material sign of Capricorn on Wednesday, things could be tricky. This pairing sets the stage for a potentially intense Valentine's Day, when the accent may be on "delivering the goods." Partners take note: forewarned is forearmed. Sunday is possibly the most auspicious morning of the week—if not the month. That's when the Moon is in a happy relationship with four other members of the solar system: the Sun (life-giving energy), Mars (action), Saturn (structure), and Neptune (inspiration). It's best to make hay while this aspect shines because everything will change in the early evening. That's when the energy begins to shift because of a difficult contact between the Moon and quirky Uranus and things could get a bit edgy.

February 14–20

This year Valentine's Day falls on Monday, when the Moon is in the super-sensitive and highly emotional sign of Cancer. This combination can create the perfect relationship crisis because this Cancer Moon is involved in two difficult aspects: a square with Jupiter and an opposition with Pluto. With feelings running high (Jupiter), the perfect storm could be brewing. Any hurt feelings will not be easily forgotten because the day after Valentine's Day the Moon gives Saturn the cold shoulder—a pattern that indicates a grudge factor may be in play. Hopefully, Friday's Leo Full Moon, which is especially powerful because it falls on the same degree in the zodiac as the fixed star Regulus (the heart of the Lion), won't throw more wood on the fire. If you are challenged during this Full Moon, it is time to have a brave heart and summon up all your courage to overcome your opponent. While the Moon is full in Leo, it is also the best day of the year to take pride in your personal accomplishments, eliminate bad habits, and rid yourself of what you no longer need. A new wave of energy enters on Sunday when the Sun finishes out its time in Aquarius and moves into Pisces. This movement indicates a shift from the rational (outgoing) to the emotional (reflective). The month that the Sun is in Pisces is the best time to focus on artistic, spiritual, or emotional pursuits. Things to avoid are lying and denying. If you tend to look at the world through rose-colored glasses, don't do it now!

February 21–27

Next to the Moon, which is actually a satellite of Earth, Mercury is the fastest-moving planet in our solar system; it's the planet that always seems to be either changing signs or changing direction. Early in the week, Mercury will begin its annual visit to Pisces. This shift out of Aquarius is the same sign change that the Sun made last week, but in the case of Mercury, it means that communications are the part of life that could become less rational and more emotional. If you are not careful, the next three weeks might be a time when you slide down the slippery slope into outright lies. On Thursday Mars follows the leader and becomes the third planet this month to exit Aquarius and enter Pisces. In watery Pisces, Mars's impulsive energy may emerge in images and dreams as well as through emotions. Although the next six weeks offer a chance to use your artistic and emotional creativity, any attempt at assertive action now could be difficult unless it is fueled by your emotions.

February 28–March 6

If you didn't get a ring during the last four weeks, when Venus was in Capricorn, you'll have to wait for another month, because Tuesday is the day Venus moves into commitment-phobic Aquarius. Although you might not be in the mood to make a commitment, the end of the week offers a wonderful moment for romance. Friday features the Pisces New Moon; it's one of the most romantic New Moons of the year. This New Moon offers the best time of the year to be in sync with your soft emotional side and your compassionate, loving nature. Fantasy is the name of the game and all you have to do is set the mood internally for the enchantment to begin. As the Moon grows bigger and brighter over the next two weeks, be sure to use the time to plant the seeds of a project or a relationship that you would like to see prosper and grow.

March 7–13

Aries is the headliner this week, and the story is about communication styles and how to let go of what you no longer need. On Wednesday, Mercury will be exiting dreamy Pisces and moving into innovative Aries. Because Mercury is on course to turn retrograde at the end of the month, its tour in Aries will be extended from the usual three weeks to two months. This is a time when you especially need to watch what you say because the impulsiveness of Mercury in Aries can indicate an outbreak of "foot in the mouth" disease. Mercury in Aries is known for great bursts of mental energy, but when the sparks die down, you might find it difficult to sustain your initial enthusiasm, or you might find that you're just plain bored. With this placement it is also wise to prepare for unexpected outbursts from yourself or from others, but luckily they tend to subside as quickly as they start. The other news story about Aries breaks on Sunday. That's the day Uranus ends its seven-year tour of Pisces and moves solidly into Aries, where it will stay until 2018. This is a significant shift because Uranus only changes signs once every seven years. The next Uranus cycle will especially affect people born under Aries and Libra (the sign opposite Aries). Under the influence of Uranus, Aries and Libra folks should get ready to rock and roll. That's because sometime over the course of the next seven years, this Uranus influence is guaranteed to remove anything that is no longer working in your life. On a more mundane note, Daylight Saving Time begins on Sunday at 2 am. Set your clocks one hour ahead (spring ahead, fall back) before you go to sleep on Saturday night.

March 14–20

The middle of this week is a "get up and go" time for those whose jobs involve sales, writing, education, or disseminating information; that's because Mercury, the planet that rules communication, has joined together with lucky Jupiter in energetic Aries. With both planets harmonizing with the Leo Moon on Wednesday, there's a golden opportunity for you to close any deal. That particular green light ends late on Thursday when the Moon moves into Virgo. The next day, the Virgo Moon bumps into minor difficulties with both Jupiter and Mercury; it also gets involved in a showdown with Mars—a sure sign that you should get ready for sparks to fly. This fiery energy leads to the Virgo Full Moon on Saturday, which will focus your attention on service to others, work, and health. You'll be able to identify any problems in these areas and make adjustments to correct them. Sunday is a day to mark on your calendar with a red circle. This is the first seasonal change in the calendar year—the first day of spring, which is the Spring Equinox. The first day of spring is calculated by the movement of the Sun into the first degree of Aries. Sunday is special because it is one of two days of the year when the hours of the day equal the hours of the night. Use this day of perfect balance between the light and the dark to take personal stock of the balance, or lack of balance, in your life. Take the time to recalibrate your internal meter so you can be as balanced in your life as the night and day.

March 21–27

On Monday, when the Sun aligns with unpredictable Uranus, already in Aries since March 11, the stage is set for a wild and unpredictable time. This highly creative combination can set the mood for new ways of personal expression. It is wise to have all systems set on "go," as this combination can also symbolize the need to act fast and to push the boundaries as far as possible. It can also reverse the direction of whatever is the current status quo. The week ends with a Saturday evening meeting between Venus and Neptune in Aquarius that, depending on your viewpoint, could either be inspiring or confusing, or both. Because the final degree of any sign carries the power of the whole sign, this could be an extreme kind of day that runs the gamut from fascinating to over-the-top to confusing. Keep an eye out for this influence in the areas of your life that have to do with love or money. On Sunday, Venus leaves both Aquarius and Neptune behind and enters emotional Pisces for the next four weeks. This is a sign change that could send your compassion meter through the roof, because Venus is over-generous in Pisces. The next month could be a period in your life when donations and charitable contributions are up, and love means giving. Venus in Pisces can also signal a time of increased creativity in the arts. On the negative side, watch out for a tendency to play the victim and throw a pity party for yourself.

March 28–April 3

It's a combat zone from now until the end of the year as explosive Uranus in Aries battles Pluto in Capricorn. This configuration echoes the mid-1960s, when the same two planets (Uranus and Pluto) were bonded together, and an intense breakdown in society was felt from the United States to China. Because Uranus energy does not recognize boundaries and insists on expression, and Pluto signifies a deep need to release underlying tensions, this is a fight that could have worldwide implications once again. Another planetary pair to watch this week is the push-pull between adventurous

Jupiter in Aries and responsible Saturn in Libra. This showdown happens once every ten years, but this time it only lasts a few weeks. You will feel it as the desire to fulfill personal pleasures pulling against your relationship responsibilities. On Wednesday, Mercury fulfills its scheduled flight plan and turns retrograde. Because this reversal means that Mercury will spend nearly three months in impulsive Aries rather than its usual three weeks, you will want to be sure to think before you speak. All Mercury retrogrades signal a time to look backwards, so you might have to go back over something that you thought was already completed. Under this influence it is best to be prepared to spend time doing things that begin with the prefix "re," such as repetition, planning a remodel, revising a project, resigning or making a retreat. While Mercury retrograde is a useful time for going over the same ground, it is not the best time to begin a new project. At the end of the week Mars follows suit and also moves into Aries. Aries is the sign where Mars is most comfortable. This happy arrangement will last until the middle of May and offsets the indications of the Mercury retrograde. The Aries New Moon joins Mars on Sunday, which could give mixed signals, confusion, and complications. While Mercury retrograde suggests that it's not a good time to make a new beginning or to seek out challenges, the Aries New Moon, which is escorted by Mars, is yelling that it's time to go, go, go! If you do choose to go with the New Moon-Mars energy, remember to apply a liberal dose of caution. Don't allow the hot vitality of Aries to push you into making an impulsive decision. If you act in haste, you are likely to repent at leisure.

April 4–10

Neptune makes the headlines this week when it leaves Aquarius and moves temporarily into its natural home sign—Pisces. Although Neptune has one last assignment with Aquarius in September, the movement of Neptune into Pisces marks an important change; it signals the beginning of a new global movement that will move the energy away from technology and toward compassion. The last time Neptune passed through Pisces was in the mid-1800s; it was then that slavery ended in the United States. Neptune's entrance into compassionate Pisces is especially important if your birthday is around February 20 or September 20, because on Sunday Pluto changes direction as it turns retrograde for the first time this year. This retrograde period will last until September, and it suggests that a window of opportunity is available for you to go back and review any intense transformations that have taken place during the last year. Pluto is especially connected to issues that involve death, separation, and loss. It is helpful, during the Pluto retrograde period, to allow yourself time to experience the process of grieving that often takes longer than you think. There is no rush, because Pluto will be in backward motion for five months.

April 11–17

The celestial stage is set for power struggles that could go viral this week, so be on your guard. This alert is due to a tense battle between Mars and Pluto over who's the leader. Whether personally or globally, Mars versus Pluto represents an intense and dangerous battle of forces. With Mars in its strongest position in Aries, tempers can flare up at a moment's notice. When Mars clashes with Pluto (in authority-minded Capricorn), there is a compulsion to secure the perimeter and take no prisoners. When these two planets lock horns, no one is willing to give an inch without a fight. There is a small hope for a peaceful resolution of some sort on Sunday, when the Libra Full Moon sheds the light of reason on this potentially destructive situation. The Libra Full Moon highlights diplomacy in relationships and brings light to any issues that might be standing in the way of a fair and equal partnership. Because Libra is a sign that values communication, this is one of the best Full Moons of the year to use your diplomatic skills to talk things out and reach a compromise.

April 18–24

This is a week of many shifts and changes in direction. On Wednesday the Sun leaves impulsive and quick-witted Aries and moves into the laid back and steady grounds of Taurus. This sign change suggests that the next month will be a time of gathering in, unlike Aries, which was a time of reaching out. The month the Sun spends in Taurus offers you a chance to work on maintaining the things you value and appreciate. There is a shift on Thursday when Venus ends its tour of emotional Pisces and shifts into fiery Aries for the next six weeks, which will affect your feelings about love and money. Venus represents receptivity and the feminine, and being in Aries, one of the most masculine signs, is definitely out of Venus's comfort zone. Since Aries underscores the self, the best use of the next six weeks could be to focus on loving yourself. On Saturday, a change of direction for Mercury ends a retrograde period and Mercury's trickster tendencies for the next few months. Mercury's direction change signals the all clear for communications, buying and selling, transportation, and signing contracts. Easter is scheduled for this Sunday, and this year it is late. Easter is always celebrated on a Sunday, but the actual date is decided according to the Spring Equinox and the date of the next Full Moon after the equinox. Although the equinox is always around March 20–21, the next Full Moon can occur anytime in March or April. This year the first Full Moon after the equinox didn't occur until last week, which means that this Easter Sunday occurs about as late in the year as it can get.

April 25–May 1

On Tuesday the Moon bonds with dreamy Neptune in Aquarius, the sign that loves to crash through boundaries. The fascinating energy of this combo can be used to help you charm and impress anyone in your social network, including colleagues, friends, lovers, and pets. This same aspect can also go against you, so it won't hurt to be on the lookout for snake-oil salesmen. Life gets real again the next day as the Sun (in Taurus) and Pluto (in Capricorn) harmonize in earthy signs. You have from Wednesday to Saturday to make a plan about what you want to bring into physical manifestation. Use this time well, because on Sunday there's a roadblock.

That's when the super power of the Moon-Venus conjunction in Aries gets in between two of the masculine big guys, Saturn and Pluto, who are battling about compromise versus control. This is a day when it is important to handle all things with kid gloves; an uncertain truce is about the best you can hope for. Later on in the day there's a tendency to go for broke when Mars conjoins Jupiter in Aries. This duo combines a wild-eyed tendency that the "sky is the limit" with an optimism that everything will work out okay in the end. Given Jupiter's luck, it probably will.

May 2–8

All is quiet on the celestial front until Tuesday, when the Sun and Moon make their monthly meeting at the New Moon and signal that it's time to start something new. The Taurus New Moon will help you to focus on financial ventures such as applying for a loan, starting a long-term relationship, or beginning a project that involves the arts. Any kind of activity that encourages natural beauty is encouraged now. Because Taurus is an earth sign, its gifts are patience, common sense, and dependability. On the negative side, your challenges under this New Moon are stubbornness and inflexibility. The Moon is very comfortable in Taurus and this New Moon is a beautiful lead-in to the annual celebration of Mother's Day on Sunday. That's when the Moon has moved to its home sign of Cancer, which, appropriately, links to the idea of mother. With this sensitive Moon in a harmonious aspect to Neptune, this could be a day filled with oceans of emotions. Because Cancer is the sign that is associated with the "good old days," make sure that any Mother's Day celebration includes home-cooked food, flowers, and sweet memories that will honor and nurture the lady that gave you life.

May 9–15

This week Mars finishes its tour in Aries and crosses into Taurus, where Mars becomes more like the tortoise and less like the hare it was while in Aries. For the next six weeks the pace will be slow and steady, but don't forget that the tortoise won the race. This Mars placement will help you focus your determination to work toward long-range goals. When Mars is in Taurus, you are slow to anger but once aroused there is absolutely no way you will back down. Beware of this tendency because you could end up butting your head against a brick wall. Wednesday through Saturday, when Mercury joins together with Venus and Jupiter in Aries, you'll have a small window of opportunity to send someone a message that is fun and new. Combined with the restless enthusiasm of Aries, this merry trio is guaranteed to energize any new undertaking, and with Mars's determination it's a sure bet that you will take it to the finish line. This window will close on Sunday when both Venus and Mercury cross over together into Taurus and meet up with Mars for the next ten days. This is a prime time to focus on personal or financial goals.

May 16–22

On Monday the unique trio of Venus, Mercury, and Mars unite in Taurus and form a positive aspect to Neptune. This is a signal to expect a beautiful day of love, peace, and harmony. Even if it doesn't turn out to be perfect day, there are no worries because with the gauzy veil of Neptune involved in the picture, it will seem like a great day anyway. Enjoy this time because the mood darkens considerably on Tuesday at the Scorpio Full Moon. Like the famous note in the Sherlock Holmes mysteries, "All is revealed, flee at once," the Scorpio Full Moon is the time that exposes all the intense emotions that have been flying under the radar for the past six months. Jealousy, hidden resentments, bruised egos, and deeply buried hurts are some of the feelings that may come flying out at you. Because Scorpio also relates to death and rebirth, Tuesday offers one of the two best times of the year (the other is the Scorpio New Moon in November) to get rid of what you no longer need. The purpose of this release is to prepare you for a rebirth. The most productive day of this week falls on Friday when the Venus-Mercury-Mars trio harmonize with the Moon-Pluto conjunction in capable Capricorn.

The next day, when the Sun leaves earth-bound Taurus and takes to the Gemini airwaves, energy shifts from down-to-earth practical to light and airy. This is the time to stretch your social and intellectual muscles. Gemini is a dual sign, and the Sun in Gemini encourages quick moves from place to place while multi-tasking along the way. Because flexibility is the name of the Gemini game, if you meet an obstacle, the best way out is to go around it. This is also the month to pump up your social life with your personal charm and your communication skills. Siblings may also loom large on the horizon. The downside of Gemini's energy is a lack of focus and a tendency toward superficiality.

May 23–29

This is a week that contains an abundance of exciting and positive energy. The only wrench in the works is on Tuesday when the Pisces Moon gets into a scrap with the Gemini Sun. This confrontation between water (Pisces) and air (Gemini) could cause emotions to get in the way of reason. Later on that old communication expert, the Gemini Sun, gets some help from unconventional Uranus. If you use this interaction wisely, it can help you to solve a challenge in a new and different way. But this same Sun/Uranus sextile should also be handled with care, because the flip side is that things could get out of control. As the Sun and Uranus part company on Friday, the Aries Moon gets in the act and bonds with Uranus. One result of this dynamic Moon-Uranus bond is that a new and unusual (Uranus) woman (Moon) enters your life. A less pleasant scenario is that you could be riding on an emotional roller coaster. Two days later the Moon moves into Taurus and makes a harmonious aspect with Pluto. This means that Sunday could be a great day for investing your energy in activities that have a long-term yield, like planting a garden or planning your retirement.

May 30–June 5

This week marks the beginning of eclipse season. There are two eclipses in June and one in July, but neither will be visible in the

United States. The signs directly affected by this eclipse season are Gemini and Sagittarius in June and Cancer and Capricorn in July. The kickoff is a solar eclipse that falls midweek on the Gemini New Moon. This emphasis in Gemini suggests new beginnings in your social and intellectual world. The most prominent aspect in the eclipse is the Gemini Sun-Moon conjunction in exact harmony with Saturn in Libra. Because both Gemini and Libra are air signs, this is an indication that emotional displays are a big no-no and that using a light and charming touch will get you what you want. Because Saturn adds structure and backbone to this mix of ideas and social gatherings, this eclipse signals the perfect moment for any kind of conference and mediation. There will be a change in the air on Friday when Neptune goes retrograde for the next six months. This movement is a flashing light that says it's time to redirect your focus to the spiritual. In a negative sense this retrograde could be a low-energy point when addictive behaviors resurface, but there is a positive side; it can be a time of heightened sensitivity in areas like the arts and spirituality. On Saturday Jupiter shifts energies again as it makes its third sign change of the year by moving from Aries to productive Taurus where it will remain for the rest of the year. This shift could have a stabilizing effect on the worldwide financial situation.

June 6–12

If you have been waiting for the right time to initiate an important conversation, Tuesday is the right day. That's when a harmonious aspect between Mercury, comfortable in its favorite sign of Gemini, and Saturn takes place. This pattern suggests that now is the time to put serious communications back on the front burner. Since both planets are in mental air signs, these communications will most likely include stimulating meetings and conversations with mentors, friends, and colleagues. Altogether, Tuesday is a perfect day to plan an event, start negotiations, win a court battle, or simply sell an idea. On Thursday Venus exits dependable Taurus and enters changeable Gemini. Because the nature of Gemini is airy, this sign change suggests that Venus-ruled areas, like love and money, have become less stable. However, if you are considering diversifying your assets in either your love life or your portfolio, the next month, while Venus is in Gemini, is a prime time to do it. On Sunday, Saturn resumes its forward motion in Libra; it's a change of direction that will make it easier for you to access the Saturn-ruled virtues of time management, patience, and perseverance. You will also be able to set boundaries and make commitments. Libra's areas of influence include one-to-one relationships, business partnerships, and courts of law.

June 13–19

The highlights this week are the lunar eclipse on Wednesday at the Full Moon and Mercury's sign change. This total lunar eclipse, which will not be visible in the United States, falls in Sagittarius, putting the spotlight on adventurous activities that involve the great outdoors and rigorous physical activities, travel, religion, and higher education. Eclipse days are times of intense energy when it is best not to schedule an important event. Because this eclipse occurs in Gemini (Sun) and Sagittarius (Moon), you might be tempted to risk playing out your dreams or living your higher purpose. You could run into problems on Wednesday if you choose excitement and opt out of your responsibilities, however. On Thursday when Mercury leaves Leo and moves into Cancer, your mental energy switches from the dramatic to the emotional. For the next three weeks, while Mercury is in sensitive Cancer, communications will be feeling-based. During this time the best way to get your message across is by using body language or another nonverbal type of communication. After Mercury makes this sign change, it moves swiftly into harmony with watery Neptune. On the plus side, this relationship sets the scene for a day of deep compassion. On the negative side, it could be a time of escapism or denial. On Sunday busy Mercury gets involved in a showdown with Pluto and that's when verbal stingers can come out, so be on your guard. Sunday is also the day the Moon moves into

Aquarius, where it is in perfect agreement with Saturn. Since Saturn corresponds to the ideal father, it's appropriate that Sunday is also Father's Day.

June 20–26

The week starts off with a sign change that promises an energy boost. On Tuesday Mars moves out of Taurus into flexible Gemini. Mars traveling through Gemini marks a period when a lower-than-usual tolerance for boredom goes hand in hand with a heightened desire for variety and change. These impulses combine to make the next six weeks ideal for an easy shift of your mental or social gears. Communication and social skills are ramped up with a focus on mental flirting rather than on getting down to business. Keeping it light and airy is the name of the game with Mars. Put a red circle around Tuesday on your calendar because that's when the second seasonal change of the year arrives. When the Sun moves into Cancer on Tuesday, summer arrives in the Northern Hemisphere; it is the longest day of the year. This event is also called the Summer Solstice because it is one of the two days a year when the Sun appears to stand still. The themes for the next four weeks are women, children, and families, as well as the housing market.

June 27–July 3

The week that leads up to Independence Day is fraught with tensions and conflicts that could cause fireworks before the national day of celebration begins. The first indication occurs on Friday with a solar eclipse at the Cancer New Moon. This eclipse is involved in one of the most difficult celestial patterns—a grand cross. Variations on this cross will be repeated periodically until the end of the year. The intense energy that is present at an eclipse indicates that Friday is not a favorable time to schedule an important event. The planets involved in this grand cross (Saturn/Uranus/Pluto) mark a time of unexpected transformations and upheavals. Because the New Moon in Cancer and the solar eclipse are part of the pattern, the areas that are spotlighted are women, children, and the housing market. On Saturday Mercury exchanges watery Cancer for fiery Leo. This points out that communications of all kinds will be heating up over the next three weeks. Although Mercury in Leo means that communications will be passionate and have a certain style, this placement can be tricky. There is a tendency for people to be know-it-alls, because the mental powers are closely tied to the ego. Taken together, these patterns all suggest that this is a week when it is wise to stay calm, cool, and collected in the face of any challenges that come your way.

July 4–10

On Monday Venus crosses into the patriotic sign of Cancer to mark Independence Day. Because Cancer is the sign of the Motherland, the fireworks display this year could be particularly emotional. Last month, when Venus was crossing through Gemini, love and money were expressed through words, but while Venus is in Cancer, your decisions in these areas will be based, for better or worse, on feelings. Saturday is important because that's the day Uranus turns retrograde. Uranus will appear to be moving in reverse for the next five months, which offers a unique opportunity to rehash any attempts to separate or break away from a relationship, a job, or any confining situation. If you take this time to step back and look at things from a different perspective, you might decide to take a different approach, to reconsider your decisions, or to let something go and pursue other options.

July 11–17

The forecast for this week is partly cloudy with a chance of clearing at the end of the week. The first storm front comes in on Wednesday. That's when the emotional Venus in Cancer (feminine/mother/lover) gets into a difficult situation with Saturn in Aries (masculine/father/warrior). The end result of this pattern can be the uncomfortable experience of feeling insecure or unworthy. The most positive way to circumvent this pattern is to temper the high expectations of Saturn with the more nurturing and loving aspects of Venus.

On Thursday and Friday the mood starts to brighten up when the Capricorn Full Moon's light reveals that the way to achieve success is by shining the spotlight on work, duty, and responsibility. As a Saturn-ruled sign, Capricorn knows that the key to achieving your dreams is a combination of ambition and hard work. If you are willing to put your nose to the grindstone, this Full Moon can be the time you can reach the top of your personal mountain.

July 18–24

The Moon bids farewell to an easy trine with the Cancer Sun Wednesday morning in preparation for a midday sign change that has the Moon slipping out of watery Pisces for a warmup in fieryAries. The Aries Moon forms an alliance with Uranus later in the evening, and the Moon-Uranus team use this opportunity to send Pluto an "out of the blue" reminder to release old patterns of thinking and move on. Although Aries is a sign that loves to start the ball rolling, this message has everyone returning to their own corner for a period of regrouping. The forecast starts to clear on Friday when the Moon settles comfortably into Taurus and the Sun leaves emotion-driven Cancer for its home ground of Leo. Because of Leo's need to be noticed, the focus for the next four weeks is on personal forms of creativity and style. If you decide to take a risk during this time, the stabilizing energy of Leo offers you the courage to do it. Besides personal and artistic creativity, children and any kind of activity that moves your fun meter to high will provide you with opportunities to get involved. The dark side of this sunny period is a tendency to be selfish and self-absorbed.

July 25–31

You can expect things to be lively this week with two sign changes and a New Moon. If you "like it hot" you will be happy to hear that Venus leaves emotional Cancer on Thursday to take a tour in fiery Leo. With Venus in Leo over the next four weeks, love is in the atmosphere and it is filled with warmth, charm, and playfulness. As soon as Venus hits Leo, it immediately makes a positive connection to Uranus that suggests passions and excitement will sizzle for several days. This aspect also contains a warning, because while fire signs generate a lot of heat, they don't offer a lot of staying power. The end result is that any fascination could fizzle out as fast as it began. Later that same day Mercury shifts out of Leo and into Virgo. This is a signal that while communications may not be as passionate, they will be more grounded. When Mercury has a showdown with dreamy Neptune, your mental focus might be compromised because that aspect tends to strengthen your right-brain intuitive abilities while weakening your logical left-brain functions. The Sun and Moon meet in Leo on Saturday to form this month's New Moon. With both lights concentrated in generous, romantic, and affectionate Leo, this can be a powerful time if you listen to your heart and act accordingly. The Leo New Moon also offers the perfect time to start creative projects in all areas of your life.

August 1–7

The word on the street this week is that it's time to shift gears. The first change is on Tuesday when Mercury shifts into reverse. While Mercury retrogrades are often hyped as annoying times of communication mix-ups and technological mishaps, they also have a good side—a chance to take a time-out. Retrograde periods coincide with introspective and reflective periods in which you take time to go back over your life with a fine-tooth comb and make adjustments. The next three weeks are fantastic for doing anything that starts with the prefix "re." This includes refinance, refine, redecorate, and relax. On Wednesday Mars shifts from rational Gemini into sensitive Cancer for the next six weeks. Since Mars rules assertive action, this is a potentially difficult time in which it seems hard to light your "fire." Fears and feelings are to blame, because there is a need to get emotionally fired-up before you can act, and you would rather play defense than offense now. When Mars is in Cancer, assertiveness with regard to women's issues, home, and family becomes a strong focus. The final shift is on Thursday when retrograde Neptune ends its four-month exploration of Pisces for one last meeting in Aquarius. Neptune will reenter Pisces in 2012 and stay there for the next fourteen years. Until that happens, Neptune in Aquarius offers one last chance to consider the impact that the Neptunian world of virtual reality and global networking has played in your life since 1998 when Neptune first entered Aquarius. The deeper consequences of this enormous shift may not be fully understood for years.

August 8–14

On Monday retrograde Mercury backs out of Virgo to make its second visit to Leo. The good news is that this reversal into Leo gives you a second chance to make good on something that didn't go your way last month during Mercury's first visit. If a house bid was rejected, you were turned down for a car loan, or you had a job interview that didn't go well in July, Mercury retrograde on a repeat visit could be a double negative that makes a positive. Get ready because the boom is about to drop on Wednesday with a crucial showdown and a double confrontation. The action starts with Mars in a standoff with the Moon-Pluto duo in Capricorn, and then Uranus in Aries strikes the match by getting in the middle. This configuration spells conflict and signals a need for a different kind of action. Whether this pattern affects you personally or just by proxy, Wednesday is certain to be a bear of a day. Thankfully, the Moon moves so quickly that it untangles itself from the mix by Saturday. That's when the energy shifts to the Aquarius Full Moon. The theme for this month's Full Moon is sudden changes or reversals that involve friends, groups and large corporations. These include attempts to break free from the status quo, as well as surprises and unexpected breakthroughs. Medicine, science, and new technologies also move into the spotlight. Because Aquarius prefers things to be cut and dried, this is a difficult time to try and hold an emotional pow-wow. Under this freedom-loving Aquarian Full Moon there is also a strong impulse to avoid drama while looking for the nearest exit.

August 15–21

Your heart might not be able to hold all the joy that Tuesday has in store. That's when the Sun, in all its Leo glory, bonds with both Mercury (communications) and Venus (love). This is the kind of pattern that can make you feel so special you might really believe you were Cleopatra or Napoleon in a past life! It's a great day for a celebration because it feels like you love everyone and everyone loves you. Saturday could also be a special day in a different way as love-driven Venus makes one last contact with magical, mysterious Neptune before it leaves Leo. Even though the two planets are on opposite sides of the zodiac this is an aspect that can still make your heart skip a beat. The downside to this picture is that there is always the danger of seeing life through rose-colored glasses when Neptune is involved. If you want to revel in fantasy, do it this Saturday, and enjoy yourself because your return trip to Earth is scheduled for Sunday. That's the day Venus floats out of the Neptunian fog and makes a hard landing in earthy Virgo; it's a sign change that's guaranteed to bring you to your senses. Over the next month that Venus spends in Virgo, you can be sure that love, finances, work, and health will be dissected, measured, and weighed. There is a more-than-likely chance that something won't be perfect, so steps must be taken to correct the problem. My favorite personification of a positive Venus in Virgo is when the character of Mary Poppins measures her waist and judges the result as "practically perfect."

August 22–28

You may feel as though life is a little foggy, because on Monday the Leo Sun moves in position opposite dreamy Neptune. This Sun/Neptune face-off could be a day when you find it is easy to space out and hard to focus on the realities of life. By Friday things should come into better focus. The Sun follows Venus into Virgo on Tuesday, which means that during the next four weeks, your interests will shift from celebrations to health, work, and service. The Sun in Virgo also directs your energies toward analyzing how to make your life better in these areas. Mercury-ruled communications, travel, and technologies will improve on Friday when Mercury turns direct. You can expect these Mercury-ruled areas of life to gradually return to normal. Sunday marks the most productive day of the week when both the Sun and Moon get together at the Virgo New Moon. This practical and grounded New Moon makes a perfect trine with Pluto in industrious Capricorn, which lets you know that you've got the right stuff to start something new. Because Virgo rules over the urge for improvement, this is also a good month to take a how-to class to fine-tune your technique.

August 29–September 4

What is luck? Does it just happen or do you have to make it happen? These are important questions to ask yourself now because Jupiter, the planet of luck, is the headliner this week. Monday starts off with a win-win situation between Jupiter and Venus that points the good-luck needle to the top of the dial and promises good fortune and abundance in love and money. But before you head off to call your partner, your bookie, or your broker, there's something else you should know. On Tuesday that same lucky planet, Jupiter, shifts into reverse and stays there until Christmas Day. Though Jupiter is retrograde, it does not mean you will be unlucky, because Jupiter is always a benefic energy. But a Jupiter retrograde period can be a good time for rethinking your beliefs—the big ones that have to do with the meaning of life, the universe, and everything in it. Pay special attention to your dreams because they can be especially vivid or prophetic during a Jupiter retrograde. At the beginning of the weekend Jupiter's retrograde motion sets off a harmonious trine to the Sun. With both the Sun and Jupiter in earth signs, this is an excellent time to make a donation or to participate in a fundraiser. Be sure to answer the door if opportunity knocks. Any offers you get now are the result of seeds you planted over the last nine months while Jupiter was moving forward.

September 5–11

The Moon moves into earthy Capricorn at the beginning of the week. On Tuesday, the Capricorn Moon squares off against Uranus before bonding with Pluto. This could be an indication of a storm brewing on the financial horizon. If you keep your head and stay grounded, this could still be your lucky day, though, because later in the day the Moon also moves into a harmonious trine to lucky Jupiter. There's a possibility that some type of communication will roll back late Thursday or Friday. That's when Mercury reenters Virgo for its second tour during the next two weeks. Mercury's second visit to Virgo indicates that there's a chance that any decisions that occurred during its last visit (July 29 to August 8) might be reversed. Because Mercury and Virgo are like two peas in a mental pod, the tendency toward analysis and detailed communications will be at maximum warp for the next two weeks. After Mercury reenters Virgo, its first stop is a harmonious earth trine with Pluto that lasts until Sunday. Pluto's ability to play detective combined with Mercury's mental acumen makes this a great week to search for buried treasure.

September 12–18

There are a couple of planetary events this week that will make you sit up and take notice. The first event occurs on Monday when the Moon becomes full in the mysterious waters of the Pisces. You can use its light to look deep into your inner core and find out just who is really there. Like the two Pisces fish swimming in opposite directions, the heightened sensitivity afforded by the Pisces Full Moon offers two different options. The first option is to pursue romance, divinely inspired creations, or devotional activities. The alternative is to lose yourself through denial, fantasy, or addictions. Even though Venus is in its favorite sign of Libra, relationships could be a source of trouble when Venus moves into a showdown with Uranus on Wednesday. Although breaking up might be hard to do, there couldn't be a better day than this to do it! On the other hand, if days of the week came with labels, the one for Friday would be: Handle With Care. This is when powerful Pluto finishes its retrograde period and slowly begins to move forward; it's a movement that will gradually unblock and release all the negative energy you've held in check since last April. While this could manifest as a completely positive outpouring of creativity, it could also it be a potential time bomb. If all goes well, you can breathe a sigh of relief on Sunday. That's when Mars exits feminine Cancer and moves into Leo where its masculinity becomes a plus instead of a minus. Mars in Leo is a power combo that will inspire confidence and creativity and encourage you to be the leader for the next eight weeks.

September 19–25

The Sun is the most important marker we have of time cycles on Earth. Sunrise and sunset mark day and night, and the Sun's movements north and south of the equator mark the change of seasons. Friday is a day to circle in red because that's the day the Sun enters the first degree of Libra, which marks the official end of summer and beginning of fall. Because today is one of only two days of the year when day and night are equal, it is also called the Fall Equinox. You can use this special day of balance between light and dark to take personal stock of the balance, or lack of, in your own life. Take time out today to recalibrate your internal meter so you can be in balance. Your ability to balance may be challenged on Sunday when the Sun moves opposite Uranus, and you may find that you need to get some space. On the same day Mercury leaves Virgo behind and moves into Libra. For the next three weeks with Mercury in rational Libra, communications will be weighed and measured with equal consideration for the issues on both sides, making it an excellent time for signing contracts, resolving relationship problems and legal disputes.

September 26–October 2

Communications and cooperation are spotlighted this week with the formation of a planetary trio—Mercury, Sun, and Moon—in Libra. Mercury has a showdown with Uranus on Tuesday, which makes it a good time for intuitive ideas, and balance through cooperation becomes easy when the Moon joins the Sun in Libra at the New Moon. On Wednesday the Sun gets a minor boost from Mercury that puts the focus on relationships, contracts, and legal agreements. Then on Friday, the Sun and Mars form a friendly relationship in spite of Mars putting out so much testosterone. Although this Libra New Moon is one where you might find that the scales are harder than usual to keep in balance because there is a T-square between Uranus, the Sun-Moon conjuction, and Pluto. Although the challenges from Uranus (new world order) and Pluto (crisis) indicate complications, if you keep your focus on reason and a sense of fair play, this could be the beginning of something big. In the relationship department, fun and romance take a back seat on Thursday when Venus bonds with heavy-duty Saturn. With this Venus-Saturn aspect, it's a time when "love hurts." It may be best to keep your focus strictly on business, at least for the present.

October 3–9

Save Thursday for something serious because that's when Mercury and Saturn join together in rational Libra. While Mercury-Saturn is a combination that does not sugarcoat reality, if you use your head and steer clear of emotions, you'll be able to work through anything. Venus, the ruler of what you love and value, exits Libra and enters Scorpio on Saturday. Even though both Venus and Scorpio are feminine energies, Venus is not at home in Scorpio's emotional energy. For while Venus is dedicated to making nice, Scorpio is a type of energy that enjoys getting down and dirty. Also, if you get your feelings hurt when Venus is in Scorpio, the Scorpio side wants to attack and punish and the Venus side hopes that by being really quiet and sweet everything will be okay. The result is that although

Scorpio has a reputation for being the sexiest sign of the zodiac, the fact is that when Venus is in Scorpio, you are often so upset that sex may be far from your mind. Don't be surprised if your feelings are on an emotional roller-coaster ride for the next month.

October 10–16

The Aries Full Moon on Tuesday marks the time of the year to bring projects or relationships to a natural conclusion. This doesn't mean that they're over for good, but rather that one cycle has ended so that the next can begin. Since this Aries Full Moon is also bonded to Uranus as well as challenged by Pluto, it's best to expect the unexpected. On Thursday Mercury exits Libra and joins Venus in Scorpio for the next three weeks. Although this means you will be more sensitive to implied criticism and slights than usual, it is also good to know that anything out of your mouth will be a "stinger." It's "all rise" on Thursday because here comes the judge in the form of the Sun and Saturn bonded in Libra. The rational objectivity of Libra makes this alignment a perfect time for arbitrations and almost always guarantees a successful resolution.

October 17–23

The Sun and Neptune are in perfect harmony in air signs on Friday. Like the wind, this combination does not recognize boundaries, and it marks a time that is definitely not reality-based. Depending on your inclination, you may feel spacey, spiritual, or shiftless. In any event, Friday will be a hard day to get things done. On Sunday the Sun marks another shift as it moves out of Libra into Scorpio. Scorpio is that time of year that tells us winter is on the way. It is a time to focus on positive ways to release any negative energy you have held on to or repressed over the last year. The most positive form of release is forgiveness, which is the gift of Scorpio. During the month that the Sun spends in Scorpio, the natural focus is on death and rebirth. This concept is symbolized by the Phoenix, the mythical bird that was reborn from the ashes of its destruction. The next four weeks offers a chance to pull inward and reflect on "the ashes" in your life. This reflection will free you to move into your own personal resurrection.

October 24–30

Be careful that you don't knock yourself out by trying to do too much during the early part of this week. On Monday the cardinal signs are active again and even though you may be able to see the right solution to the problems that come your way, suggesting a solution can result in trouble. This is because the Moon in rational Libra is involved again in a face-off with Uranus (reasoning with a rebel) and trying to give Pluto (power struggles between leadership and management) a cold shoulder. On Wednesday the Sun and Moon come together in Scorpio at the New Moon. Every New Moon marks the best time of the month to start something new, and the keyword for the Scorpio New Moon is "release." The Scorpio New Moon is one of the two most transformational Moons of the year (the other is the Scorpio Full Moon in spring). You can begin by making it your intention to release any negativity. Then let go of your personal garbage. Follow up your intention by physically getting rid of something. By following through on this intention, you will be able to free up space for new people and things to enter your life. On Friday the life-giving Sun gets a nod from powerful Pluto, which makes this a day to lend a helping hand to someone through social activism.

October 31–November 6

This year Halloween falls on Monday and it looks like it will be a very mellow night with more emphasis on treats than tricks. This treat comes from the Capricorn Moon harmonious meeting with the spooky Scorpio Sun—it is a sure sign that even the scariest creatures will be enveloped in a safety net. On that same day Venus and Mercury join forces to celebrate their last days in Scorpio. Because the scorpion has a stinger it does not hesitate to use when it feels threatened, it's best to be on your guard with any communication because you may get one that is nasty-nice. Besides the usual chit-chat, be on the lookout for incoming texts, e-mails, tweets, blogs, and voice mails that might contain hidden negativity. This energy does a total turnaround on Wednesday when Venus and Mercury team up and leave Scorpio for Sagittarius, where nothing is hidden. Because Sagittarius is honest to the point of bluntness, the only danger for the next four weeks is that if you ask a question, you will get more than you bargained for. Venus and Mercury joined in Sagittarius suggest that you are up for an adventure whether you are making love or making a judgment call. But be careful you don't get burned. Because this fire sign has a tendency to be overly optimistic and naïve. You might forget that every action also has a consequence. Clock time changes from Daylight Saving to Standard Time on Sunday at 2 am local time, so remember to turn your clocks back (spring ahead, fall back) one hour.

November 7–13

The blinders come off when Neptune ends its five-month retrograde and starts to move forward on Wednesday; it marks a major shift in how you have been seeing, or not seeing, the world. Neptune's forward movement tells you that it's time to recognize any cover-ups or negative codependencies that have affected you since last June, when Neptune turned retrograde. The most positive effect of this planetary shift is that it can bring greater clarity into your life that will recharge your spiritual and artistic batteries. The next day is the high point of the month as the Sun and Moon align on opposite sides of the Earth to create the Taurus Full Moon. The Taurus Full Moon offers an opportunity to bring any matters that have to do with what you value, from your garden to your bankbook, to a successful conclusion. The Sun in Scorpio and Moon in Taurus make this a time that is both practical and emotional; it's also one of the most creative Full Moons of the year. The fixed nature of both signs ensures that whatever is set at this Full Moon will have a longlasting effect. On Thursday Mars leaves the drama of Leo behind when it moves into practical Virgo. Since Mars will be in Virgo until the end of the year, this is a natural time for your assertive energies to be channeled into making adjustments in existing systems, fixing technical glitches, and reaching out to help others. The downside is that it demands perfection and has a tendency to be overly critical and spin out on details. If you can keep the big picture in mind, this is a time when you can get a lot done.

November 14–20

The week begins with another battle in the ongoing Uranus/Pluto saga that started last April. Things start to heat up on Monday when the Moon in Cancer gets in the middle. The good news is that with all three planets in signs that encourage you to take charge, you have everything you need to come up with the answers to whatever problems you face. Wednesday will be a productive day because that's the day Mars and Jupiter are humming the same tune in earth signs. Given any kind of project, whether it is creating a system, a company, a relationship, or a building, you can be sure the job will get done when a couple of planets are in earth signs. If you're looking for a day when you can light a mental or physical fire under someone, then Thursday is your day. The charisma of the Leo Moon in perfect sync with both Mercury and Venus is the only match you'll need. This magic lasts until Sunday when the Moon shifts into Virgo and then bumps up against Mercury and Venus. This meeting tells you to be on the lookout for irritability and missed cues. Everything will work out fine.

November 21–27

This week promises to be a busy one because it includes a sign change, a direction change, the beginning of the second eclipse season, and Thanksgiving Day. On Tuesday the Sun leads off by exiting the emotional depths of Scorpio to enter the fiery and adventurous energy field of Sagittarius for the next month. Get ready to rock and roll because this is the beginning of a month of exciting adventures. Whether you're an armchair traveler or you take to the skies, now is the time to think big. On Wednesday Mercury changes direction and starts its three-week retrograde period. This reversal means that Mercury will finish out the year in Sagittarius, which sends up a big red flag. Because Mercury in Sagittarius has a tendency to exaggerate and to be too optimistic, there is a chance that during this time you will make a bad judgment call. This placement could also cause mix-ups and delays in travel around the holiday. On Friday, there will be a New Moon and a partial solar eclipse. Because this New Moon solar eclipse occurs with four planets in Sagittarius, it looks like Thanksgiving could be a super-charged day when too much might not be enough. If you are discriminating, though, and keep on an even keel, you will sail safely through this week's challenges.

November 28–December 4

If you are in the mood to do your financials, Thursday is the day to follow the money. That's when Venus bonds with Pluto in fiscally responsible Capricorn. Because Pluto is linked to digging around in dark places, this day can be a gift if you want to research an unauthorized purchase or uncover a mistake in your checkbook. Since Venus is also linked to relationship issues, this proximity to the god of the Underworld can be a little scary. If you have something to hide regarding your relationship, you better make sure it's well out of sight. It's also football season and if you're the betting type, Sunday is not the day to try to beat the odds. The reason is that Mercury, the planet that helps you analyze the odds, is in trouble in three different ways. The first problem is that Mercury does not do well in Sagittarius because Sagittarius tends to be overly optimistic and always see the glass as half full. When Mercury is in this sign, there is a big tendency to ignore the facts and go with the possibilities. The second reason is that Mercury is retrograde, which makes this a better time to re-do or to go back and read the fine print, but it is not a good time to take a risk. The last reason is that Mercury is in a position that is so close to the Sun that the ability to send and receive messages has gone up in smoke. Despite all this, with both the Sun and Mercury in happy-go-lucky Sagittarius, even if you take a chance and lose, you'll probably still be a happy camper.

December 5–11

Monday is an excellent day if you feel like making love or making money. That's the day when Venus and Mars have a love fest in earthy signs, which offers you a chance to get down with the physical world. Friday, when Uranus ends its six-month retrograde period and begins to look to its future in assertive Aries, is the time to move ahead with new inventions or revolutionary ideas that break with the past. The high point of the week occurs on Saturday with the Full Moon in Gemini that includes a total lunar eclipse. This eclipse is the only one that will be visible over the United States this year. The Sagittarius Sun and Gemini Moon focus the light of this Full Moon lunar eclipse on the way knowledge is most widely distributed in the modern world, which is through the media. Since the Full Moon signifies completion, the intense energy that surrounds this eclipse may be saying that social networking via technology has reached its tipping point. It is beyond the scope of this forecast to guess what the next generation of technology will be. Due to the intense alignment of the Sun, Moon, and earth during an eclipse, Saturday is not a favorable day to schedule an important event.

December 12–18

On Tuesday, Mercury puts away its bag of tricks for this year as its retrograde period comes to an end. This movement signals the end of glitches in communication, transportation, and technology and signals that things will gradually be returning to normal. However, there is still a warning in place. Even though Mercury is moving forward, it is still traveling through Sagittarius, which means that your judgment may be compromised. Although Sagittarius is the most optimistic sign of the zodiac, it is also the least discriminating. Remember that if something seems too good to be true, it usually is. Sunday brings one of the last difficult configurations of the year—the Libra Moon, which is involved in a showdown with Uranus, also gets into a conflict with Pluto. This pattern lets you know that if you try to settle a fight by getting someone to smoke the peace pipe, Sunday is not going to be your day.

December 19–25

On Tuesday, Venus leaves practical Capricorn for Aquarius, and conservative feelings about love and money give way to a need for greater independence and experimentation. Wednesday marks the first day of winter—the Winter Solstice. This event occurs when the Sun moves into the first degree of Capricorn. It is called the Winter Solstice because it is one of two days in every year when the Sun (sol) appears to standstill (stice). The Winter Solstice is good news if you are a night person, because it is the shortest day of the year. Enjoy the darkness because tomorrow the days start to get longer. The themes for the next month, when the Sun is traveling through Capricorn, are duty, responsibility, and setting long-term goals. On Thursday, a harmonious trine from Jupiter to the Sun is a blessing from the stars to Earth. The New Moon in Capricorn occurs on Christmas Eve. This earthy New Moon favors new beginnings for practical activities like business plans, investments, and careers. Capricorn will also turn your attention to people in authority, like fathers or bosses, and also toward security issues and making long-term commitments. On Christmas day Jupiter ends its four-month retrograde period and turns direct. This is a joyful sign that marks the return of the light, and also a return to hope and optimism about the future.

December 26–31

On Thursday the Sun in stately Capricorn makes use of its once-a-year meeting with Pluto to deliver the message that problems facing people around the world are reaching a breaking point. The Sun joined to Pluto in Capricorn is an indication that this is the time to lay the groundwork for permanent solutions rather than quick fixes. Capricorn also suggests that a practical approach and a sober attitude are the best means to find the way out. On Saturday the year ends on the same note as it began; this is a time of personal and global challenge. During the day the Aries Moon bonds with Uranus and confronts Pluto, and during the night of New Year's Eve, there is a confrontation between the Sun in Capricorn and the Moon in Aries. Although the two brightest lights in the sky are in conflict, it is comforting to know that the battle is being fought in upbeat signs (Aries and Capricorn) that encourage constructive solutions. This emphasis on positive change could be a key to the problems the world faces today. The Capricorn Sun is also a reminder to honor the past, while the Aries Moon offers the courage to face the future. In the words of T. S. Elliot, "The end is where we start from."

About the Astrologer

Pam Ciampi is a certified professional astrologer with over thirty years of experience. Pam holds a certified professional astrologer diploma from International Society for Astrological Research (ISAR) and has membership in the National Council for Geocosmic Research (NCGR) and the American Federation of Astrologers (AFA). Pam was president of the San Diego Astrological Society from 1998 to 2005, and is currently serving as the president of the San Diego chapter of NCGR. Besides her busy private practice, Pam also teaches ongoing intermediate astrology classes in the San Diego area. Pam can be reached at pciampi@sbcglobal.net. Her Web site is: www.pciampi-astrology.com.

Finding Opportunity Periods

by Jim Shawvan

There are times when the most useful things you can do are ordinary tasks such as laundry, cooking, listening to music, reading, learning, meditating, etc. There are other times when the universe opens the gates of opportunity. Meetings, decisions, or commitments during these "Opportunity Periods" can lead to new and positive developments in your life. Most people are unaware of these subtle changes in the energies, so they wind up doing laundry when they could be signing an important contract, or they go out to try to meet a new sweetheart when the energies for such a thing are totally blocked.

I developed the Opportunity Periods system over more than thirty years, as I tested first one hypothesis and then another in real life. In about 1998, when I studied classical astrology with Lee Lehman, the system got some added zing, including William Lilly's idea that the Moon when void-of-course in the signs of the Moon and Jupiter "performeth somewhat." For those who want to understand the details of the system, they are explained in outline form below. If you simply want to use the system, this calendar gives all the information you need (you don't need to learn the technicalities).

An Opportunity Period is a period in which the aspects of the transiting Moon to other transiting planets show no interference with the free flow of decision and action.

Opportunity Periods apply to everyone in the world all at once; although, if the astrological influences on your own chart are putting blocks in your path, you may not be able to use every Opportunity

Signs of the Moon and Jupiter

- Taurus: the Moon's exaltation
- Cancer: the Moon's domicile and Jupiter's exaltation
- Sagittarius: Jupiter's fiery domicile
- Pisces: Jupiter's watery domicile

Period to the fullest. Nevertheless, you are always better off taking important actions and decisions during an Opportunity Period.

Steps to Find Your Opportunity Periods

Under Sun's Beams

Step 1: Determine whether the Moon is or is not "under Sun's beams," i.e., less than 17 degrees from the Sun. If it is, go to Step 7. If not, continue to Step 2.

Moon Void-of-Course

Step 2: Determine when the Moon goes void-of-course (v/c). The Moon is said to be void-of-course from the time it makes the last Ptolemaic aspect—conjunction, sextile, square, trine, or opposition—in a sign until it enters the next sign.

In eight of the twelve signs of the zodiac, Moon-void periods are NOT Opportunity Periods. In the other four signs, however, they are! According to seventeenth-century astrologer William Lilly, the Moon in the signs of the Moon and Jupiter "performeth somewhat." Lee Lehman says that she has taken this to the bank many times—and so have I.

Stressful or Easy Aspect

Step 3: Determine whether the aspect on which the Moon goes void is a stressful or an easy aspect. Every square is stressful, and every trine and every sextile is easy. Conjunctions and oppositions require judgment according to the nature of the planet the Moon is aspecting, and according to your individual ability to cope with the energies of that planet. For example, the Moon applying to a conjunction of Jupiter, Venus, or Mercury is easy, whereas, for most purposes, the Moon applying to a conjunction of Saturn, Mars, Neptune, Pluto, or Uranus is stressful. However, if you are a person for whom Uranus or Pluto is a familiar and more or less comfortable energy, you may find that the period before the Moon's conjunction to that planet is an Opportunity Period for you. (Since this is true for relatively few people, such periods are not marked as Opportunity Periods in this calendar.)

Oppositions can work if the Moon is applying to an opposition of Jupiter, Venus, Mercury, or the Sun (just before the Full Moon). The Moon applying to conjunction with the Sun (New Moon) presents a whole set of issues on its own. See Step 7.

Easy Equals Opportunity

Step 4: If the aspect on which the Moon goes void is an easy aspect, there is an Opportunity Period before the void period. If the aspect on which the Moon goes void is a stressful aspect, there is no Opportunity Period preceding the void period in that sign. To determine the beginning of the Opportunity Period, find the last stressful aspect the Moon makes in the sign. The Opportunity Period runs from the last stressful aspect to the last aspect (assuming that the last aspect is an easy one). If the Moon makes no stressful aspects at all while in the sign, then the Opportunity Period begins as soon as the Moon enters the sign, and ends at the last aspect.

When Is an Aspect Over?

Step 5: When is an aspect over? There are three different answers to this question, and I recommend observation to decide this question. I also recommend caution.

- An aspect is over (in electional astrology) as soon as it is no longer exact. For example, if the Moon's last stressful aspect in a sign is a square to Saturn at 1:51 pm, the Opportunity Period (if there is one) would be considered to begin immediately. This is the way the Opportunity Periods are shown in this calendar.

- Lee Lehman says an aspect is effective (for electional purposes) until it is no longer partile. An aspect is said to be partile if the two planets are in the same degree numerically. For example, a planet at 0 Aries 00' 00" is in partile trine to a planet at 0 Leo 59' 59", but it is not in partile conjunction to another planet at 29 Pisces 59' 59", even though the orb of the conjunction is only one second of arc ($\frac{1}{3,600}$ of a degree.

- An aspect is effective until the Moon has separated from the exact aspect by a full degree, which takes about two hours. This is the most cautious viewpoint. If you have doubts about the wisdom of signing a major contract while the Moon is still within one degree of a nasty aspect, then for your own peace of mind you should give it two hours, to get the one-degree separating orb.

Translating Light and Translating Darkness

Step 6: One should avoid starting important matters when the Moon is translating light from a stressful aspect with a malefic planet to an ostensibly easy aspect with another malefic planet—or even a series of such aspects uninterrupted by any aspects to benefic planets. I refer to this as "translating darkness." Translation of light is a concept used primarily in horary astrology, and it is discussed in great detail in books and on Web sites on that subject. For example, the Moon's last difficult aspect is a square to Saturn, and there is an apparent Opportunity Period because the Moon's next aspect is a trine to Mars, on which the Moon goes void-of-course.

The problem is this: the Moon is translating light from one malefic to another, and this vitiates what would otherwise be an Opportunity Period. The same would be true if the sequence were, for example, Moon square Saturn, then Moon trine Mars, then Moon sextile Neptune—an unbroken series of malefics.

For the purpose of this system, we may regard all of the following planets as malefics: Mars, Saturn, Uranus, Neptune, and Pluto. I can almost hear the howls of protest from the folks who believe that there is no such thing as a malefic planet or a bad aspect. On the level of spiritual growth, that is doubtless true, but this calendar is meant to be used to make your everyday life easier. Anyone who urges others to suffer more than absolutely necessary in the name of spirituality is indulging in great spiritual arrogance themselves.

New Moon, Balsamic Phase, and Cazimi Notes

Step 7: Notes on the period around the New Moon: waxing, waning, Balsamic, under beams, combust, and Cazimi.

As it separates from conjunction with the Sun (New Moon) and moves towards opposition (Full Moon), the Moon is said to be waxing, or increasing in light. Traditionally, the period of the waxing Moon is considered favorable for electional purposes.

Then after the Full Moon, as the Moon applies to conjunction with the Sun, it is said to be waning, or decreasing in light. Traditionally, this is regarded as a poor choice for electional purposes, and the closer the Moon gets to the Sun, the worse it is said to be. In practice, I find that problems only seem to occur as the Moon gets very close to the Sun.

When the Moon is applying to conjunction with the Sun (New Moon) and is less than 45 degrees away from the Sun, the Moon is said to be in its Balsamic phase. This phase is associated with giving things up and is considered especially unfavorable for starting things you wish to increase.

Any planet within 17 degrees of the Sun is said to be under Sun's beams. Traditionally, this weakens the planet, particularly for electional and horary purposes.

Any planet within 8 degrees of the Sun is said to be combust. Traditionally, this weakens the planet even more, particularly in electional and horary work.

Any planet whose center is within 17 minutes of arc of the center of the Sun in celestial longitude is said to be Cazimi. Oddly, this is considered the highest form of accidental dignity. In other words, a planet is thought to be weak when under Sun's beams, weaker still when combust, but—surprisingly—very powerful and benefic when Cazimi!

The average speed of the Moon is such that it remains Cazimi for about an hour—that is, half an hour before and half an hour after the exact conjunction with the Sun (New Moon). Other things being equal, you can use the Cazimi Moon to start something if you really want it to succeed.

However, please do not attempt to use the Cazimi Moon at the time of a solar eclipse, nor if the Moon is moving from the Cazimi into a stressful aspect. Cazimi is powerful, but it cannot override the difficulties shown by a solar eclipse, nor those shown by, say, the Moon's application to a square of Saturn.

If you really need to start something around the time of the New Moon, and you cannot use the Cazimi (see above), it is a good idea to wait until the first Opportunity Period after the

Moon has begun waxing. Even if the Moon is still under Sun's beams at that time, it is better than starting the new project while the Moon is still waning. However, if you can reasonably do so, it is best to wait for the first Opportunity Period after the Moon is no longer under Sun's beams (i.e., after the Moon has separated from the Sun by at least 17 degrees). For the principles to use at that time, see Step 2.

About the Astrologer

Jim Shawvan developed the system of Opportunity Periods over a period of three decades, out of his interest in electional astrology—the art of picking times for important actions such as getting married, opening a business, or incorporating a company (or even matters of only medium importance). Jim began the study of astrology in 1969; he teaches classes in predictive astrology and has lectured numerous times to the San Diego Astrological Society and other astrological groups and conferences.

Jim's articles have appeared in the Mountain Astrologer and other publications, a number of which are linked at his Web site (www.jshawvan.homestead .com). He predicted the delay in the results of the U.S. presidential election of 2000; and in early 2001, he predicted that, in response to anti-American terrorism, the U.S. would be at war in Afghanistan in the first two years of George W. Bush's presidency.

Jim studied cultural anthropology and structural linguistics at Cornell University, and later became a computer programmer and systems analyst. From 1989 to 1997, he was the technical astrologer at Neil Michelsen's Astro Communications Services, handling the most difficult questions and orders. He holds the Certified Astrological Professional certificate issued by the International Society for Astrological Research (ISAR).

Jim offers consultations in the areas of electional, horary, karmic, natal, predictive, relationship, relocation, and travel astrology. Consultations are done by phone or in person, and are taped. The client receives both the cassette and the charts.

Contact Jim Shawvan and Right Place Consulting at jshawvan@yahoo .com or through his Web site: www.jshawvan.homestead.com.

Business Guide

Collections

Try to make collections on days when your Sun is well aspected. Avoid days when Mars or Saturn are aspected. If possible, the Moon should be in a cardinal sign: Aries, Cancer, Libra, or Capricorn. It is more difficult to collect when the Moon is in Taurus or Scorpio.

Employment, Promotion

Choose a day when your Sun is favorably aspected or the Moon is in your tenth house. Good aspects of Venus or Jupiter are beneficial.

Loans

Moon in the first and second quarters favors the lender; in the third and fourth it favors the borrower. Good aspects of Jupiter or Venus to the Moon are favorable to both, as is Moon in Leo, Sagittarius, Aquarius, or Pisces.

New Ventures

Things usually get off to a better start during the increase of the Moon. If there is impatience, anxiety, or deadlock, it can often be broken at the Full Moon. Agreements can be reached then.

Partnerships

Agreements and partnerships should be made on a day that is favorable to both parties. Mars, Neptune, Pluto, and Saturn should not be square or opposite the Moon. It is best to make an agreement or partnership when the Moon is in a mutable sign, especially Gemini or Virgo. The other signs are not favorable, with the possible exception of Leo or Capricorn. Begin partnerships when the Moon is increasing in light, as this is a favorable time for starting new ventures.

Public Relations

The Moon rules the public, so this must be well aspected, particularly by the Sun, Mercury, Uranus, or Neptune.

Selling

Selling is favored by good aspects of Venus, Jupiter, or Mercury to the Moon. Avoid aspects to Saturn. Try to get the planetary ruler of your product well aspected by Venus, Jupiter, or the Moon.

Signing Important Papers

Sign contracts or agreements when the Moon is increasing in a fruitful sign. Avoid days when Mars, Saturn, Neptune, or Pluto are afflicting the Moon. Don't sign anything if your Sun is badly afflicted.

Calendar Pages
How to Use Your Daily Planetary Guide

Both Eastern and Pacific times are given in the datebook. The Eastern times are listed in the left-hand column. The Pacific times are in the right-hand column in bold typeface. Note: Adjustments have been made for Daylight Saving Time. The void-of-course Moon is listed to the right of the daily aspect at the exact time that it occurs. It is indicated by "v/c." On days when it occurs for only one time zone and not the other, it is indicated next to the appropriate column and then repeated on the next day for the other time zone. The monthly ephemeris on pages 188–199 is shown for midnight, Greenwich Mean Time (GMT).

Symbol Key			
Planets	☉ Sun	♃	Jupiter
	☽ Moon	♄	Saturn
	☿ Mercury	♅	Uranus
	♀ Venus	♆	Neptune
	♂ Mars	♇	Pluto
Signs	♈ Aries	♎	Libra
	♉ Taurus	♏	Scorpio
	♊ Gemini	♐	Sagittarius
	♋ Cancer	♑	Capricorn
	♌ Leo	♒	Aquarius
	♍ Virgo	♓	Pisces
Aspects	♂ Conjunction (0°)	△	Trine (120°)
	✶ Sextile (60°)	⊼	Quincunx (150°)
	☐ Square (90°)	☍	Opposition (180°)
Motion	℞ Retrograde	D	Direct
Moon Phase	● New Moon	◑	First Quarter
	○ Full Moon	◐	Fourth Quarter

December 2010

Mercury Note: Mercury goes direct on December 29 or 30, depending on the time zone. However, Mercury remains in its Storm, moving less than 40 minutes of arc per day, until January 4.

27 Mon
2nd ♍
☽ 6 ♎ 19

☽ ♍ ☍ ♃ ♓		5:49 am	**2:49 am**	
☽ ♍ ⚻ ♆ ♒		6:54 am	**3:54 am**	
☽ ♍ ☍ ♅ ♓		7:21 am	**4:21 am**	v/c
☽ ♍ ⚻ ⚷ ♒		8:14 am	**5:14 am**	
☽ enters ♎		12:38 pm	**9:38 am**	
☽ ♎ ☐ ♇ ♑		9:25 pm	**6:25 pm**	
☽ ♎ ☐ ☉ ♑		11:18 pm	**8:18 pm**	

28 Tue
3rd ♍

OP: After Moon conjoins Saturn today until v/c Moon on Wednesday. Good work can be done now, but with Mars square Saturn it may feel like an uphill struggle. Remember to focus on follow-up and not on innovation while Mercury remains in its retrograde and then in its Storm.

☽ ♎ ☐ ♂ ♑		3:42 pm	**12:42 pm**
☽ ♎ ☌ ♄ ♎		4:40 pm	**1:40 pm**
☽ ♎ ✶ ☿ ♐		10:11 pm	**7:11 pm**

29 Wed
4th ♎

☽ ♎ ⚻ ♃ ♓		9:20 am	**6:20 am**	
☽ ♎ △ ♆ ♒		10:05 am	**7:05 am**	v/c
♂ ♑ ☐ ♄ ♎		10:29 am	**7:29 am**	
☽ ♎ ⚻ ♅ ♓		10:30 am	**7:30 am**	
☽ ♎ △ ⚷ ♒		11:31 am	**8:31 am**	
☽ enters ♏		3:49 pm	**12:49 pm**	
☽ ♏ ✶ ♇ ♑			**9:56 pm**	
☿ D in ♐			**11:21 pm**	

30 Thu
4th ♎

☽ ♏ ✶ ♇ ♑		12:56 am	
☿ D in ♐		2:21 am	
☽ ♏ ✶ ☉ ♑		6:51 am	**3:51 am**
☽ ♏ ✶ ♂ ♑		10:39 pm	**7:39 pm**

☽♏ ☌ ♀♏	8:11 am	**5:11 am**
☽♏ △ ♃♓	2:11 pm	**11:11 am**
☽♏ □ ♆♒	2:33 pm	**11:33 am**
☽♏ △ ♅♓	2:57 pm	**11:57 am** v/c
☽♏ □ ⚷♒	4:07 pm	**1:07 pm**
☽ enters ♐	8:21 pm	**5:21 pm**

Fri 31
4th ♏
New Year's Eve

☽♐ ⚹ ♄♎	11:21 pm

Sat 1
4th ♐
New Year's Day
Kwanzaa ends

☽♐ ⚹ ♄♎	2:21 am	
☽♐ ☌ ☿♐	9:02 am	**6:02 am**
☽♐ ⚹ ♆♒	8:45 pm	**5:45 pm**
☽♐ □ ♃♓	8:49 pm	**5:49 pm**
☽♐ □ ♅♓	9:08 pm	**6:08 pm** v/c
☽♐ ⚹ ⚷♒	10:28 pm	**7:28 pm**
☽ enters ♑		**11:39 pm**

Sun 2
4th ♐

OP: After Moon squares Uranus until Moon enters Capricorn. Sagittarius is one of four signs in which the v/c Moon is actually good news (see p. 70). However, there are three reasons to be cautious right now: Mercury is still slow, the Moon is Balsamic, and we are between eclipses. Use this period only for following up on plans begun before Mercury went retrograde on December 10.

Eastern Time plain / **Pacific Time bold**

DECEMBER 2010						
S	M	T	W	T	F	S
			1	2	3	4
5	6	7	8	9	10	11
12	13	14	15	16	17	18
19	20	21	22	23	24	25
26	27	28	29	30	31	

JANUARY 2011						
S	M	T	W	T	F	S
						1
2	3	4	5	6	7	8
9	10	11	12	13	14	15
16	17	18	19	20	21	22
23	24	25	26	27	28	29
30	31					

FEBRUARY						
S	M	T	W	T	F	S
		1	2	3	4	5
6	7	8	9	10	11	12
13	14	15	16	17	18	19
20	21	22	23	24	25	26
27	28					

January

Mercury Note: Mercury finally leaves its Storm on Tuesday. Now we can begin evaluating all the "bright ideas" that we got while Mercury was retrograde and while it was slow. It helps if you wrote each new idea down with the date and time when it occurred to you.

3 Mon 4th ♐	☽ enters ♑	2:39 am	
	☽♑ ☌ ♇♑	12:42 pm	**9:42 am**

4 Tue 4th ♑ ● 13 ♑ 39 Solar Eclipse (Partial)	♀♏ □ ♆♒	3:27 am	**12:27 am**
	☽♑ ☌ ☉♑	4:03 am	**1:03 am**
	♃♓ ☌ ♅♓	7:53 am	**4:53 am**
	♀♏ △ ♅♓	8:33 am	**5:33 am**
	♀♏ △ ♃♓	8:39 am	**5:39 am**
	☽♑ □ ♄♎	10:00 am	**7:00 am**
	☽♑ ☌ ♂♑	6:49 pm	**3:49 pm**

5 Wed 1st ♑ **OP: After Moon sextiles Uranus (see "Translating Darkness" on p. 73) until v/c Moon.** The Moon is just moving away from yesterday's eclipse and is still under Sun's beams, so use this period with caution.	♀♏ □ ⚷♒	4:07 am	**1:07 am**
	☽♑ ✶ ♅♓	5:30 am	**2:30 am**
	☽♑ ✶ ♃♓	5:42 am	**2:42 am**
	☽♑ ✶ ♀♏	7:15 am	**4:15 am** v/c
	☽ enters ♒	11:08 am	**8:08 am**

6 Thu 1st ♒	☽♒ △ ♄♎	7:59 pm	**4:59 pm**

♀ enters ♐   7:30 am **4:30 am**   **FRI 7**   1st ≈
☉♑□ ♄♎   9:00 am **6:00 am**
☽≈ ⚹ ☿♐   9:43 am **6:43 am**
☽≈ ☌ ♆≈   3:51 pm **12:51 pm** v/c
☽≈ ☌ ⚷≈   5:57 pm **2:57 pm**
☽ enters ♓   9:57 pm **6:57 pm**
☽♓ □ ♀♐   11:16 pm **8:16 pm**

☽♓ ⚹ ♇♑   9:09 am **6:09 am**   **SAT 8**   1st ♓

☽♓ ⚻ ♄♎   8:03 am **5:03 am**   **SUN 9**   1st ♓
☽♓ ⚹ ☉♑   12:20 pm **9:20 am**
☽♓ ⚹ ♂♑   **10:25 pm**

Eastern Time plain / **Pacific Time bold**

DECEMBER 2010								JANUARY 2011								FEBRUARY					
S	M	T	W	T	F	S		S	M	T	W	T	F	S		S	M	T	W	T	F	S
			1	2	3	4								1				1	2	3	4	5
5	6	7	8	9	10	11		2	3	4	5	6	7	8		6	7	8	9	10	11	12
12	13	14	15	16	17	18		9	10	11	12	13	14	15		13	14	15	16	17	18	19
19	20	21	22	23	24	25		16	17	18	19	20	21	22		20	21	22	23	24	25	26
26	27	28	29	30	31			23	24	25	26	27	28	29		27	28					
								30	31													

10 MON
1st ♓

OP: After Moon conjoins Uranus until Moon enters Aries. A very short OP before the Moon conjoins Jupiter—really too short to be usable—is followed by a slightly longer one during v/c Moon in Pisces, one of the four signs in which a void Moon is good news.

☽ ♓	✶	♂ ♑	1:25 am		
☽ ♓	□	☿ ♐	3:20 am	**12:20 am**	
☽ ♓	☌	♅ ♓	4:43 am	**1:43 am**	
☽ ♓	☌	♃ ♓	6:12 am	**3:12 am**	v/c
☽ enters ♈			10:24 am	**7:24 am**	
☿ ♐	✶	♆ ♒	3:03 pm	**12:03 pm**	
☽ ♈	△	♀ ♐	5:27 pm	**2:27 pm**	
☿ ♐	□	♅ ♓	7:13 pm	**4:13 pm**	
☽ ♈	□	♇ ♑	9:54 pm	**6:54 pm**	

11 TUE
1st ♈

☿ ♐	□	♃ ♓	3:37 pm	**12:37 pm**
☿ ♐	✶	⚷ ♒	5:08 pm	**2:08 pm**
☽ ♈	☍	♄ ♎	8:47 pm	**5:47 pm**

12 WED
1st ♈

◐ 21 ♈ 54

OP: After Moon squares Mars until v/c Moon. You can get a lot accomplished as the Moon approaches its trine to Mercury.

♂ ♑	✶	♅ ♓	5:30 am	**2:30 am**	
☽ ♈	□	☉ ♑	6:31 am	**3:31 am**	
☽ ♈	✶	♆ ♒	4:52 pm	**1:52 pm**	
☽ ♈	□	♂ ♑	6:00 pm	**3:00 pm**	
☽ ♈	✶	⚷ ♒	7:13 pm	**4:13 pm**	
☽ ♈	△	☿ ♐	9:47 pm	**6:47 pm**	v/c
☽ enters ♉			10:37 pm	**7:37 pm**	

13 THU
2nd ♉

☿ enters ♑			6:25 am	**3:25 am**
☽ ♉	△	♇ ♑	9:59 am	**6:59 am**
☽ ♉	⊼	♀ ♐	11:05 am	**8:05 am**
♂ ♑	✶	♃ ♓	7:35 pm	**4:35 pm**

☽ ♉ ⊼ ♄ ♎	7:58 am	**4:58 am**
☽ ♉ △ ☉ ♑	10:16 pm	**7:16 pm**

FRI 14
2nd ♉

☽ ♉ □ ♆ ♒	3:06 am	**12:06 am**
☽ ♉ ✶ ♅ ♓	3:25 am	**12:25 am**
☽ ♉ □ ⚷ ♒	5:26 am	**2:26 am**
☽ ♉ ✶ ♃ ♓	6:01 am	**3:01 am**
☽ ♉ △ ♂ ♑	7:47 am	**4:47 am** v/c
☽ enters ♊	8:23 am	**5:23 am**
☽ ♊ ⊼ ☿ ♑	1:33 pm	**10:33 am**
♂ enters ♒	5:41 pm	**2:41 pm**
☽ ♊ ⊼ ♇ ♑	7:15 pm	**4:15 pm**
☽ ♊ ☍ ♀ ♐		**10:08 pm**

SAT 15
2nd ♉

OP: After Moon sextiles Uranus (see "Translating Darkness" on p. 73) until Moon enters Gemini. Two short OP's back to back, the second being the v/c Moon in Taurus, one of four signs in which this is good news.

☽ ♊ ☍ ♀ ♐	1:08 am	
☽ ♊ △ ♄ ♎	3:46 pm	**12:46 pm**

SUN 16
2nd ♊

Eastern Time plain / **Pacific Time bold**

DECEMBER 2010

S	M	T	W	T	F	S
			1	2	3	4
5	6	7	8	9	10	11
12	13	14	15	16	17	18
19	20	21	22	23	24	25
26	27	28	29	30	31	

JANUARY 2011

S	M	T	W	T	F	S
						1
2	3	4	5	6	7	8
9	10	11	12	13	14	15
16	17	18	19	20	21	22
23	24	25	26	27	28	29
30	31					

FEBRUARY

S	M	T	W	T	F	S
		1	2	3	4	5
6	7	8	9	10	11	12
13	14	15	16	17	18	19
20	21	22	23	24	25	26
27	28					

17 MON
2nd ♊
BIRTHDAY OF MARTIN LUTHER KING, JR. (OBSERVED)

☽ ♊ ⚻ ☉ ♑	9:27 am	**6:27 am**
☽ ♊ △ ♆ ♒	9:41 am	**6:41 am**
☽ ♊ □ ♅ ♓	9:59 am	**6:59 am**
☽ ♊ △ ⚷ ♒	11:58 am	**8:58 am**
☽ ♊ □ ♃ ♓	12:57 pm	**9:57 am** v/c
☽ enters ♋	2:29 pm	**11:29 am**
☉ ♑ ✶ ♅ ♓	4:56 pm	**1:56 pm**
☽ ♋ ⚻ ♂ ♒	5:10 pm	**2:10 pm**
☽ ♋ ☍ ☿ ♑		**9:45 pm**
☽ ♋ ☍ ♇ ♑		**9:45 pm**
☿ ♑ ☌ ♇ ♑		**9:50 pm**

18 TUE
2nd ♋

☽ ♋ ☍ ☿ ♑	12:45 am	
☽ ♋ ☍ ♇ ♑	12:45 am	
☿ ♑ ☌ ♇ ♑	12:50 am	
☽ ♋ ⚻ ♀ ♐	10:29 am	**7:29 am**
☽ ♋ □ ♄ ♎	7:53 pm	**4:53 pm**

19 WED
2nd ♋
○ 6 ♎ 19
OP: After Moon trines Uranus (see "Translating Darkness" on p. 73) until Moon enters Leo. Cancer is another of the four signs in which the v/c Moon is good news.

☽ ♋ ⚻ ♆ ♒	12:50 pm	**9:50 am**
☽ ♋ △ ♅ ♓	1:08 pm	**10:08 am**
☽ ♋ ⚻ ⚷ ♒	3:06 pm	**12:06 pm**
☽ ♋ ☍ ☉ ♑	4:21 pm	**1:21 pm**
☽ ♋ △ ♃ ♓	4:26 pm	**1:26 pm** v/c
☽ enters ♌	5:16 pm	**2:16 pm**
☉ ♑ ✶ ♃ ♓	5:39 pm	**2:39 pm**
☽ ♌ ☍ ♂ ♒	10:42 pm	**7:42 pm**

20 THU
3rd ♌

☽ ♌ ⚻ ♇ ♑	3:09 am	**12:09 am**
☉ enters ♒	5:19 am	**2:19 am**
☽ ♌ ⚻ ☿ ♑	8:03 am	**5:03 am**
☽ ♌ △ ♀ ♐	4:17 pm	**1:17 pm**
☽ ♌ ✶ ♄ ♎	9:25 pm	**6:25 pm**

Fri 21
3rd ♌

☽♌ ☍ ♆≈	1:57 pm **10:57 am** v/c
☽♌ ⊼ ♅♓	2:15 pm **11:15 am**
☽♌ ☍ ♅≈	4:16 pm **1:16 pm**
☽♌ ⊼ ♃♓	5:57 pm **2:57 pm**
☽ enters ♍	6:10 pm **3:10 pm**
☽♍ ⊼ ☉≈	8:53 pm **5:53 pm**
☽♍ ⊼ ♂≈	**11:14 pm**

Sat 22
3rd ♍

☽♍ ⊼ ♂≈	2:14 am
☽♍ △ ♇♑	4:00 am **1:00 am**
♃ enters ♈	12:11 pm **9:11 am**
☽♍ △ ☿♑	1:43 pm **10:43 am**
☽♍ □ ♀♐	8:47 pm **5:47 pm**

Sun 23
3rd ♍

♀♐ ✳ ♄♎	2:19 pm **11:19 am**
☽♍ ⊼ ♆≈	2:49 pm **11:49 am**
☽♍ ☍ ♅♓	3:08 pm **12:08 pm** v/c
☽♍ ⊼ ♅≈	5:15 pm **2:15 pm**
☽ enters ♎	6:59 pm **3:59 pm**
☽♎ ☍ ♃♈	7:22 pm **4:22 pm**
☽♎ △ ☉≈	**10:25 pm**

Eastern Time plain / **Pacific Time bold**

DECEMBER 2010						
S	M	T	W	T	F	S
			1	2	3	4
5	6	7	8	9	10	11
12	13	14	15	16	17	18
19	20	21	22	23	24	25
26	27	28	29	30	31	

JANUARY 2011						
S	M	T	W	T	F	S
						1
2	3	4	5	6	7	8
9	10	11	12	13	14	15
16	17	18	19	20	21	22
23	24	25	26	27	28	29
30	31					

FEBRUARY						
S	M	T	W	T	F	S
		1	2	3	4	5
6	7	8	9	10	11	12
13	14	15	16	17	18	19
20	21	22	23	24	25	26
27	28					

JANUARY

Saturn Note: Saturn goes retrograde on Tuesday or Wednesday, depending on your time zone, and remains retrograde until mid-June.

24 MON
3rd ♎

OP: After Moon conjoins Saturn until v/c Moon. Good for intuition and artistic creativity.

☽♎ △ ☉♒	1:25 am	
☽♎ □ ♇♑	5:07 am	**2:07 am**
☽♎ △ ♂♒	5:59 am	**2:59 am**
☽♎ ☌ ♄♎	11:36 pm	**8:36 pm**
☽♎ ✶ ♀♐		**11:22 pm**

25 TUE

☽♎ ✶ ♀♐	2:22 am	
☽♎ △ ♆♒	5:04 pm	**2:04 pm** v/c
☽♎ ⚻ ♅♓	5:23 pm	**2:23 pm**
☽♎ △ ⚷♒	7:42 pm	**4:42 pm**
☽ enters ♏	9:15 pm	**6:15 pm**
☽♏ ⚻ ♃♈	10:20 pm	**7:20 pm**
♄ ℞ in ♎		**10:10 pm**

26 WED
3rd ♎
3rd ♏
◑ 6 ♏ 13

♄ ℞ in ♎	1:10 am	
☿♑ □ ♄♎	4:58 am	**1:58 am**
☽♏ ✶ ♇♑	7:57 am	**4:57 am**
☽♏ □ ☉♒	7:57 am	**4:57 am**
☽♏ □ ♂♒	11:48 am	**8:48 am**

27 THU
4th ♏

☽♏ ✶ ☿♑	5:50 am	**2:50 am**
☽♏ □ ♆♒	9:39 pm	**6:39 pm**
☽♏ △ ♅♓	10:01 pm	**7:01 pm** v/c
☽♏ □ ⚷♒		**9:32 pm**
☽ enters ♐		**10:55 pm**

Fri 28
4th ♏

☽♏ □ ♅ ≈	12:32 am	
☽ enters ♐	1:55 am	
☽♐ △ ♃ ♈	3:48 am	**12:48 am**
☽♐ ✶ ☉ ≈	5:35 pm	**2:35 pm**
☽♐ ✶ ♂ ≈	8:34 pm	**5:34 pm**

Sat 29
4th ♐

| ☽♐ ✶ ♄ ♎ | 9:17 am | **6:17 am** |
| ☽♐ ♂ ♀ ♐ | 10:18 pm | **7:18 pm** |

Sun 30
4th ♐

☽♐ ✶ ♆ ≈	4:46 am	**1:46 am**
☽♐ □ ♅ ♓	5:10 am	**2:10 am** v/c
☽♐ ✶ ♇ ≈	7:54 am	**4:54 am**
☽ enters ♑	9:04 am	**6:04 am**
☽♑ □ ♃ ♈	11:53 am	**8:53 am**
☽♑ ♂ ♇ ♑	9:02 pm	**6:02 pm**

Eastern Time plain / **Pacific Time bold**

DECEMBER 2010						
S	M	T	W	T	F	S
			1	2	3	4
5	6	7	8	9	10	11
12	13	14	15	16	17	18
19	20	21	22	23	24	25
26	27	28	29	30	31	

JANUARY 2011						
S	M	T	W	T	F	S
						1
2	3	4	5	6	7	8
9	10	11	12	13	14	15
16	17	18	19	20	21	22
23	24	25	26	27	28	29
30	31					

FEBRUARY						
S	M	T	W	T	F	S
		1	2	3	4	5
6	7	8	9	10	11	12
13	14	15	16	17	18	19
20	21	22	23	24	25	26
27	28					

31 Mon
4th ♑

OP: After Moon squares Saturn until v/c Moon. OK for follow-through, but with the Moon becoming Balsamic, avoid starting major projects now.

☽ ♑ □ ♄ ♎	5:40 pm	**2:40 pm**

1 Tue
4th ♑

☽ ♑ ☌ ☿ ♑	11:41 am	**8:41 am**
☽ ♑ ✶ ♅ ♓	2:32 pm	**11:32 am** v/c
☽ enters ♒	6:21 pm	**3:21 pm**
☽ ♒ ✶ ♃ ♈	10:12 pm	**7:12 pm**
♀ ♐ ✶ ♆ ♒		**11:35 pm**

2 Wed
4th ♒
● 13 ♒ 54
Chinese New Year (rabbit)
Groundhog Day

♀ ♐ ✶ ♆ ♒	2:35 am	
♀ ♐ □ ♅ ♓	7:47 am	**4:47 am**
☿ ♑ ✶ ♅ ♓	11:15 am	**8:15 am**
☽ ♒ ☌ ☉ ♒	9:31 pm	**6:31 pm**
☽ ♒ ☌ ♂ ♒	10:16 pm	**7:16 pm**

3 Thu
1st ♒

☽ ♒ △ ♄ ♎	3:57 am	**12:57 am**
☿ enters ♒	5:19 pm	**2:19 pm**
♀ ♐ ✶ ♅ ♒	6:02 pm	**3:02 pm**
♀ enters ♑		**9:58 pm**
☽ ♒ ☌ ♆ ♒		**10:11 pm** v/c

♀ enters ♑	12:58 am		
☽≈ ♂ ♆≈	1:11 am		v/c
☽≈ ♂ ⚷≈	4:48 am	**1:48 am**	
☽ enters ♓	5:24 am	**2:24 am**	
☽♓ ✶ ♀♑	5:52 am	**2:52 am**	
☉≈♂ ♂≈	11:40 am	**8:40 am**	
☽♓ ✶ ♇♑	6:24 pm	**3:24 pm**	

FRI 4
1st ≈

☿≈ ✶ ♃♈	10:30 am	**7:30 am**
☽♓ ⊼ ♄♎	3:44 pm	**12:44 pm**
☉≈△ ♄♎		**10:40 pm**

SAT 5
1st ♓

☉≈△ ♄♎	1:40 am	
♂≈ △ ♄♎	12:16 pm	**9:16 am**
☽♓ ♂ ♅♓	2:13 pm	**11:13 am** v/c
♀♑ □ ♃♈	2:39 pm	**11:39 am**
☽ enters ♈	5:45 pm	**2:45 pm**
☽♈ ♂ ♃♈	11:50 pm	**8:50 pm**
☽♈ □ ♀♑		**9:38 pm**

SUN 6
1st ♓

OP: After Moon conjoins Uranus until Moon enters Aries. Use this short v/c Moon period in Pisces for helping others, creativity, appreciation of the arts, or contemplation.

Eastern Time plain / **Pacific Time bold**

JANUARY 2011						
S	M	T	W	T	F	S
						1
2	3	4	5	6	7	8
9	10	11	12	13	14	15
16	17	18	19	20	21	22
23	24	25	26	27	28	29
30	31					

FEBRUARY						
S	M	T	W	T	F	S
		1	2	3	4	5
6	7	8	9	10	11	12
13	14	15	16	17	18	19
20	21	22	23	24	25	26
27	28					

MARCH						
S	M	T	W	T	F	S
		1	2	3	4	5
6	7	8	9	10	11	12
13	14	15	16	17	18	19
20	21	22	23	24	25	26
27	28	29	30	31		

7 MON
1st ♈

☽♈□♀♑	12:38 am	
☽♈⚹☿♒	4:52 am	**1:52 am**
☽♈□♇♑	7:05 am	**4:05 am**

8 TUE
1st ♈

OP: After Moon sextiles Mars until v/c Moon. An entire day with the energy of the Aries Moon at your back should help you to get a lot done.

☽♈☍♄♎	4:20 am	**1:20 am**
☽♈⚹♂♒	7:16 am	**4:16 am**
☽♈⚹☉♒	9:09 am	**6:09 am**
⚷ enters ♓	3:00 pm	**12:00 pm**
☽♈⚹♆♒		**11:31 pm** v/c

9 WED
1st ♈

☽♈⚹♆♒	2:31 am	v/c
☽ enters ♉	6:22 am	**3:22 am**
☽♉⚹⚷♓	6:28 am	**3:28 am**
☽♉△♀♑	7:32 pm	**4:32 pm**
☽♉△♇♑	7:40 pm	**4:40 pm**
♀♑☌♇♑	8:52 pm	**5:52 pm**
☽♉□☿♒		**11:40 pm**

10 THU
1st ♉
◐ 22 ♉ 13 (Pacific)

☽♉□☿♒	2:40 am	
☽♉⚻♄♎	4:09 pm	**1:09 pm**
☽♉□♂♒	11:13 pm	**8:13 pm**
☽♉□☉♒		**11:18 pm**

☽ ♉ □ ☉ ♒	2:18 am	
☽ ♉ □ ♆ ♒	1:50 pm **10:50 am**	
☽ ♉ ⚹ ♅ ♓	2:27 pm **11:27 am** v/c	
☽ enters ♊	5:20 pm **2:20 pm**	
☽ ♊ □ ⚷ ♓	5:45 pm **2:45 pm**	
☽ ♊ ⚹ ♃ ♈	**10:04 pm**	

FRI 11
1st ♉
◑ 22 ♉ 13 (Eastern)

OP: After Moon sextiles Uranus until Moon enters Gemini.
Short but usable.

☽ ♊ ⚹ ♃ ♈	1:04 am	
☽ ♊ ⚼ ♇ ♑	6:06 am **3:06 am**	
☽ ♊ ⚼ ♀ ♑	11:38 am **8:38 am**	
☽ ♊ △ ☿ ♒	9:08 pm **6:08 pm**	
☽ ♊ △ ♄ ♎	**10:10 pm**	

SAT 12
2nd ♊

☽ ♊ △ ♄ ♎	1:10 am	
☽ ♊ △ ♂ ♒	11:32 am **8:32 am**	
☽ ♊ △ ☉ ♒	3:28 pm **12:28 pm**	
☽ ♊ △ ♆ ♒	9:42 pm **6:42 pm**	
☽ ♊ □ ♅ ♓	10:19 pm **7:19 pm** v/c	
☽ enters ♋	**9:48 pm**	
☽ ♋ △ ⚷ ♓	**10:28 pm**	

SUN 13
2nd ♊

Eastern Time plain / **Pacific Time bold**

JANUARY 2011						
S	M	T	W	T	F	S
						1
2	3	4	5	6	7	8
9	10	11	12	13	14	15
16	17	18	19	20	21	22
23	24	25	26	27	28	29
30	31					

FEBRUARY						
S	M	T	W	T	F	S
		1	2	3	4	5
6	7	8	9	10	11	12
13	14	15	16	17	18	19
20	21	22	23	24	25	26
27	28					

MARCH						
S	M	T	W	T	F	S
		1	2	3	4	5
6	7	8	9	10	11	12
13	14	15	16	17	18	19
20	21	22	23	24	25	26
27	28	29	30	31		

14 MON
2nd ♊
VALENTINE'S DAY

☽ enters ♋		12:48 am	
☽ ♋ △ ⚷ ♓		1:28 am	
☿ ♒ △ ♄ ♎		3:48 am	**12:48 am**
☽ ♋ □ ♃ ♈		8:52 am	**5:52 am**
☽ ♋ ☍ ♇ ♑		12:46 pm	**9:46 am**
☽ ♋ ☍ ♀ ♑		10:42 pm	**7:42 pm**

15 TUE
2nd ♋

☽ ♋ □ ♄ ♎		6:11 am	**3:11 am**
☽ ♋ ⚻ ☿ ♒		9:52 am	**6:52 am**
☽ ♋ ⚻ ♂ ♒		6:58 pm	**3:58 pm**
☽ ♋ ⚻ ☉ ♒		11:30 pm	**8:30 pm**
☽ ♋ ⚻ ♆ ♒			**10:29 pm**
☽ ♋ △ ♅ ♓			**11:06 pm** v/c

16 WED
2nd ♋

☽ ♋ ⚻ ♆ ♒		1:29 am	
☽ ♋ △ ♅ ♓		2:06 am	v/c
☽ enters ♌		4:14 am	**1:14 am**
☽ ♌ ⚻ ⚷ ♓		5:05 am	**2:05 am**
☽ ♌ △ ♃ ♈		12:29 pm	**9:29 am**
☽ ♌ ⚻ ♇ ♑		3:28 pm	**12:28 pm**

17 THU
2nd ♌

☽ ♌ ⚻ ♀ ♑		4:54 am	**1:54 am**
☉ ♒ ♂ ♆ ♒		4:56 am	**1:56 am**
☽ ♌ ✳ ♄ ♎		7:35 am	**4:35 am**
☽ ♌ ☍ ☿ ♒		5:35 pm	**2:35 pm**
☽ ♌ ☍ ♂ ♒		10:30 pm	**7:30 pm**
☽ ♌ ☍ ♆ ♒			**11:08 pm**
☽ ♌ ⚻ ♅ ♓			**11:46 pm**

☽♌ ☍ ♆♒	2:08 am	
☽♌ ⊼ ♅♓	2:46 am	
☽♌ ☍ ☉♒	3:36 am **12:36 am** v/c	
☽ enters ♍	4:39 am **1:39 am**	
☽♍ ☍ ⚷♓	5:41 am **2:41 am**	
☽♍ ⊼ ♃♈	1:17 pm **10:17 am**	
♀♑ □ ♄♎	2:21 pm **11:21 am**	
☽♍ △ ♇♑	3:31 pm **12:31 pm**	
☉ enters ♓	7:25 pm **4:25 pm**	

Fri 18
2nd ♌
○ 29 ♌ 20

☽♍ △ ♀♑	8:27 am **5:27 am**	
☉♓ ♂ ⚷♓	1:08 pm **10:08 am**	
☽♍ ⊼ ☿♒	11:12 pm **8:12 pm**	
☽♍ ⊼ ♂♒	**9:29 pm**	
☽♍ ⊼ ♆♒	**10:37 pm**	
☽♍ ☍ ♅♓	**11:18 pm** v/c	

Sat 19
3rd ♍

☽♍ ⊼ ♂♒	12:29 am	
☽♍ ⊼ ♆♒	1:37 am	
☽♍ ☍ ♅♓	2:18 am	v/c
☽ enters ♎	4:01 am **1:01 am**	
☽♎ ⊼ ⚷♓	5:16 am **2:16 am**	
☽♎ ⊼ ☉♓	6:20 am **3:20 am**	
☽♎ ☍ ♃♈	1:24 pm **10:24 am**	
☽♎ □ ♇♑	3:02 pm **12:02 pm**	
☿♒ ♂ ♂♒	5:44 pm **2:44 pm**	
☿♒ ♂ ♆♒	8:07 pm **5:07 pm**	
♂♒ ♂ ♆♒	11:17 pm **8:17 pm**	

Sun 20
3rd ♍

Eastern Time plain / **Pacific Time bold**

JANUARY 2011						
S	M	T	W	T	F	S
						1
2	3	4	5	6	7	8
9	10	11	12	13	14	15
16	17	18	19	20	21	22
23	24	25	26	27	28	29
30	31					

FEBRUARY						
S	M	T	W	T	F	S
		1	2	3	4	5
6	7	8	9	10	11	12
13	14	15	16	17	18	19
20	21	22	23	24	25	26
27	28					

MARCH						
S	M	T	W	T	F	S
		1	2	3	4	5
6	7	8	9	10	11	12
13	14	15	16	17	18	19
20	21	22	23	24	25	26
27	28	29	30	31		

February

21 Mon

3rd ♎︎

Presidents' Day

OP: After Moon squares Venus until v/c Moon. Great for work, and even better for socializing into the evening.

☽♎︎ ☌ ♄♎︎	6:37 am	**3:37 am**
☽♎︎ □ ♀♑︎	12:19 pm	**9:19 am**
☿ enters ♓︎	3:53 pm	**12:53 pm**
☽♎︎ △ ♆♒︎		**11:07 pm**
☽♎︎ ⚻ ♅♓︎		**11:52 pm**

22 Tue

3rd ♎︎

☽♎︎ △ ♆♒︎	2:07 am	
☽♎︎ ⚻ ♅♓︎	2:52 am	
☽♎︎ △ ♂♒︎	3:35 am	**12:35 am** v/c
☿♓︎ ☌ ⚷♓︎	4:10 am	**1:10 am**
☽ enters ♏︎	4:29 am	**1:29 am**
☽♏︎ △ ⚷♓︎	6:01 am	**3:01 am**
☽♏︎ △ ☿♓︎	6:16 am	**3:16 am**
☽♏︎ △ ☉♓︎	10:33 am	**7:33 am**
☽♏︎ ⚻ ♃♈︎	3:05 pm	**12:05 pm**
☽♏︎ ✶ ♇♑︎	4:06 pm	**1:06 pm**
♂ enters ♓︎	8:06 pm	**5:06 pm**

23 Wed

3rd ♏︎

☽♏︎ ✶ ♀♑︎	7:10 pm	**4:10 pm**

24 Thu

3rd ♏︎

☽ 6 ♐︎ 00

♂♓︎ ☌ ⚷♓︎	4:19 am	**1:19 am**
☽♏︎ □ ♆♒︎	5:23 am	**2:23 am**
☽♏︎ △ ♅♓︎	6:14 am	**3:14 am** v/c
☽ enters ♐︎	7:46 am	**4:46 am**
☽♐︎ □ ⚷♓︎	9:40 am	**6:40 am**
☽♐︎ □ ♂♓︎	9:58 am	**6:58 am**
☽♐︎ □ ☿♓︎	5:45 pm	**2:45 pm**
☽♐︎ □ ☉♓︎	6:26 pm	**3:26 pm**
☽♐︎ △ ♃♈︎	7:58 pm	**4:58 pm**

☉♓ ♂ ☿♓	3:48 am **12:48 am**	
☿♓ ⚹ ♇♑	12:06 pm **9:06 am**	
☽♐ ⚹ ♄♎	1:20 pm **10:20 am**	
♃♈ ☐ ♇♑	3:40 pm **12:40 pm**	
☉♓ ⚹ ♇♑	7:17 pm **4:17 pm**	

Fri 25
4th ♐

☽♐ ⚹ ♆♒	12:09 pm **9:09 am**	
☽♐ ☐ ♅♓	1:08 pm **10:08 am** v/c	
☽ enters ♑	2:32 pm **11:32 am**	
☽♑ ⚹ ⚷♓	4:51 pm **1:51 pm**	
☽♑ ⚹ ♂♓	8:31 pm **5:31 pm**	

Sat 26
4th ♐

☽♑ ♂ ♇♑	3:54 am **12:54 am**	
☽♑ ☐ ♃♈	4:30 am **1:30 am**	
☽♑ ⚹ ☉♓	6:40 am **3:40 am**	
☽♑ ⚹ ☿♓	10:48 am **7:48 am**	
☽♑ ☐ ♄♎	9:36 pm **6:36 pm**	

Sun 27
4th ♑

OP: After Moon squares Saturn until v/c Moon. The fourth-quarter Moon warns us to follow up on projects already begun, rather than starting anything new.

Eastern Time plain / **Pacific Time bold**

JANUARY 2011						
S	M	T	W	T	F	S
						1
2	3	4	5	6	7	8
9	10	11	12	13	14	15
16	17	18	19	20	21	22
23	24	25	26	27	28	29
30	31					

FEBRUARY						
S	M	T	W	T	F	S
		1	2	3	4	5
6	7	8	9	10	11	12
13	14	15	16	17	18	19
20	21	22	23	24	25	26
27	28					

MARCH						
S	M	T	W	T	F	S
		1	2	3	4	5
6	7	8	9	10	11	12
13	14	15	16	17	18	19
20	21	22	23	24	25	26
27	28	29	30	31		

28 MON
4th ♑

OP: After Moon squares Saturn until v/c Moon. The fourth-quarter Moon warns us to follow up on projects already begun, rather than starting anything new.

☽♑ ☌ ♀♑	9:57 pm	**6:57 pm**	
☽♑ ⚹ ♅♓	11:03 pm	**8:03 pm** v/c	
☽ enters ♒		**9:14 pm**	

1 TUE
4th ♑

☽ enters ♒	12:14 am	
♀♑ ⚹ ♅♓	9:49 am	**6:49 am**
☽♒ ⚹ ♃♈	3:53 pm	**12:53 pm**
♀ enters ♒	9:39 pm	**6:39 pm**

2 WED
4th ♒

☿♓ ⚻ ♄♎	8:03 am	**5:03 am**
☽♒ △ ♄♎	8:10 am	**5:10 am**

3 THU
4th ♒

☽♒ ☌ ♆♒	9:36 am	**6:36 am** v/c
☽ enters ♓	11:47 am	**8:47 am**
☽♓ ☌ ♀♓	2:55 pm	**11:55 am**
♂♓ ⚹ ♇♑	9:52 pm	**6:52 pm**
☽♓ ⚹ ♇♑		**11:10 pm**
☽♓ ☌ ♂♓		**11:28 pm**

☽ ♓ ✶ ♇ ♑	2:10 am	
☽ ♓ ♂ ♂ ♓	2:28 am	
☽ ♓ ♂ ☉ ♓	3:46 pm **12:46 pm**	
☽ ♓ ⊼ ♄ ♎	8:00 pm **5:00 pm**	

Fri 4
4th ♓
● 13 ♓ 03

☽ ♓ ♂ ☿ ♓	7:56 am **4:56 am**	
☽ ♓ ♂ ♅ ♓	11:34 pm **8:34 pm** v/c	
☽ enters ♈	**9:14 pm**	

Sat 5
1st ♓

☽ enters ♈	12:14 am	
☽ ♈ ✶ ♀ ♒	11:09 am **8:09 am**	
☽ ♈ □ ♇ ♑	2:50 pm **11:50 am**	
☉ ♓ ⊼ ♄ ♎	3:26 pm **12:26 pm**	
☽ ♈ ♂ ♃ ♈	6:43 pm **3:43 pm**	

Sun 6
1st ♓

Eastern Time plain / **Pacific Time bold**

FEBRUARY						
S	M	T	W	T	F	S
		1	2	3	4	5
6	7	8	9	10	11	12
13	14	15	16	17	18	19
20	21	22	23	24	25	26
27	28					

MARCH						
S	M	T	W	T	F	S
		1	2	3	4	5
6	7	8	9	10	11	12
13	14	15	16	17	18	19
20	21	22	23	24	25	26
27	28	29	30	31		

APRIL						
S	M	T	W	T	F	S
					1	2
3	4	5	6	7	8	9
10	11	12	13	14	15	16
17	18	19	20	21	22	23
24	25	26	27	28	29	30

7 Mon
1st ♈

♊ ♈ ☍ ♄ ♎   8:21 am   **5:21 am**

8 Tue
1st ♈
Mardi Gras
Fat Tuesday

☽ ♈ ✳ ♆ ♒   11:04 am   **8:04 am** v/c
☽ enters ♉   12:52 pm   **9:52 am**
☽ ♉ ✳ ⚷ ♓   4:42 pm   **1:42 pm**

9 Wed
1st ♉
Ash Wednesday

☽ ♉ △ ♇ ♑   3:27 am   **12:27 am**
☽ ♉ □ ♀ ♒   6:23 am   **3:23 am**
☿ ♓ ☌ ♅ ♓   11:05 am   **8:05 am**
☽ ♉ ✳ ♂ ♓   12:05 pm   **9:05 am**
☿ enters ♈   12:47 pm   **9:47 am**
☽ ♉ ⊼ ♄ ♎   8:20 pm   **5:20 pm**

10 Thu
1st ♉

☽ ♉ ✳ ☉ ♓   3:43 am   **12:43 am**
♀ ♒ ✳ ♃ ♈   7:25 am   **4:25 am**
☽ ♉ □ ♆ ♒   10:57 pm   **7:57 pm**
☽ ♉ ✳ ♅ ♓   **9:26 pm** v/c
☽ enters ♊   **9:31 pm**

Fri 11
1st ♉

☽ ♉ ✶ ♅ ♓	12:26 am		v/c
☽ enters ♊	12:31 am		
☽ ♊ □ ⚷ ♓	4:33 am	**1:33 am**	
☽ ♊ ✶ ☿ ♈	6:55 am	**3:55 am**	
☽ ♊ ⚹ ♇ ♑	2:41 pm	**11:41 am**	
♅ enters ♈	7:49 pm	**4:49 pm**	
☽ ♊ ✶ ♃ ♈	8:31 pm	**5:31 pm**	
☽ ♊ △ ♀ ♒	11:38 pm	**8:38 pm**	
☽ ♊ □ ♂ ♓		**11:51 pm**	

Sat 12
1st ♊
● 22 ♊ 03

☽ ♊ □ ♂ ♓	2:51 am		
☽ ♊ △ ♄ ♎	6:30 am	**3:30 am**	
☽ ♊ □ ☉ ♓	6:45 pm	**3:45 pm**	

OP: After Moon squares Sun until v/c Moon. A great time to go dancing or have a party.

Sun 13
2nd ♊

DAYLIGHT SAVING TIME BEGINS AT 2:00 AM

☽ ♊ △ ♆ ♒	9:10 am	**6:10 am**	v/c
☽ enters ♋	10:29 am	**7:29 am**	
☽ ♋ □ ♅ ♈	10:39 am	**7:39 am**	
☿ ♈ □ ♇ ♑	1:32 pm	**10:32 am**	
☽ ♋ △ ⚷ ♓	2:34 pm	**11:34 am**	
☽ ♋ ☍ ♇ ♑	11:50 pm	**8:50 pm**	
☽ ♋ □ ☿ ♈		**10:22 pm**	

	FEBRUARY					
S	M	T	W	T	F	S
		1	2	3	4	5
6	7	8	9	10	11	12
13	14	15	16	17	18	19
20	21	22	23	24	25	26
27	28					

	MARCH					
S	M	T	W	T	F	S
		1	2	3	4	5
6	7	8	9	10	11	12
13	14	15	16	17	18	19
20	21	22	23	24	25	26
27	28	29	30	31		

	APRIL					
S	M	T	W	T	F	S
					1	2
3	4	5	6	7	8	9
10	11	12	13	14	15	16
17	18	19	20	21	22	23
24	25	26	27	28	29	30

March

14 Mon
2nd ♋

OP: After Moon trines Mars until Moon enters Leo. Work can be productive, and time spent with family and friends on Monday evening will be gratifying.

☽ ♋	□	☿ ♈	1:22 am	
☽ ♋	□	♃ ♈	6:13 am	**3:13 am**
♂ ♓	⊼	♄ ♎	9:54 am	**6:54 am**
☽ ♋	⊼	♀ ♒	1:29 pm	**10:29 am**
☽ ♋	□	♄ ♎	2:14 pm	**11:14 am**
☽ ♋	△	♂ ♓	2:32 pm	**11:32 am**
♀ ♒	△	♄ ♎	9:34 pm	**6:34 pm**

15 Tue
2nd ♋

☽ ♋	△	☉ ♓	6:05 am	**3:05 am** v/c
☽ ♋	⊼	♆ ♒	2:27 pm	**11:27 am**
☽ enters ♌			3:33 pm	**12:33 pm**
☽ ♌	△	♅ ♈	3:55 pm	**12:55 pm**
☽ ♌	⊼	♇ ♓	7:34 pm	**4:34 pm**
☿ ♈	♂	♃ ♈	9:26 pm	**6:26 pm**

16 Wed
2nd ♌

☽ ♌	⊼	♇ ♑	3:57 am	**12:57 am**
☽ ♌	△	♃ ♈	10:40 am	**7:40 am**
☽ ♌	△	☿ ♈	12:04 pm	**9:04 am**
☽ ♌	✶	♄ ♎	5:01 pm	**2:01 pm**
☽ ♌	⊼	♂ ♓	8:25 pm	**5:25 pm**
☽ ♌	♂	♀ ♒	9:05 pm	**6:05 pm**

17 Thu
2nd ♌

St. Patrick's Day

☽ ♌	⊼	☉ ♓	11:36 am	**8:36 am**
☽ ♌	♂	♆ ♒	3:58 pm	**12:58 pm** v/c
☽ enters ♍			4:53 pm	**1:53 pm**
☽ ♍	⊼	♅ ♈	5:25 pm	**2:25 pm**
☽ ♍	♂	♇ ♓	8:52 pm	**5:52 pm**

☽ ♍ △ ♇ ♑	4:36 am	**1:36 am**
☿ ♈ ☍ ♄ ♎	9:55 am	**6:55 am**
☽ ♍ ⚻ ♃ ♈	11:43 am	**8:43 am**
☽ ♍ ⚻ ☿ ♈	5:30 pm	**2:30 pm**
☽ ♍ ☍ ♂ ♓	10:50 pm	**7:50 pm**
☽ ♍ ⚻ ♀ ♒		**9:56 pm**

Fri 18

2nd ♍

OP: After Moon opposes Mars until v/c Moon. Friday evening may be big for clubs and parties. Those who don't sleep in too late on Saturday can get some important things done.

☽ ♍ ⚻ ♀ ♒	12:56 am	
☽ ♍ ☍ ☉ ♓	2:10 pm	**11:10 am** v/c
☽ ♍ ⚻ ♆ ♒	3:16 pm	**12:16 pm**
☽ enters ♎	4:03 pm	**1:03 pm**
☽ ♎ ☍ ♅ ♈	4:45 pm	**1:45 pm**
☽ ♎ ⚻ ⚷ ♓	8:08 pm	**5:08 pm**

Sat 19

2nd ♍

○ 28 ♍ 48

☽ ♎ □ ♇ ♑	3:37 am	**12:37 am**
☽ ♎ ☍ ♃ ♈	11:22 am	**8:22 am**
☽ ♎ ☌ ♄ ♎	3:27 pm	**12:27 pm**
☉ enters ♈	7:21 pm	**4:21 pm**
☽ ♎ ☍ ☿ ♈	8:47 pm	**5:47 pm**
☽ ♎ ⚻ ♂ ♓		**9:20 pm**

Sun 20

3rd ♎

Purim

OP: After Moon conjoins Saturn today until v/c Moon on Monday. This evening would be an excellent time to finish preparing your income tax return, to avoid doing so during the upcoming Mercury retrograde. Follow that with a relaxed Monday—sort of a role reversal.

Eastern Time plain / **Pacific Time bold**

FEBRUARY						
S	M	T	W	T	F	S
		1	2	3	4	5
6	7	8	9	10	11	12
13	14	15	16	17	18	19
20	21	22	23	24	25	26
27	28					

MARCH						
S	M	T	W	T	F	S
		1	2	3	4	5
6	7	8	9	10	11	12
13	14	15	16	17	18	19
20	21	22	23	24	25	26
27	28	29	30	31		

APRIL						
S	M	T	W	T	F	S
					1	2
3	4	5	6	7	8	9
10	11	12	13	14	15	16
17	18	19	20	21	22	23
24	25	26	27	28	29	30

MARCH

21 MON
3rd ♎

OP: After Moon conjoins Saturn on Sunday until v/c Moon today.

☽♎ ⊼ ♂♓	12:20 am	
☽♎ △ ♀♒	3:54 am	**12:54 am**
☉♈ ♂ ♅♈	8:24 am	**5:24 am**
☽♎ △ ♆♒	2:35 pm	**11:35 am** v/c
☽ enters ♏	3:17 pm	**12:17 pm**
☽♏ ⊼ ♅♈	4:10 pm	**1:10 pm**
☽♏ ⊼ ☉♈	4:42 pm	**1:42 pm**
☽♏ △ ⚷♓	7:41 pm	**4:41 pm**

22 TUE
3rd ♏

☽♏ ✶ ♇♑	3:14 am	**12:14 am**
☽♏ ⊼ ♃♈	12:05 pm	**9:05 am**
☽♏ ⊼ ☿♈		**10:02 pm**

23 WED
3rd ♏

☽♏ ⊼ ☿♈	1:02 am	
☽♏ △ ♂♓	3:42 am	**12:42 am**
☽♏ □ ♀♒	9:09 am	**6:09 am**
☽♏ □ ♆♒	4:08 pm	**1:08 pm** v/c
☽ enters ♐	4:45 pm	**1:45 pm**
☽♐ △ ♅♈	5:55 pm	**2:55 pm**
☽♐ □ ⚷♓	9:40 pm	**6:40 pm**
☽♐ △ ☉♈	10:03 pm	**7:03 pm**

24 THU
3rd ♐

☽♐ △ ♃♈	3:57 pm	**12:57 pm**
☽♐ ✶ ♄♎	6:14 pm	**3:14 pm**

Mercury Note: Mercury enters its Storm on Friday—the period in which it moves less than 40 minutes of arc per day. The Storm, like the coming retrograde, is not a good time to start new projects, though it can be excellent for following through on matters already under way.

Fri 25
3rd ♐

☽ ♐ △ ☿ ♈	8:23 am	**5:23 am**
☽ ♐ □ ♂ ♓	11:08 am	**8:08 am**
☽ ♐ ⚹ ♀ ♒	7:02 pm	**4:02 pm**
☽ ♐ ⚹ ♆ ♒	9:25 pm	**6:25 pm** v/c
☽ enters ♑	9:57 pm	**6:57 pm**
☽ ♑ □ ♅ ♈	11:26 pm	**8:26 pm**

OP: After Moon squares Mars until Moon enters Capricorn. You can be very productive now as long as you don't try to be original!

Sat 26
3rd ♑
◑ 5 ♑ 29

☽ ♑ ⚹ ♇ ♓	3:31 am	**12:31 am**
☽ ♑ □ ☉ ♈	8:07 am	**5:07 am**
☽ ♑ ☌ ♇ ♑	11:48 am	**8:48 am**
♀ ♒ ☌ ♆ ♒	9:39 pm	**6:39 pm**
☽ ♑ □ ♃ ♈		**9:01 pm**
☽ ♑ □ ♄ ♎		**10:04 pm**
♀ enters ♓		**11:53 pm**

Sun 27
4th ♑

☽ ♑ □ ♃ ♈	12:01 am	
☽ ♑ □ ♄ ♎	1:04 am	
♀ enters ♓	2:53 am	
☽ ♑ □ ☿ ♈	7:00 pm	**4:00 pm**
☽ ♑ ⚹ ♂ ♓	11:17 pm	**8:17 pm** v/c

OP: After Moon squares Mercury until v/c Moon. Short but usable.

Eastern Time plain / **Pacific Time bold**

FEBRUARY						
S	M	T	W	T	F	S
		1	2	3	4	5
6	7	8	9	10	11	12
13	14	15	16	17	18	19
20	21	22	23	24	25	26
27	28					

MARCH						
S	M	T	W	T	F	S
		1	2	3	4	5
6	7	8	9	10	11	12
13	14	15	16	17	18	19
20	21	22	23	24	25	26
27	28	29	30	31		

APRIL						
S	M	T	W	T	F	S
					1	2
3	4	5	6	7	8	9
10	11	12	13	14	15	16
17	18	19	20	21	22	23
24	25	26	27	28	29	30

March

Mercury Note: Mercury goes retrograde on March 30 and remains so until April 23. During the Storms and the retrograde, if you get a "bright idea", write it down and note the date and time. Wait until May to get perspective on those ideas.

28 Mon
4th ♑

☽ enters ♒	7:00 am	**4:00 am**
☉♈□ ♇♑	8:13 am	**5:13 am**
☽♒ ✶ ♅♈	8:50 am	**5:50 am**
♃♈ ☍ ♄♎	5:55 pm	**2:55 pm**
☽♒ ✶ ☉♈	10:52 pm	**7:52 pm**

29 Tue
4th ♒

☽♒ △ ♄♎	11:12 am	**8:12 am**
☽♒ ✶ ♃♈	11:40 am	**8:40 am**
♀♓ ☌ ⚷♓	7:15 pm	**4:15 pm**

30 Wed
4th ♒

OP: When Moon enters Pisces until Moon enters Aries. Two OP's back to back, the second being the v/c Moon in Pisces. Fourth-quarter Moon and Mercury retrograde tell us to take it easy right now.

☽♒ ✶ ☿♈	7:16 am	**4:16 am**
☿℞ in ♈	4:48 pm	**1:48 pm**
☽♒ ☌ ♆♒	6:21 pm	**3:21 pm** v/c
☽ enters ♓	6:38 pm	**3:38 pm**
☽♓ ☌ ⚷♓		**10:16 pm**

31 Thu
4th ♓

☽♓ ☌ ⚷♓	1:16 am	
☽♓ ☌ ♀♓	4:29 am	**1:29 am**
☽♓ ✶ ♇♑	9:44 am	**6:44 am** v/c
☽♓ ⊼ ♄♎	11:06 pm	**8:06 pm**

♂ enters ♈   **9:51 pm**

FRI 1
4th ♓
APRIL FOOLS' DAY

♂ enters ♈   12:51 am
☽ enters ♈   7:16 am **4:16 am**
☽♈ ☌ ♂♈   7:43 am **4:43 am**
♀♓ ⚹ ♇♑   8:30 am **5:30 am**
☽♈ ☌ ♅♈   9:45 am **6:45 am**
☽♈ □ ♇♑   10:26 pm **7:26 pm**

SAT 2
4th ♓

☽♈ ☌ ☉♈   10:32 am **7:32 am**
☽♈ ☍ ♄♎   11:22 am **8:22 am**
☽♈ ☌ ♃♈   3:08 pm **12:08 pm**
♂♈ ☌ ♅♈   4:52 pm **1:52 pm**
☉♈ ☍ ♄♎   7:56 pm **4:56 pm**

SUN 3
4th ♈
● 13 ♈ 30

OP: After Moon opposes Saturn until v/c Moon on Monday. The Moon is still combust and under Sun's beams, and the Sun opposes Saturn as well. Caution is advised.

Eastern Time plain / **Pacific Time bold**

MARCH						
S	M	T	W	T	F	S
		1	2	3	4	5
6	7	8	9	10	11	12
13	14	15	16	17	18	19
20	21	22	23	24	25	26
27	28	29	30	31		

APRIL						
S	M	T	W	T	F	S
					1	2
3	4	5	6	7	8	9
10	11	12	13	14	15	16
17	18	19	20	21	22	23
24	25	26	27	28	29	30

MAY						
S	M	T	W	T	F	S
1	2	3	4	5	6	7
8	9	10	11	12	13	14
15	16	17	18	19	20	21
22	23	24	25	26	27	28
29	30	31				

4 MON
1st ♈

OP: When Moon enters Taurus until Moon enters Gemini. Two OP's back to back, the second being the v/c Moon in Taurus. This is a great time to just enjoy life.

☽ ♈ ♂ ☿ ♈	6:04 am	**3:04 am** v/c
♆ enters ♓	9:50 am	**6:50 am**
☽ enters ♉	7:46 pm	**4:46 pm**
☽ ♉ ⚹ ♆ ♓	7:47 pm	**4:47 pm**
☽ ♉ ⚹ ⚷ ♓		**11:56 pm**

5 TUE
1st ♉

☽ ♉ ⚹ ⚷ ♓	2:56 am	
☽ ♉ △ ♇ ♑	10:47 am	**7:47 am**
☽ ♉ ⚹ ♀ ♓	7:02 pm	**4:02 pm** v/c
☽ ♉ ⚻ ♄ ♎	11:10 pm	**8:10 pm**

6 WED
1st ♉

☉ ♈ ♂ ♃ ♈	10:40 am	**7:40 am**

7 THU
1st ♉

☽ enters ♊	7:22 am	**4:22 am**
☽ ♊ □ ♆ ♓	7:31 am	**4:31 am**
♀ ♓ ⚻ ♄ ♎	10:09 am	**7:09 am**
☽ ♊ ⚹ ♅ ♈	10:19 am	**7:19 am**
☽ ♊ □ ⚷ ♓	2:38 pm	**11:38 am**
☽ ♊ ⚹ ♂ ♈	3:56 pm	**12:56 pm**
☽ ♊ ⚻ ♇ ♑	10:01 pm	**7:01 pm**

☽ ♊ △ ♄ ♎	9:40 am	**6:40 am**
☽ ♊ □ ♀ ♓	12:21 pm	**9:21 am**
☽ ♊ ⚹ ♃ ♈	4:21 pm	**1:21 pm**
☽ ♊ ⚹ ☉ ♈	7:48 pm	**4:48 pm**
☽ ♊ ⚹ ☿ ♈	10:24 pm	**7:24 pm** v/c

FRI 8
1st ♊

OP: After Moon squares Venus until v/c Moon. Busy and productive, good for review and follow-up.

♇ ℞ in ♑	4:50 am	**1:50 am**
☉ ♈ ☌ ☿ ♈	3:36 pm	**12:36 pm**
☽ enters ♋	5:02 pm	**2:02 pm**
☽ ♋ △ ♆ ♓	5:19 pm	**2:19 pm**
☽ ♋ □ ♅ ♈	8:06 pm	**5:06 pm**
☽ ♋ △ ⚷ ♓		**9:12 pm**

SAT 9
1st ♊

☽ ♋ △ ⚷ ♓	12:12 am	
☽ ♋ □ ♂ ♈	4:52 am	**1:52 am**
☽ ♋ ☍ ♇ ♑	7:01 am	**4:01 am**
☽ ♋ □ ♄ ♎	5:45 pm	**2:45 pm**
☽ ♋ □ ♃ ♈		**10:26 pm**
☽ ♋ △ ♀ ♓		**11:15 pm**

SUN 10
1st ♋

Eastern Time plain / **Pacific Time bold**

MARCH						
S	M	T	W	T	F	S
		1	2	3	4	5
6	7	8	9	10	11	12
13	14	15	16	17	18	19
20	21	22	23	24	25	26
27	28	29	30	31		

APRIL						
S	M	T	W	T	F	S
					1	2
3	4	5	6	7	8	9
10	11	12	13	14	15	16
17	18	19	20	21	22	23
24	25	26	27	28	29	30

MAY						
S	M	T	W	T	F	S
1	2	3	4	5	6	7
8	9	10	11	12	13	14
15	16	17	18	19	20	21
22	23	24	25	26	27	28
29	30	31				

11 MON
1st ♋
◗ 21 ♋ 16

OP: After Moon in Cancer squares Sun until v/c Moon in Leo. Two OPs back to back: The first is the v/c Moon in Cancer, and the second starts with the Moon's entry into Leo. A highly productive time if we're following up on matters begun before Mercury's Storm and retrograde.

☽♋□♃♈	1:26 am	
☽♋△♀♓	2:15 am	
☽♋□☿♈	3:03 am	**12:03 am**
☽♋□☉♈	8:05 am	**5:05 am** v/c
♂♈□♇♑	4:41 pm	**1:41 pm**
☽ enters ♌	11:37 pm	**8:37 pm**
☿♈☌♃♈	11:59 pm	**8:59 pm**
☽♌⚻♆♓	11:59 pm	**8:59 pm**
☽♌△♅♈		**11:43 pm**

12 TUE
2nd ♌

☽♌△♅♈	2:43 am	
☽♌⚻⚷♓	6:33 am	**3:33 am**
☽♌⚻♇♑	12:43 pm	**9:43 am**
☽♌△♂♈	1:54 pm	**10:54 am**
☽♌✶♄♎	10:28 pm	**7:28 pm**

13 WED
2nd ♌

☽♌△☿♈	4:48 am	**1:48 am**
☽♌△♃♈	6:50 am	**3:50 am**
☽♌⚻♀♓	11:33 am	**8:33 am**
☽♌△☉♈	3:58 pm	**12:58 pm** v/c
☽ enters ♍		**11:40 pm**

14 THU
2nd ♌

OP: After Moon trines Pluto until v/c Moon. If you're submitting your tax returns on Friday, wait until after the Moon goes v/c to file them. Many astrologers find that if they mail their returns during the v/c Moon, they're less likely to get unwanted responses from the IRS.

☽ enters ♍	2:40 am	
☽♍☍♆♓	3:07 am	**12:07 am**
☽♍⚻♅♈	5:46 am	**2:46 am**
☽♍☍⚷♓	9:20 am	**6:20 am**
☽♍△♇♑	2:57 pm	**11:57 am**
☽♍⚻♂♈	6:50 pm	**3:50 pm**

☽ ♍ ⊼ ☿ ♈	3:59 am **12:59 am**		**Fri 15**
☽ ♍ ⊼ ♃ ♈	8:52 am **5:52 am**		2nd ♍
☽ ♍ ☍ ♀ ♓	4:49 pm **1:49 pm** v/c	
☽ ♍ ⊼ ☉ ♈	8:08 pm **5:08 pm**	
☽ enters ♎	**11:59 pm**	

☽ enters ♎	2:59 am	**Sat 16**
☽ ♎ ⊼ ♆ ♓	3:29 am **12:29 am**	2nd ♍
☽ ♎ ☍ ♅ ♈	6:07 am **3:07 am**
☽ ♎ ⊼ ⚷ ♓	9:33 am **6:33 am**
☽ ♎ □ ♇ ♑	2:49 pm **11:49 am**
☽ ♎ ☍ ♂ ♈	9:09 pm **6:09 pm**
☽ ♎ ☌ ♄ ♎	11:17 pm **8:17 pm**
☽ ♎ ☍ ☿ ♈	**10:49 pm**

OP: **After Moon conjoins Saturn until v/c Moon.** A pleasant weekend ahead.

☽ ♎ ☍ ☿ ♈	1:49 am	**Sun 17**
☽ ♎ ☍ ♃ ♈	9:05 am **6:05 am**	2nd ♎
☽ ♎ ⊼ ♀ ♓	8:16 pm **5:16 pm**	○ 27 ♎ 44
☽ ♎ ☍ ☉ ♈	10:44 pm **7:44 pm** v/c	Palm Sunday
☽ enters ♏	**11:19 pm**
☽ ♏ △ ♆ ♓	**11:54 pm**

OP: **When Moon enters Scorpio today until v/c Moon on Tuesday (Pacific) or Wednesday (Eastern).** We should be able to think clearly, though Mercury retrograde is getting old by now, and Mars opposing Saturn guarantees that not everything goes easily.

Eastern Time plain / **Pacific Time bold**

	MARCH								APRIL								MAY					
S	M	T	W	T	F	S		S	M	T	W	T	F	S		S	M	T	W	T	F	S
		1	2	3	4	5							1	2		1	2	3	4	5	6	7
6	7	8	9	10	11	12		3	4	5	6	7	8	9		8	9	10	11	12	13	14
13	14	15	16	17	18	19		10	11	12	13	14	15	16		15	16	17	18	19	20	21
20	21	22	23	24	25	26		17	18	19	20	21	22	23		22	23	24	25	26	27	28
27	28	29	30	31				24	25	26	27	28	29	30		29	30	31				

18 MON
3rd ♎

OP: When Moon enters Scorpio on Sunday until v/c Moon on Tuesday (Pacific) or Wednesday (Eastern). We should be able to think clearly, though Mercury retrograde is getting old by now, and Mars opposing Saturn guarantees that not everything goes easily.

☽ enters ♏	2:19 am	
☽♏ △ ♆♓	2:54 am	
☽♏ ⊼ ♅♈	5:38 am	**2:38 am**
☽♏ △ ⚷♓	9:04 am	**6:04 am**
♂♈ ☍ ♄♎	12:02 pm	**9:02 am**
☽♏ ✶ ♇♑	2:14 pm	**11:14 am**
☽♏ ⊼ ♂♈	11:16 pm	**8:16 pm**
☽♏ ⊼ ☿♈		**9:07 pm**

19 TUE
3rd ♏
PASSOVER BEGINS

☽♏ ⊼ ☿♈	12:07 am	
☽♏ ⊼ ♃♈	9:43 am	**6:43 am**
☿♈ ☌ ♂♈	10:58 am	**7:58 am**
☽♏ △ ♀♓		**9:53 pm** v/c
☽♏ ⊼ ☉♈		**11:35 pm**
☽ enters ♐		**11:50 pm**

20 WED
3rd ♏

OP: After Moon sextiles Saturn until Moon enters Capricorn. Two OPs back to back, the second being the v/c Moon in Sagittarius. Things can go smoothly on Thursday, though we're still in review mode.

☽♏ △ ♀♓	12:53 am	v/c
☽♏ ⊼ ☉♈	2:35 am	
☽ enters ♐	2:50 am	
☽♐ □ ♆♓	3:31 am	**12:31 am**
☉ enters ♉	6:17 am	**3:17 am**
☽♐ △ ♅♈	6:29 am	**3:29 am**
☽♐ □ ⚷♓	10:04 am	**7:04 am**
☉♉ ✶ ♆♓	4:43 pm	**1:43 pm**
☽♐ ✶ ♄♎		**9:00 pm**
♀ enters ♈		**9:06 pm**
☽♐ △ ☿♈		**9:53 pm**

21 THU
3rd ♐

☽♐ ✶ ♄♎	12:00 am	
♀ enters ♈	12:06 am	
☽♐ △ ☿♈	12:53 am	
☽♐ △ ♂♈	3:48 am	**12:48 am**
☽♐ △ ♃♈	12:57 pm	**9:57 am** v/c

Mercury Note: Mercury goes direct on Saturday, but remains in its Storm until May 2. We're not out of the woods yet.

☽ enters ♑	6:24 am	**3:24 am**
☽♑ ✶ ♆♓	7:14 am	**4:14 am**
☽♑ □ ♀♈	9:25 am	**6:25 am**
☽♑ △ ☉♉	10:11 am	**7:11 am**
☽♑ □ ♅♈	10:33 am	**7:33 am**
☽♑ ✶ ⚷♓	2:22 pm	**11:22 am**
☽♑ ☌ ♇♑	7:51 pm	**4:51 pm**
♀♈ ☌ ♅♈	10:28 pm	**7:28 pm**

Fri 22
3rd ♐
Earth Day
Good Friday | Orthodox Good Friday

☽♑ □ ♄♎	4:56 am	**1:56 am**
☽♑ □ ☿♈	5:47 am	**2:47 am**
☿ D in ♈	6:04 am	**3:04 am**
☽♑ □ ♂♈	12:42 pm	**9:42 am**
☽♑ □ ♃♈	8:13 pm	**5:13 pm** v/c

Sat 23
3rd ♑

☽ enters ♒	1:59 pm	**10:59 am**
☽♒ ✶ ♅♈	6:39 pm	**3:39 pm**
☉♉ ✶ ⚷♓	9:50 pm	**6:50 pm**
☽♒ □ ☉♉	10:47 pm	**7:47 pm**
☽♒ ✶ ♀♈	11:13 pm	**8:13 pm**

Sun 24
3rd ♑
◑ 4 ♒ 34
Easter | Orthodox Easter
OP: After Moon squares Sun today until v/c Moon on Tuesday. Stay cautious—Mercury is still in its Storm and the Moon is in its fourth quarter.

Eastern Time plain / **Pacific Time bold**

MARCH						
S	M	T	W	T	F	S
		1	2	3	4	5
6	7	8	9	10	11	12
13	14	15	16	17	18	19
20	21	22	23	24	25	26
27	28	29	30	31		

APRIL						
S	M	T	W	T	F	S
					1	2
3	4	5	6	7	8	9
10	11	12	13	14	15	16
17	18	19	20	21	22	23
24	25	26	27	28	29	30

MAY						
S	M	T	W	T	F	S
1	2	3	4	5	6	7
8	9	10	11	12	13	14
15	16	17	18	19	20	21
22	23	24	25	26	27	28
29	30	31				

25 MON
4th ♒︎

OP: After Moon squares Sun on Sunday until v/c Moon on Tuesday. Stay cautious—Mercury is still in its Storm and the Moon is in its fourth quarter.

☽ ♒︎ △ ♄ ♎︎	1:45 pm	**10:45 am**
☽ ♒︎ ✶ ☿ ♈︎	3:27 pm	**12:27 pm**
☽ ♒︎ ✶ ♂ ♈︎		**11:13 pm**

26 TUE
4th ♒︎

OP: After Moon conjoins Neptune until Moon enters Aries. Two OPs back to back, the second being the v/c Moon in Pisces. Do what you can, knowing that things will only start to become clear after the New Moon next Monday.

☽ ♒︎ ✶ ♂ ♈︎	2:13 am	
☽ ♒︎ ✶ ♃ ♈︎	7:28 am	**4:28 am** v/c
☽ enters ♓︎		**9:57 pm**
☽ ♓︎ ♂ ♆ ♓︎		**11:05 pm**

27 WED
4th ♒︎

☽ enters ♓︎	12:57 am	
☽ ♓︎ ♂ ♆ ♓︎	2:05 am	
♀ ♈︎ □ ♇ ♑︎	3:21 am	**12:21 am**
☽ ♓︎ ♂ ⚷ ♓︎	10:16 am	**7:16 am**
☽ ♓︎ ✶ ☉ ♉︎	3:25 pm	**12:25 pm**
☽ ♓︎ ✶ ♇ ♑︎	3:53 pm	**12:53 pm** v/c
☉ ♉︎ △ ♇ ♑︎	9:00 pm	**6:00 pm**
☽ ♓︎ ⚻ ♄ ♎︎		**10:18 pm**

28 THU
4th ♓︎

| ☽ ♓︎ ⚻ ♄ ♎︎ | 1:18 am | |

☽ enters ♈	1:33 pm	**10:33 am**	
☽♈ ☌ ♅♈	6:59 pm	**3:59 pm**	

FRI 29
4th ♓

☽♈ □ ♇♑	4:31 am	**1:31 am**	
☽♈ ☌ ♀♈	12:54 pm	**9:54 am**	
☽♈ ☍ ♄♎	1:41 pm	**10:41 am**	
☽♈ ☌ ☿♈	8:13 pm	**5:13 pm**	
♀♈ ☍ ♄♎	8:14 pm	**5:14 pm**	
♂♈ ☌ ♃♈		**9:26 pm**	

SAT 30
4th ♈

♂♈ ☌ ♃♈	12:26 am		
☽♈ ☌ ♃♈	10:51 am	**7:51 am**	
☽♈ ☌ ♂♈	11:20 am	**8:20 am** v/c	
☽ enters ♉		**10:58 pm**	

SUN 1
4th ♈

Eastern Time plain / **Pacific Time bold**

APRIL						
S	M	T	W	T	F	S
					1	2
3	4	5	6	7	8	9
10	11	12	13	14	15	16
17	18	19	20	21	22	23
24	25	26	27	28	29	30

MAY						
S	M	T	W	T	F	S
1	2	3	4	5	6	7
8	9	10	11	12	13	14
15	16	17	18	19	20	21
22	23	24	25	26	27	28
29	30	31				

JUNE						
S	M	T	W	T	F	S
			1	2	3	4
5	6	7	8	9	10	11
12	13	14	15	16	17	18
19	20	21	22	23	24	25
26	27	28	29	30		

2 MON

4th ♈

● 12 ♉ 31 (Pacific)

OP: This Cazimi Moon is usable ½ hour before and ½ hour after the Sun-Moon conjunction (Pacific time). If you are awake for this, use it for following up on decisions made way back before Mercury went retrograde. Technically, the Cazimi is followed by an OP with v/c Moon in Taurus, but the Moon is combust, so use that period only for follow-through.

☽ enters ♉	1:58 am	
☽ ♉ ⚹ ♆ ♓	3:16 am	**12:16 am**
☉ ♉ ⊼ ♄ ♎	9:34 am	**6:34 am**
☽ ♉ ⚹ ⚷ ♓	11:35 am	**8:35 am**
☽ ♉ △ ♇ ♑	4:39 pm	**1:39 pm**
☽ ♉ ⊼ ♄ ♎		**10:23 pm**
☽ ♉ ☌ ☉ ♉		**11:51 pm** v/c

3 TUE

4th ♉

● 12 ♉ 31 (Eastern)

OP: This Cazimi Moon is usable ½ hour before and ½ hour after the Sun-Moon conjunction (Eastern time).

☽ ♉ ⊼ ♄ ♎	1:23 am	
☽ ♉ ☌ ☉ ♉	2:51 am v/c	

4 WED

1st ♉

☽ enters ♊	1:09 pm	**10:09 am**
☽ ♊ □ ♆ ♓	2:30 pm	**11:30 am**
☽ ♊ ⚹ ♅ ♈	6:49 pm	**3:49 pm**
☽ ♊ □ ⚷ ♓	10:40 pm	**7:40 pm**

5 THU

1st ♊

CINCO DE MAYO

OP: After Moon trines Saturn until v/c Moon. This is the most promising OP we've had since March. It should be easy to think clearly and get things done for a change.

☽ ♊ ⊼ ♇ ♑	3:22 am	**12:22 am**
☽ ♊ △ ♄ ♎	11:38 am	**8:38 am**
☽ ♊ ⚹ ♀ ♈		**9:09 pm**
☽ ♊ ⚹ ☿ ♈		**10:49 pm**

☽ ♊ ✶ ♀ ♈	12:09 am	
☽ ♊ ✶ ☿ ♈	1:49 am	
☽ ♊ ✶ ♃ ♈	10:29 am	**7:29 am**
☽ ♊ ✶ ♂ ♈	4:12 pm	**1:12 pm** v/c
☽ enters ♋	10:32 pm	**7:32 pm**
☽ ♋ △ ♆ ♓	11:53 pm	**8:53 pm**

FRI 6
1st ♊

☽ ♋ □ ♅ ♈	4:11 am	**1:11 am**
☽ ♋ △ ⚷ ♓	7:50 am	**4:50 am**
☽ ♋ ☍ ♇ ♑	12:10 pm	**9:10 am**
☽ ♋ □ ♄ ♎	7:56 pm	**4:56 pm**

SAT 7
1st ♋

☽ ♋ ✶ ☉ ♉	7:00 am	**4:00 am**
☽ ♋ □ ♀ ♈	1:52 pm	**10:52 am**
☽ ♋ □ ☿ ♈	2:10 pm	**11:10 am**
☽ ♋ □ ♃ ♈	7:04 pm	**4:04 pm**
☽ ♋ □ ♂ ♈		**11:52 pm** v/c

SUN 8
1st ♋
MOTHER'S DAY

Eastern Time plain / **Pacific Time bold**

APRIL						
S	M	T	W	T	F	S
					1	2
3	4	5	6	7	8	9
10	11	12	13	14	15	16
17	18	19	20	21	22	23
24	25	26	27	28	29	30

MAY						
S	M	T	W	T	F	S
1	2	3	4	5	6	7
8	9	10	11	12	13	14
15	16	17	18	19	20	21
22	23	24	25	26	27	28
29	30	31				

JUNE						
S	M	T	W	T	F	S
			1	2	3	4
5	6	7	8	9	10	11
12	13	14	15	16	17	18
19	20	21	22	23	24	25
26	27	28	29	30		

9 Mon
1st ♋

☽ ♋ □ ♂ ♈	2:52 am	v/c
☽ enters ♌	5:35 am	**2:35 am**
☽ ♌ ⊼ ♆ ♓	6:57 am	**3:57 am**
☽ ♌ △ ♅ ♈	11:10 am	**8:10 am**
☿ ♈ ♂ ♀ ♈	11:44 am	**8:44 am**
☽ ♌ ⊼ ⚷ ♓	2:36 pm	**11:36 am**
☽ ♌ ⊼ ♇ ♑	6:33 pm	**3:33 pm**
☽ ♌ ✶ ♄ ♎		**10:46 pm**

10 Tue
1st ♌
☽ 19 ♌ 13
Census Day (Canada)

OP: After Moon squares Sun until v/c Moon. If you want to meet someone new, Tuesday evening would be a great time to go out and socialize. For the best results, arrive well before the Moon trines Mercury.

☽ ♌ ✶ ♄ ♎	1:46 am	
☽ ♌ □ ☉ ♉	4:33 pm	**1:33 pm**
☽ ♌ △ ☿ ♈	11:48 pm	**8:48 pm**
☽ ♌ △ ♀ ♈		**9:07 pm**
☽ ♌ △ ♃ ♈		**9:52 pm** v/c

11 Wed
2nd ♌

OP: After Moon trines Pluto until v/c Moon. You have all day Thursday to accomplish a great deal.

☽ ♌ △ ♀ ♈	12:07 am	
☽ ♌ △ ♃ ♈	12:52 am	v/c
♂ enters ♉	3:03 am	**12:03 am**
☽ enters ♍	9:59 am	**6:59 am**
☽ ♍ △ ♂ ♉	10:22 am	**7:22 am**
♀ ♈ ♂ ♃ ♈	10:42 am	**7:42 am**
☽ ♍ ☍ ♆ ♓	11:19 am	**8:19 am**
☽ ♍ ⊼ ♅ ♈	3:27 pm	**12:27 pm**
☿ ♈ ♂ ♃ ♈	3:57 pm	**12:57 pm**
☽ ♍ ☍ ⚷ ♓	6:38 pm	**3:38 pm**
☽ ♍ △ ♇ ♑	10:14 pm	**7:14 pm**

12 Thu
2nd ♍

♂ ♉ ✶ ♆ ♓	4:28 am	**1:28 am**
☽ ♍ △ ☉ ♉	10:52 pm	**7:52 pm** v/c

Fri 13
2nd ♍

☽♍ ⚻ ♃♈	4:01 am	**1:01 am**
☽♍ ⚻ ☿♈	6:37 am	**3:37 am**
☽♍ ⚻ ♀♈	7:03 am	**4:03 am**
☽ enters ♎	11:56 am	**8:56 am**
☽♎ ⚻ ♆♓	1:16 pm	**10:16 am**
☽♎ ⚻ ♂♉	3:00 pm	**12:00 pm**
☽♎ ☍ ♅♈	5:20 pm	**2:20 pm**
☽♎ ⚻ ⚷♓	8:21 pm	**5:21 pm**
☽♎ □ ♇♑	11:41 pm	**8:41 pm**

Sat 14
2nd ♎

☽♎ ☌ ♄♎	6:06 am	**3:06 am**

OP: After Moon conjoins Saturn until v/c Moon. Today is a great day to meet someone new, or just to be with friends. The good vibes continue on Sunday morning.

Sun 15
2nd ♎

☽♎ ⚻ ☉♉	3:03 am	**12:03 am**	
☽♎ ☍ ♃♈	5:28 am	**2:28 am**	
☽♎ ☍ ☿♈	11:51 am	**8:51 am**	
☽♎ ☍ ♀♈	12:01 pm	**9:01 am**	v/c
☽ enters ♏	12:31 pm	**9:31 am**	
☽♏ △ ♆♓	1:52 pm	**10:52 am**	
☽♏ ⚻ ♅♈	6:00 pm	**3:00 pm**	
☽♏ ☍ ♂♉	6:08 pm	**3:08 pm**	
♀ enters ♉	6:12 pm	**3:12 pm**	
☿ enters ♉	7:18 pm	**4:18 pm**	
☽♏ △ ⚷♓	8:56 pm	**5:56 pm**	
☽♏ ✶ ♇♑		**9:07 pm**	

OP: After Moon sextiles Pluto this evening until v/c Moon on Tuesday. The energy level is high on Monday, but people are mostly acting smooth and tactful. It's easy to get a lot done.

Eastern Time plain / **Pacific Time bold**

APRIL						
S	M	T	W	T	F	S
					1	2
3	4	5	6	7	8	9
10	11	12	13	14	15	16
17	18	19	20	21	22	23
24	25	26	27	28	29	30

MAY						
S	M	T	W	T	F	S
1	2	3	4	5	6	7
8	9	10	11	12	13	14
15	16	17	18	19	20	21
22	23	24	25	26	27	28
29	30	31				

JUNE						
S	M	T	W	T	F	S
			1	2	3	4
5	6	7	8	9	10	11
12	13	14	15	16	17	18
19	20	21	22	23	24	25
26	27	28	29	30		

16 MON
2nd ♏

OP: After Moon sextiles Pluto on Sunday until v/c Moon on Tuesday. The energy level is high today, but people are tactful. It will be easy to get a lot done.

☽ ♏ ✶ ♇ ♑	12:07 am		
☿ ♉ ♂ ♀ ♉	5:25 am	**2:25 am**
☿ ♉ ✶ ♆ ♓	10:17 am	**7:17 am**
♀ ♉ ✶ ♆ ♓	10:52 am	**7:52 am**

17 TUE
2nd ♏
○ 26 ♏ 13

☽ ♏ ⚻ ♃ ♈	6:56 am	**3:56 am**
☽ ♏ ☍ ☉ ♉	7:09 am	**4:09 am** v/c
☽ enters ♐	1:22 pm	**10:22 am**
☽ ♐ □ ♆ ♓	2:47 pm	**11:47 am**
☽ ♐ ⚻ ♀ ♉	5:19 pm	**2:19 pm**
☽ ♐ ⚻ ☿ ♉	5:47 pm	**2:47 pm**
☽ ♐ △ ♅ ♈	7:08 pm	**4:08 pm**
☽ ♐ ⚻ ♂ ♉	9:49 pm	**6:49 pm**
☽ ♐ □ ⚷ ♓	10:05 pm	**7:05 pm**

18 WED
3rd ♐

OP: After Moon sextiles Saturn until Moon enters Capricorn. Two OP's back to back, the second being the v/c Moon in Sagittarius. Potentially a very productive period.

♂ ♉ ✶ ⚷ ♓	3:19 am	**12:19 am**
☽ ♐ ✶ ♄ ♎	7:41 am	**4:41 am**

19 THU
3rd ♐

☽ ♐ △ ♃ ♈	10:17 am	**7:17 am** v/c
☿ ♉ ✶ ⚷ ♓	1:11 pm	**10:11 am**
☽ ♐ ⚻ ☉ ♉	1:28 pm	**10:28 am**
☽ enters ♑	4:16 pm	**1:16 pm**
☽ ♑ ✶ ♆ ♓	5:47 pm	**2:47 pm**
☽ ♑ □ ♅ ♈	10:30 pm	**7:30 pm**
☽ ♑ △ ♀ ♉		**10:26 pm**
☽ ♑ ✶ ⚷ ♓		**10:34 pm**
♀ ♉ ✶ ⚷ ♓		**11:56 pm**

☽♑△♀♉	1:26 am	
☽♑⚹⚷♓	1:34 am	
♀♉⚹⚷♓	2:56 am	
☽♑△☿♉	3:05 am	**12:05 am**
☽♑△♂♉	4:12 am	**1:12 am**
☽♑☌♇♑	4:46 am	**1:46 am**
☽♑□♄♎	11:33 am	**8:33 am**
♂♉△♇♑	2:22 pm	**11:22 am**
☿♉△♇♑	5:54 pm	**2:54 pm**
☿♉☌♂♉	9:20 pm	**6:20 pm**

Fri 20
3rd ♑

☉ enters ♊	5:21 am	**2:21 am**
♀♉△♇♑	2:04 pm	**11:04 am**
☽♑□♃♈	5:04 pm	**2:04 pm** v/c
☽ enters ♒	10:32 pm	**7:32 pm**
☽♒△☉♊	11:55 pm	**8:55 pm**

Sat 21
3rd ♑

☉♊□♆♓	3:31 am	**12:31 am**
☽♒⚹♅♈	5:22 am	**2:22 am**
☽♒□♀♉	2:12 pm	**11:12 am**
☽♒□♂♉	2:46 pm	**11:46 am**
☽♒□☿♉	5:53 pm	**2:53 pm**
☽♒△♄♎	7:01 pm	**4:01 pm**
☿♉⊼♄♎		**11:30 pm**

Sun 22
3rd ♒

OP: After Moon squares Mercury today until v/c Moon on Tuesday. Many people will be feeling very sexy now, as Venus conjoins Mars. Both Sunday and Monday evenings are good times to find a new lover.

Eastern Time plain / **Pacific Time bold**

APRIL						
S	M	T	W	T	F	S
					1	2
3	4	5	6	7	8	9
10	11	12	13	14	15	16
17	18	19	20	21	22	23
24	25	26	27	28	29	30

MAY						
S	M	T	W	T	F	S
1	2	3	4	5	6	7
8	9	10	11	12	13	14
15	16	17	18	19	20	21
22	23	24	25	26	27	28
29	30	31				

JUNE						
S	M	T	W	T	F	S
			1	2	3	4
5	6	7	8	9	10	11
12	13	14	15	16	17	18
19	20	21	22	23	24	25
26	27	28	29	30		

23 Mon
3rd ♒

☿ ♉ ⊼ ♄ ♎	2:30 am	
♀ ♉ ☌ ♂ ♉	4:25 am	**1:25 am**

OP: After Moon squares Mercury on Sunday until v/c Moon on Tuesday. Many people will be feeling very sexy now, as Venus conjoins Mars. Both Sunday and Monday evenings are good times to find a new lover.

24 Tue
3rd ♒
◑ 3 ♓ 16

☽ ♒ ⚹ ♃ ♈	3:40 am	**12:40 am** v/c
☽ enters ♓	8:24 am	**5:24 am**
☽ ♓ ☌ ♆ ♓	10:11 am	**7:11 am**
♀ ♉ ⊼ ♄ ♎	2:47 pm	**11:47 am**
☽ ♓ □ ☉ ♊	2:52 pm	**11:52 am**
☽ ♓ ☌ ⚷ ♓	7:04 pm	**4:04 pm**
☽ ♓ ⚹ ♇ ♑	10:20 pm	**7:20 pm**
☉ ♊ ⚹ ♅ ♈		**11:47 pm**

OP: After Moon squares Sun until Moon enters Aries. Two OP's back to back, the second being the v/c Moon in Pisces. Rest now and get active later. Both Tuesday and Wednesday evenings are great for going out and socializing.

25 Wed
4th ♓

☉ ♊ ⚹ ♅ ♈	2:47 am	
☽ ♓ ⚹ ♂ ♉	5:22 am	**2:22 am**
☽ ♓ ⊼ ♄ ♎	5:47 am	**2:47 am**
☽ ♓ ⚹ ♀ ♉	7:31 am	**4:31 am**
♂ ♉ ⊼ ♄ ♎	11:49 am	**8:49 am**
☽ ♓ ⚹ ☿ ♉	2:15 pm	**11:15 am** v/c

26 Thu
4th ♓

☉ ♊ □ ⚷ ♓	8:18 pm	**5:18 pm**
☽ enters ♈	8:36 pm	**5:36 pm**

Fri 27
4th ♈

☽♈ ☌ ♅♈	4:19 am	**1:19 am**
☽♈ ✶ ☉♊	8:32 am	**5:32 am**
☽♈ □ ♇♑	10:41 am	**7:41 am**
☽♈ ☍ ♄♎	6:10 pm	**3:10 pm**

OP: After Moon opposes Saturn until v/c Moon. Aries is full of energy, but the fourth quarter Moon is telling us to take it easy.

Sat 28
4th ♈

| ☉♊ ⚻ ♇♑ | 10:38 am | **7:38 am** |

Sun 29
4th ♈

☽♈ ☌ ♃♈	6:28 am	**3:28 am** v/c
☽ enters ♉	9:02 am	**6:02 am**
☽♉ ✶ ♆♓	10:52 am	**7:52 am**
☽♉ ✶ ⚷♓	7:51 pm	**4:51 pm**
☽♉ △ ♇♑	10:46 pm	**7:46 pm**

Eastern Time plain / **Pacific Time bold**

		APRIL				
S	M	T	W	T	F	S
					1	2
3	4	5	6	7	8	9
10	11	12	13	14	15	16
17	18	19	20	21	22	23
24	25	26	27	28	29	30

		MAY				
S	M	T	W	T	F	S
1	2	3	4	5	6	7
8	9	10	11	12	13	14
15	16	17	18	19	20	21
22	23	24	25	26	27	28
29	30	31				

		JUNE				
S	M	T	W	T	F	S
			1	2	3	4
5	6	7	8	9	10	11
12	13	14	15	16	17	18
19	20	21	22	23	24	25
26	27	28	29	30		

30 Mon
4th ♉
MEMORIAL DAY (OBSERVED)

OP: After Moon conjoins Mars until Moon enters Gemini. Two OP's back to back, the second being the v/c Moon in Taurus. Have a special dinner this evening, and expect to be busy on Tuesday.

☽ ♉	⊼	♄ ♎		6:05 am	**3:05 am**
☽ ♉	♂	♂ ♉		1:43 pm	**10:43 am**
☽ ♉	♂	♀ ♉		9:23 pm	**6:23 pm**

31 Tue
4th ♉

☽ ♉	♂	☿ ♉	11:37 am	**8:37 am** v/c
☽ enters ♊			7:56 pm	**4:56 pm**
☽ ♊	□	♆ ♓	9:43 pm	**6:43 pm**

1 Wed
4th ♊
● 11 ♊ 02
Solar Eclipse (Partial)

☽ ♊	✶	♅ ♈	3:34 am	**12:34 am**
☉ ♊	△	♄ ♎	5:15 am	**2:15 am**
☽ ♊	□	⚷ ♓	6:25 am	**3:25 am**
☽ ♊	⊼	♇ ♑	9:05 am	**6:05 am**
☽ ♊	△	♄ ♎	4:08 pm	**1:08 pm**
☽ ♊	♂	☉ ♊	5:03 pm	**2:03 pm**

2 Thu
1st ♊

☿ enters ♊		4:02 pm	**1:02 pm**

☿ Ⅱ □ ♆ ♓	3:05 am	**12:05 am**	
♆ ℞ in ♓	3:27 am	**12:27 am**	
☽ Ⅱ ✶ ♃ ♈	4:08 am	**1:08 am**	v/c
☽ enters ♋	4:36 am	**1:36 am**	
☽ ♋ △ ♆ ♓	6:19 am	**3:19 am**	
☽ ♋ □ ♅ ♈	12:04 pm	**9:04 am**	
☽ ♋ △ ⚷ ♓	2:42 pm	**11:42 am**	
☽ ♋ ☍ ♇ ♑	5:08 pm	**2:08 pm**	
☽ ♋ □ ♄ ♎	11:56 pm	**8:56 pm**	

FRI 3
1st Ⅱ

♃ enters ♉	9:56 am	**6:56 am**	
☽ ♋ ✶ ♂ ♉	1:48 pm	**10:48 am**	
☿ Ⅱ ✶ ♅ ♈	3:57 pm	**12:57 pm**	
☽ ♋ ✶ ♀ ♉		**10:33 pm**	v/c

SAT 4
1st ♋

OP: **After Moon sextiles Mars until Moon enters Leo.** Two OP's back to back, the second being the v/c Moon in Cancer. Saturday evening provides yet another chance to meet someone new.

☽ ♋ ✶ ♀ ♉	1:33 am		v/c
☿ Ⅱ □ ⚷ ♓	8:12 am	**5:12 am**	
☽ enters ♌	11:03 am	**8:03 am**	
☽ ♌ □ ♃ ♉	11:26 am	**8:26 am**	
☽ ♌ ⚻ ♆ ♓	12:42 pm	**9:42 am**	
☽ ♌ △ ♅ ♈	6:20 pm	**3:20 pm**	
☽ ♌ ⚻ ⚷ ♓	8:47 pm	**5:47 pm**	
☿ Ⅱ ⚻ ♇ ♑	10:43 pm	**7:43 pm**	
☽ ♌ ⚻ ♇ ♑	11:01 pm	**8:01 pm**	
☽ ♌ ✶ ☿ Ⅱ	11:04 pm	**8:04 pm**	

SUN 5
1st ♋

Eastern Time plain / **Pacific Time bold**

	MAY								JUNE								JULY					
S	M	T	W	T	F	S		S	M	T	W	T	F	S		S	M	T	W	T	F	S
1	2	3	4	5	6	7					1	2	3	4							1	2
8	9	10	11	12	13	14		5	6	7	8	9	10	11		3	4	5	6	7	8	9
15	16	17	18	19	20	21		12	13	14	15	16	17	18		10	11	12	13	14	15	16
22	23	24	25	26	27	28		19	20	21	22	23	24	25		17	18	19	20	21	22	23
29	30	31						26	27	28	29	30				24	25	26	27	28	29	30
																31						

6 Mon
1st ♌

☽	♌	⚹	♄	♎	5:36 am	**2:36 am**
☽	♌	⚹	☉	♊	2:48 pm	**11:48 am**
☽	♌	□	♂	♉	10:01 pm	**7:01 pm**

7 Tue
1st ♌

☽	♌	□	♀	♉	11:27 am	**8:27 am** v/c
☽ enters ♍					3:33 pm	**12:33 pm**
☿	♊	△	♄	♎	4:40 pm	**1:40 pm**
☽	♍	△	♃	♉	4:42 pm	**1:42 pm**
☽	♍	☍	♆	♓	5:08 pm	**2:08 pm**
☽	♍	⚻	♅	♈	10:42 pm	**7:42 pm**
☽	♍	☍	⚷	♓		**9:58 pm**

8 Wed
1st ♍
◐ 17 ♍ 56

OP: After Moon squares Sun until v/c Moon. Usable by night owls.

☽	♍	☍	⚷	♓	12:58 am	
☽	♍	△	♇	♑	3:03 am	**12:03 am**
☽	♍	□	☿	♊	12:31 pm	**9:31 am**
⚷ ℞ in ♓					3:07 pm	**12:07 pm**
☽	♍	□	☉	♊	10:11 pm	**7:11 pm**
♃	♉	⚹	♆	♓	10:39 pm	**7:39 pm**

9 Thu
2nd ♍

☽	♍	△	♂	♉	4:13 am	**1:13 am** v/c
♀ enters ♊					10:23 am	**7:23 am**
☽ enters ♎					6:31 pm	**3:31 pm**
☽	♎	△	♀	♊	7:16 pm	**4:16 pm**
☽	♎	⚻	♆	♓	8:03 pm	**5:03 pm**
☽	♎	⚻	♃	♉	8:21 pm	**5:21 pm**
☽	♎	☍	♅	♈		**10:34 pm**

Fri 10
2nd ♎

☽♎☌♅♈	1:34 am	
☽♎⊼♂♓	3:42 am	**12:42 am**
♀♊□♆♓	4:24 am	**1:24 am**
☽♎□♇♑	5:39 am	**2:39 am**
☽♎☌♄♎	12:00 pm	**9:00 am**
☽♎△☿♊		**9:02 pm**

OP: **After Moon conjoins Saturn until v/c Moon.** Friday evening is great if you need to catch up on work, and equally good for just chatting with friends.

Sat 11
2nd ♎

☽♎△☿♊	12:02 am	
☽♎△☉♊	4:04 am	**1:04 am** v/c
☽♎⊼♂♉	9:05 am	**6:05 am**
☽ enters ♏	8:33 pm	**5:33 pm**
☽♏△♆♓	10:04 pm	**7:04 pm**
☽♏☍♃♉	11:04 pm	**8:04 pm**
☽♏⊼♀♊		**10:55 pm**

Sun 12
2nd ♏

☽♏⊼♀♊	1:55 am	
☽♏⊼♅♈	3:38 am	**12:38 am**
☽♏△♂♓	5:40 am	**2:40 am**
☽♏⚹♇♑	7:31 am	**4:31 am**
☉♊☌☿♊	7:44 pm	**4:44 pm**
♀♊⚹♅♈	10:36 pm	**7:36 pm**
♄ D in ♎	11:51 pm	**8:51 pm**

Eastern Time plain / **Pacific Time bold**

MAY						
S	M	T	W	T	F	S
1	2	3	4	5	6	7
8	9	10	11	12	13	14
15	16	17	18	19	20	21
22	23	24	25	26	27	28
29	30	31				

JUNE						
S	M	T	W	T	F	S
			1	2	3	4
5	6	7	8	9	10	11
12	13	14	15	16	17	18
19	20	21	22	23	24	25
26	27	28	29	30		

JULY						
S	M	T	W	T	F	S
					1	2
3	4	5	6	7	8	9
10	11	12	13	14	15	16
17	18	19	20	21	22	23
24	25	26	27	28	29	30
31						

13 Mon
2nd ♏

☽♏ ⚻ ☉♊	9:35 am	**6:35 am**	
☽♏ ⚻ ☿♊	11:00 am	**8:00 am**	
☽♏ ☍ ♂♉	1:43 pm	**10:43 am** v/c
♀♊ □ ⚷♓	10:11 pm	**7:11 pm**	
☽ enters ♐	10:38 pm	**7:38 pm**	
☽♐ □ ♆♓		**9:09 pm**	
☽♐ ⚻ ♃♉		**10:53 pm**	

14 Tue
2nd ♐
Flag Day

OP: **After Moon trines Uranus until v/c Moon.** The total lunar eclipse on Wednesday prevents this period from being as usable as it would otherwise be. You should still be able to follow through on matters already begun.

☽♐ □ ♆♓	12:09 am		
☽♐ ⚻ ♃♉	1:53 am		
☽♐ △ ♅♈	5:53 am	**2:53 am**	
☽♐ □ ⚷♓	7:52 am	**4:52 am**	
☽♐ ☍ ♀♊	8:47 am	**5:47 am**	
☽♐ ✶ ♄♎	4:18 pm	**1:18 pm**	
♀♊ ⚻ ♇♑	7:10 pm	**4:10 pm**	

15 Wed
2nd ♐
○ 24 ♐ 23
Lunar Eclipse (Total)

☽♐ ☍ ☉♊	4:14 pm	**1:14 pm**	
☽♐ ⚻ ♂♉	7:33 pm	**4:33 pm**	
☽♐ ☍ ☿♊	11:31 pm	**8:31 pm** v/c
☽ enters ♑		**10:59 pm**	

16 Thu
3rd ♐

☽ enters ♑	1:59 am		
☽♑ ✶ ♆♓	3:31 am	**12:31 am**	
☽♑ △ ♃♉	6:05 am	**3:05 am**	
☽♑ □ ♅♈	9:36 am	**6:36 am**	
☽♑ ✶ ⚷♓	11:33 am	**8:33 am**	
☽♑ ☌ ♇♑	1:23 pm	**10:23 am**	
☿ enters ♋	3:09 pm	**12:09 pm**	
☽♑ ⚻ ♀♊	5:38 pm	**2:38 pm**	
☽♑ □ ♄♎	8:24 pm	**5:24 pm**	
☿♋ △ ♆♓		**9:52 pm**	

☿♋△♆♓	12:52 am	
☿♋✶♃♉	8:35 pm **5:35 pm**	
♀♊△♄♎	**9:31 pm**	
☽♑⊼☉♊	**10:41 pm**	

Fri 17
3rd ♑

♀♊△♄♎	12:31 am	
☽♑⊼☉♊	1:41 am	
☽♑△♂♉	4:07 am **1:07 am** v/c	
☽ enters ♒	7:47 am **4:47 am**	
☽♒□♃♉	12:55 pm **9:55 am**	
☽♒⊼☿♋	3:51 pm **12:51 pm**	
☽♒✶♅♈	3:55 pm **12:55 pm**	
☿♋□♅♈	4:11 pm **1:11 pm**	

Sat 18
3rd ♑

☽♒△♄♎	3:19 am **12:19 am**	
☿♋△⚷♓	4:04 am **1:04 am**	
☽♒△♀♊	6:08 am **3:08 am**	
☿♋☍♇♑	3:18 pm **12:18 pm**	

Sun 19
3rd ♒
FATHER'S DAY

Eastern Time plain / **Pacific Time bold**

MAY

S	M	T	W	T	F	S
1	2	3	4	5	6	7
8	9	10	11	12	13	14
15	16	17	18	19	20	21
22	23	24	25	26	27	28
29	30	31				

JUNE

S	M	T	W	T	F	S
			1	2	3	4
5	6	7	8	9	10	11
12	13	14	15	16	17	18
19	20	21	22	23	24	25
26	27	28	29	30		

JULY

S	M	T	W	T	F	S
					1	2
3	4	5	6	7	8	9
10	11	12	13	14	15	16
17	18	19	20	21	22	23
24	25	26	27	28	29	30
31						

20 Mon
3rd ≈

☽ ≈ △ ☉ ♊	3:02 pm **12:02 pm**
☽ ≈ □ ♂ ♉	4:23 pm **1:23 pm** v/c
☽ enters ♓	4:45 pm **1:45 pm**
☽ ♓ ♂ ♆ ♓	6:24 pm **3:24 pm**
♂ enters ♊	10:50 pm **7:50 pm**
☽ ♓ ✶ ♃ ♉	11:02 pm **8:02 pm**

21 Tue
3rd ♓

SUMMER SOLSTICE

OP: After Moon squares Venus until Moon enters Aries. Just keep your head above water. With Mars square Neptune and also Mercury square Saturn now, there will be a lot of nasty headlines.

☽ ♓ ♂ ⚷ ♓	3:21 am **12:21 am**
☽ ♓ ✶ ♇ ♑	5:15 am **2:15 am**
☽ ♓ △ ☿ ♋	1:09 pm **10:09 am**
☉ enters ♋	1:16 pm **10:16 am**
☽ ♓ ⊼ ♄ ♎	1:24 pm **10:24 am**
☿ ♋ □ ♄ ♎	2:42 pm **11:42 am**
☽ ♓ □ ♀ ♊	10:51 pm **7:51 pm** v/c
♂ ♊ □ ♆ ♓	**11:45 pm**

22 Wed
3rd ♓

♂ ♊ □ ♆ ♓	2:45 am
☉ ♋ △ ♆ ♓	10:07 am **7:07 am**

23 Thu
3rd ♓
◑ 1 ♈ 41

☽ enters ♈	4:24 am **1:24 am**
☽ ♈ □ ☉ ♋	7:48 am **4:48 am**
☽ ♈ ✶ ♂ ♊	7:49 am **4:49 am**
☽ ♈ ♂ ♅ ♈	1:23 pm **10:23 am**
☽ ♈ □ ♇ ♑	5:08 pm **2:08 pm**
☽ ♈ ☍ ♄ ♎	**10:41 pm**

☽♈☍♄♎	1:41 am	
☽♈□☿♋	1:29 pm **10:29 am**	

FRI 24
4th ♈

OP: After Moon squares Mercury until v/c Moon. Great for conviviality, customer contacts, and sales.

☽♈⚹♀♊	6:07 pm **3:07 pm** v/c	

☽ enters ♉	4:53 pm **1:53 pm**
☽♉⚹♆♓	6:28 pm **3:28 pm**
☉♋⚹♃♉	7:54 pm **4:54 pm**
☽♉☌♃♉	**10:07 pm**
☽♉⚹☉♋	**10:29 pm**

SAT 25
4th ♈

OP: When Moon enters Taurus today until Moon enters Gemini next Tuesday. The fourth-quarter Moon warns against starting new projects now, but Saturday evening and Sunday can be great for socializing and entertaining.

☽♉☌♃♉	1:07 am
☽♉⚹☉♋	1:29 am
☽♉⚹⚷♓	3:33 am **12:33 am**
☽♉△♇♑	5:22 am **2:22 am**
☉♋□♅♈	6:13 am **3:13 am**
☽♉⚻♄♎	2:00 pm **11:00 am**

SUN 26
4th ♉

Eastern Time plain / **Pacific Time bold**

MAY						
S	M	T	W	T	F	S
1	2	3	4	5	6	7
8	9	10	11	12	13	14
15	16	17	18	19	20	21
22	23	24	25	26	27	28
29	30	31				

JUNE						
S	M	T	W	T	F	S
			1	2	3	4
5	6	7	8	9	10	11
12	13	14	15	16	17	18
19	20	21	22	23	24	25
26	27	28	29	30		

JULY						
S	M	T	W	T	F	S
					1	2
3	4	5	6	7	8	9
10	11	12	13	14	15	16
17	18	19	20	21	22	23
24	25	26	27	28	29	30
31						

27 MON
4th ♉

☉♋△ ⚷♓	3:08 am	**12:08 am**
♂♊⚹ ♅♈	6:26 am	**3:26 am**
☽♉⚹ ☿♋	12:24 pm	**9:24 am** v/c
☉♋☍ ♇♑		**10:19 pm**

28 TUE
4th ♉

☉♋☍ ♇♑	1:19 am	
☽ enters ♊	3:56 am	**12:56 am**
☽♊□ ♆♓	5:24 am	**2:24 am**
♂♊□ ⚷♓	9:27 am	**6:27 am**
☽♊⚹ ♅♈	12:35 pm	**9:35 am**
☽♊□ ⚷♓	2:05 pm	**11:05 am**
☽♊♂ ♂♊	2:22 pm	**11:22 am**
☽♊⚻ ♇♑	3:47 pm	**12:47 pm**
☽♊△ ♄♎		**9:16 pm**

29 WED
4th ♊

☽♊△ ♄♎	12:16 am	
♂♊⚻ ♇♑	2:47 pm	**11:47 am**

OP: After Moon trines Saturn until v/c Moon. Wednesday evening has great vibes, but the Balsamic Moon makes it unlikely that you'll meet someone now who will become important in your life. Just enjoy yourself.

30 THU
4th ♊

☽♊♂ ♀♊	3:33 am	**12:33 am** v/c
☽ enters ♋	12:13 pm	**9:13 am**
☽♋△ ♆♓	1:33 pm	**10:33 am**
☽♋□ ♅♈	8:28 pm	**5:28 pm**
☽♋⚹ ♃♉	9:11 pm	**6:11 pm**
☽♋△ ⚷♓	9:45 pm	**6:45 pm**
☽♋☍ ♇♑	11:21 pm	**8:21 pm**

☽♋ ☌ ☉♋	4:54 am	**1:54 am**	
☽♋ □ ♄♎	7:37 am	**4:37 am** v/c	
☿ enters ♌		**10:38 pm**	

Fri 1
4th ♋
● New Moon 9 ♋ 12
Solar Eclipse (Partial)

OP: After Moon squares Saturn until Moon enters Leo. The Moon remains under Sun's beams almost until the end of this OP. Your thinking should be clearer by Saturday afternoon.

☿ enters ♌	1:38 am		
☿♌ ⚻ ♆♓	11:43 am	**8:43 am**	
♃♉ ✶ ⚷♓	2:13 pm	**11:13 am**	
☽ enters ♌	5:43 pm	**2:43 pm**	
☽♌ ⚻ ♆♓	6:56 pm	**3:56 pm**	
☽♌ ☌ ☿♌	7:55 pm	**4:55 pm**	
☉♋ □ ♄♎	8:17 pm	**5:17 pm**	
☽♌ △ ♅♈		**10:37 pm**	
☽♌ ⚻ ⚷♓		**11:45 pm**	
☽♌ □ ♃♉		**11:55 pm**	

Sat 2
1st ♋

☽♌ △ ♅♈	1:37 am		
☽♌ ⚻ ⚷♓	2:45 am		
☽♌ □ ♃♉	2:55 am		
☽♌ ⚻ ♇♑	4:16 am	**1:16 am**	
☽♌ ✶ ♂♊	9:00 am	**6:00 am**	
☽♌ ✶ ♄♎	12:25 pm	**9:25 am** v/c	
♀ enters ♋		**9:17 pm**	

Sun 3
1st ♌

OP: After Moon squares Jupiter until v/c Moon. If you have something important to do on Sunday morning, you can be responsible and get it done.

Eastern Time plain / **Pacific Time bold**

JUNE						
S	M	T	W	T	F	S
			1	2	3	4
5	6	7	8	9	10	11
12	13	14	15	16	17	18
19	20	21	22	23	24	25
26	27	28	29	30		

JULY						
S	M	T	W	T	F	S
					1	2
3	4	5	6	7	8	9
10	11	12	13	14	15	16
17	18	19	20	21	22	23
24	25	26	27	28	29	30
31						

AUGUST						
S	M	T	W	T	F	S
	1	2	3	4	5	6
7	8	9	10	11	12	13
14	15	16	17	18	19	20
21	22	23	24	25	26	27
28	29	30	31			

4 M‌ON

1st ♌
I‌NDEPENDENCE D‌AY

♀ enters ♋	12:17 am	
♀♋ △ ♆♓	1:26 pm	**10:26 am**
☿♌ △ ♅♈	8:47 pm	**5:47 pm**
☽ enters ♍	9:15 pm	**6:15 pm**
☽♍ ☍ ♆♓	10:23 pm	**7:23 pm**
☽♍ ✶ ♀♋	11:14 pm	**8:14 pm**

5 T‌UE

1st ♍
OP: After Moon squares Mars until v/c Moon. Short but productive.

☽♍ ⚻ ♅♈	4:59 am	**1:59 am**
☿♌ ⚻ ⚷♓	5:53 am	**2:53 am**
☽♍ ☍ ⚷♓	5:59 am	**2:59 am**
☽♍ △ ♃♉	6:49 am	**3:49 am**
☽♍ △ ♇♑	7:27 am	**4:27 am**
☿♌ □ ♃♉	2:09 pm	**11:09 am**
☽♍ □ ♂♊	2:50 pm	**11:50 am**
☿♌ ⚻ ♇♑	7:08 pm	**4:08 pm**
☽♍ ✶ ☉♋	8:19 pm	**5:19 pm** v/c

6 W‌ED

1st ♍

♂♊ △ ♄♎	8:16 am	**5:16 am**
☽ enters ♎	11:54 pm	**8:54 pm**
☽♎ ⚻ ♆♓		**9:57 pm**

7 T‌HU

1st ♎
◑ 15 ♎ 47 (Pacific)

☽♎ ⚻ ♆♓	12:57 am	
☽♎ □ ♀♋	6:37 am	**3:37 am**
☽♎ ☍ ♅♈	7:35 am	**4:35 am**
☽♎ ⚻ ⚷♓	8:28 am	**5:28 am**
☽♎ ⚻ ♃♉	9:56 am	**6:56 am**
☽♎ □ ♇♑	9:56 am	**6:56 am**
♃♉ △ ♇♑	10:06 am	**7:06 am**
☽♎ ✶ ☿♌	2:37 pm	**11:37 am**
♀♋ □ ♅♈	5:44 pm	**2:44 pm**
☽♎ ☌ ♄♎	6:20 pm	**3:20 pm**
☽♎ △ ♂♊	8:00 pm	**5:00 pm**
☽♎ □ ☉♋		**11:29 pm** v/c

Uranus Note: Uranus goes retrograde on Saturday and remains so until early December.

☽ ♎ □ ☉ ♋	2:29 am		v/c
♀ ♋ △ ⚷ ♓	3:45 am	**12:45 am**	
♀ ♋ ☍ ♇ ♑	8:31 pm	**5:31 pm**	
♀ ♋ ✶ ♃ ♉		**11:06 pm**	
☽ enters ♏		**11:31 pm**	

Fri 8

1st ♎

◗ 15 ♎ 47 (Eastern)

♀ ♋ ✶ ♃ ♉	2:06 am		
☽ enters ♏	2:31 am		
☽ ♏ △ ♆ ♓	3:32 am	**12:32 am**	
☿ ♌ ✶ ♄ ♎	4:19 am	**1:19 am**	
☽ ♏ ⚹ ♅ ♈	10:16 am	**7:16 am**	
☽ ♏ △ ⚷ ♓	11:04 am	**8:04 am**	
☽ ♏ ✶ ♇ ♑	12:33 pm	**9:33 am**	
☽ ♏ ☍ ♃ ♉	1:11 pm	**10:11 am**	
☽ ♏ △ ♀ ♋	2:07 pm	**11:07 am**	
♅ ℞ in ♈	8:35 pm	**5:35 pm**	
☽ ♏ □ ☿ ♌	11:06 pm	**8:06 pm**	
☽ ♏ ⚹ ♂ ♊		**10:27 pm**	

Sat 9

2nd ♎

OP: After Moon squares Mercury until v/c Moon. Usable for night owls.

☽ ♏ ⚹ ♂ ♊	1:27 am		
☽ ♏ △ ☉ ♋	9:05 am	**6:05 am**	v/c

Sun 10

2nd ♏

Eastern Time plain / **Pacific Time bold**

JUNE						
S	M	T	W	T	F	S
			1	2	3	4
5	6	7	8	9	10	11
12	13	14	15	16	17	18
19	20	21	22	23	24	25
26	27	28	29	30		

JULY						
S	M	T	W	T	F	S
					1	2
3	4	5	6	7	8	9
10	11	12	13	14	15	16
17	18	19	20	21	22	23
24	25	26	27	28	29	30
31						

AUGUST						
S	M	T	W	T	F	S
	1	2	3	4	5	6
7	8	9	10	11	12	13
14	15	16	17	18	19	20
21	22	23	24	25	26	27
28	29	30	31			

11 MON
2nd ♏

☽ enters ♐		5:47 am	**2:47 am**
☽ ♐ □ ♆ ♓		6:44 am	**3:44 am**
☽ ♐ △ ♅ ♈		1:40 pm	**10:40 am**
☽ ♐ □ ⚷ ♓		2:23 pm	**11:23 am**
☽ ♐ ⊼ ♃ ♉		5:11 pm	**2:11 pm**
☽ ♐ ⊼ ♀ ♋		10:36 pm	**7:36 pm**
☿ ♌ ✶ ♂ ♊		11:28 pm	**8:28 pm**
☽ ♐ ✶ ♄ ♎			**10:05 pm**

12 TUE
2nd ♐

OP: After Moon opposes Mars until Moon enters Capricorn. Wait two hours after the opposition before making any important decisions. The usable portion of this OP is entirely within the v/c Moon in Sagittarius.

☽ ♐ ✶ ♄ ♎		1:05 am	
☽ ♐ ☍ ♂ ♊		7:56 am	**4:56 am**
☽ ♐ △ ☿ ♌		8:21 am	**5:21 am** v/c
☽ ♐ ⊼ ☉ ♋		4:52 pm	**1:52 pm**

13 WED
2nd ♐

♀ ♋ □ ♄ ♎		3:35 am	**12:35 am**
☽ enters ♑		10:14 am	**7:14 am**
☽ ♑ ✶ ♆ ♓		11:08 am	**8:08 am**
☽ ♑ □ ♅ ♈		6:20 pm	**3:20 pm**
☽ ♑ ✶ ⚷ ♓		6:58 pm	**3:58 pm**
☽ ♑ ☌ ♇ ♑		8:34 pm	**5:34 pm**
☽ ♑ △ ♃ ♉		10:32 pm	**7:32 pm**

14 THU
2nd ♑

○ 22 ♑ 28 (Pacific)

OP: After Moon squares Saturn until v/c Moon. A high-energy Full Moon day.

☽ ♑ □ ♄ ♎		6:19 am	**3:19 am**
☽ ♑ ☍ ♀ ♋		8:55 am	**5:55 am**
☽ ♑ ⊼ ♂ ♊		4:09 pm	**1:09 pm**
☽ ♑ ⊼ ☿ ♌		7:09 pm	**4:09 pm**
☽ ♑ ☍ ☉ ♋			**11:40 pm** v/c

☽ ♑ ☌ ☉♋ 2:40 am v/c
☽ enters ≈ 4:30 pm **1:30 pm**
☽ ≈ ⚹ ♅♈ **9:56 pm**

Fri 15
2nd ♑
○ 22 ♑ 28 (Eastern)

☽ ≈ ⚹ ♅♈ 12:56 am
☽ ≈ □ ♃♉ 5:54 am **2:54 am**
☽ ≈ △ ♄♎ 1:41 pm **10:41 am**
☽ ≈ ⊼ ♀♋ 10:04 pm **7:04 pm**
☽ ≈ △ ♂♊ **11:56 pm**

Sat 16
3rd ≈

OP: After Moon squares Jupiter until v/c Moon. An energetic mood, good for sports and for dancing.

☽ ≈ △ ♂♊ 2:56 am
☽ ≈ ☍ ☿♌ 8:23 am **5:23 am** v/c
☽ ≈ ⊼ ☉♋ 3:20 pm **12:20 pm**
☽ enters ♓ **10:13 pm**
☽ ♓ ☌ ♆♓ **11:02 pm**

Sun 17
3rd ≈

Eastern Time plain / **Pacific Time bold**

	JUNE					
S	M	T	W	T	F	S
			1	2	3	4
5	6	7	8	9	10	11
12	13	14	15	16	17	18
19	20	21	22	23	24	25
26	27	28	29	30		

	JULY					
S	M	T	W	T	F	S
					1	2
3	4	5	6	7	8	9
10	11	12	13	14	15	16
17	18	19	20	21	22	23
24	25	26	27	28	29	30
31						

	AUGUST					
S	M	T	W	T	F	S
	1	2	3	4	5	6
7	8	9	10	11	12	13
14	15	16	17	18	19	20
21	22	23	24	25	26	27
28	29	30	31			

18 Mon
3rd ♒

☽ enters ♓	1:13 am	
☽ ♓ ☌ ♆ ♓	2:02 am	
☽ ♓ ☌ ♅ ♓	10:26 am	**7:26 am**
☽ ♓ ⚹ ♇ ♑	12:17 pm	**9:17 am**
☽ ♓ ⚹ ♃ ♉	3:51 pm	**12:51 pm**
☽ ♓ ☌ ♄ ♎	11:39 pm	**8:39 pm**

19 Tue
3rd ♓

OP: After Moon squares Mars until Moon enters Aries. Tuesday evening consider doing something to help others, being creative, or at least enjoying the arts.

☽ ♓ △ ♀ ♋	2:43 pm	**11:43 am**
☽ ♓ □ ♂ ♊	4:45 pm	**1:45 pm**
☽ ♓ ☌ ☿ ♌		**9:19 pm**

20 Wed
3rd ♓

☽ ♓ ☌ ☿ ♌	12:19 am	
☽ ♓ △ ☉ ♋	7:15 am	**4:15 am** v/c
☽ enters ♈	12:25 pm	**9:25 am**
☽ ♈ ☌ ♅ ♈	9:30 pm	**6:30 pm**
☽ ♈ □ ♇ ♑	11:45 pm	**8:45 pm**

21 Thu
3rd ♈

☽ ♈ ☍ ♄ ♎	11:53 am	**8:53 am**

Mercury Note: Mercury enters its Storm (moving less than 40 minutes of arc per day) on Sunday, as it slows down before going retrograde. The Storm acts like the retrograde. Don't start any new projects now—just follow through with the items that are already on your plate.

☽♈⚹♂♊	8:45 am	**5:45 am**
☽♈□♀♋	9:57 am	**6:57 am**

☽♈△☿♌	5:34 pm	**2:34 pm** v/c
☉ enters ♌		**9:12 pm**
☽ enters ♉		**9:58 pm**
☽♉□☉♌		**10:02 pm**
☽♉⚹♆♓		**10:36 pm**

Fri 22
3rd ♈

◑ 0 ♉ 02 (Pacific)

OP: After Moon squares Venus until v/c Moon. Make a list of your plans now as a reference before Mercury enters its Storm and then goes retrograde.

☉ enters ♌	12:12 am	
☽ enters ♉	12:58 am	
☽♉□☉♌	1:02 am	
☽♉⚹♆♓	1:36 am	
☉♌⚻♆♓	7:54 am	**4:54 am**
☽♉⚹⚷♓	10:10 am	**7:10 am**
☽♉△♇♑	12:12 pm	**9:12 am**
☽♉♂♃♉	5:19 pm	**2:19 pm**
☽♉⚻♄♎		**9:41 pm**

Sat 23
3rd ♈

◑ 0 ♉ 02 (Eastern)

☽♉⚻♄♎	12:41 am	

Sun 24
4th ♉

Eastern Time plain / **Pacific Time bold**

JUNE						
S	M	T	W	T	F	S
			1	2	3	4
5	6	7	8	9	10	11
12	13	14	15	16	17	18
19	20	21	22	23	24	25
26	27	28	29	30		

JULY						
S	M	T	W	T	F	S
					1	2
3	4	5	6	7	8	9
10	11	12	13	14	15	16
17	18	19	20	21	22	23
24	25	26	27	28	29	30
31						

AUGUST						
S	M	T	W	T	F	S
	1	2	3	4	5	6
7	8	9	10	11	12	13
14	15	16	17	18	19	20
21	22	23	24	25	26	27
28	29	30	31			

25 Mon
4th ♉

OP: After Moon squares Mercury until Moon enters Gemini.
Short but usable OP.

☽ ♉ ✶ ♀ ♋	4:44 am	**1:44 am**
☽ ♉ □ ☿ ♌	9:12 am	**6:12 am** v/c
☽ enters ♊	12:34 pm	**9:34 am**
☽ ♊ □ ♆ ♓	1:04 pm	**10:04 am**
☽ ♊ ✶ ☉ ♌	5:37 pm	**2:37 pm**
☽ ♊ ✶ ♅ ♈	9:13 pm	**6:13 pm**
☽ ♊ □ ⚷ ♓	9:15 pm	**6:15 pm**
☽ ♊ ⚻ ♇ ♑	11:16 pm	**8:16 pm**

26 Tue
4th ♊

☽ ♊ △ ♄ ♎	11:35 am	**8:35 am**

27 Wed
4th ♊

OP: After Moon conjoins Mars until v/c Moon. Fourth-quarter
Moon and Mercury Storm both suggest following through on
projects already begun. This can be a highly productive day.

☽ ♊ ☌ ♂ ♊	12:55 pm	**9:55 am**
☉ ♌ ⚻ ⚷ ♓	2:55 pm	**11:55 am**
☉ ♌ △ ♅ ♈	3:43 pm	**12:43 pm**
☽ ♊ ✶ ☿ ♌	8:35 pm	**5:35 pm** v/c
☽ enters ♋	9:11 pm	**6:11 pm**
☽ ♋ △ ♆ ♓	9:33 pm	**6:33 pm**

28 Thu
4th ♋

OP: After Moon squares Saturn until Moon enters Leo on
Friday. With Mercury slowing down and opposing Neptune,
thinking clearly may be a challenge now. Take care of ordinary
business.

☽ ♋ △ ⚷ ♓	5:09 am	**2:09 am**
☽ ♋ □ ♅ ♈	5:15 am	**2:15 am**
☽ ♋ ☍ ♇ ♑	7:08 am	**4:08 am**
♀ enters ♌	10:59 am	**7:59 am**
☽ ♋ ✶ ♃ ♉	12:50 pm	**9:50 am**
☿ enters ♍	1:59 pm	**10:59 am**
♀ ♌ ⚻ ♆ ♓	2:33 pm	**11:33 am**
☉ ♌ ⚻ ♇ ♑	5:30 pm	**2:30 pm**
☽ ♋ □ ♄ ♎	7:03 pm	**4:03 pm** v/c
☿ ♍ ☍ ♆ ♓		**9:00 pm**

☿ ♍ ☍ ♆ ♓   12:00 am
☽ enters ♌   **11:16 pm**
☽ ♌ ⊼ ♆ ♓   **11:31 pm**

Fri 29
4th ♋

☽ enters ♌   2:16 am
☽ ♌ ⊼ ♆ ♓   2:31 am
☽ ♌ ♂ ♀ ♌   6:03 am   **3:03 am**
☽ ♌ ⊼ ⚷ ♓   9:36 am   **6:36 am**
☽ ♌ △ ♅ ♈   9:47 am   **6:47 am**
☽ ♌ ⊼ ♇ ♑   11:32 am   **8:32 am**
☽ ♌ ♂ ☉ ♌   2:40 pm   **11:40 am**
☽ ♌ □ ♃ ♉   5:22 pm   **2:22 pm**
☽ ♌ ✶ ♄ ♎   11:09 pm   **8:09 pm**

Sat 30
4th ♋
● 7 ♌ 16

OP: **After Moon squares Jupiter until v/c Moon.** Mercury is at a crawl now, and the Moon is still under "Sun's beams."

♀ ♌ ⊼ ⚷ ♓   9:22 pm   **6:22 pm**
♀ ♌ △ ♅ ♈   **9:09 pm**
☽ ♌ ✶ ♂ ♊   **11:20 pm** v/c

Sun 31
1st ♌

Eastern Time plain / **Pacific Time bold**

	JUNE					
S	M	T	W	T	F	S
			1	2	3	4
5	6	7	8	9	10	11
12	13	14	15	16	17	18
19	20	21	22	23	24	25
26	27	28	29	30		

	JULY					
S	M	T	W	T	F	S
					1	2
3	4	5	6	7	8	9
10	11	12	13	14	15	16
17	18	19	20	21	22	23
24	25	26	27	28	29	30
31						

	AUGUST					
S	M	T	W	T	F	S
	1	2	3	4	5	6
7	8	9	10	11	12	13
14	15	16	17	18	19	20
21	22	23	24	25	26	27
28	29	30	31			

AUGUST

Mercury Note: Mercury goes retrograde on Tuesday and remains so until August 26, after which it will still be in its Storm until August 30. Projects begun during this entire period may not work out as planned. It's best to use this time for review, editing, escrows, etc.

1 MON
1st ♌

RAMADAN BEGINS

OP: After Moon conjoins Mercury (which opposes Neptune) until v/c Moon. Thinking big is better than trying to handle details right now, but sticking to routine is best of all.

♀♌ △ ♅♈	12:09 am	
☽♌ ⚹ ♂♊	2:20 am	v/c
☽ enters ♍	4:41 am	**1:41 am**
☽♍ ☍ ♆♓	4:51 am	**1:51 am**
☽♍ ☌ ☿♍	6:28 am	**3:28 am**
☉♌ □ ♃♉	10:41 am	**7:41 am**
☽♍ ☍ ⚷♓	11:38 am	**8:38 am**
☽♍ ⚻ ♅♈	11:54 am	**8:54 am**
☽♍ △ ♇♑	1:35 pm	**10:35 am**
☽♍ △ ♃♉	7:38 pm	**4:38 pm** v/c
♀♌ ⚻ ♇♑	7:49 pm	**4:49 pm**

2 TUE
1st ♍

☿℞ in ♍	11:50 pm	**8:50 pm**

3 WED
1st ♍

♂ enters ♋	5:22 am	**2:22 am**
☽ enters ♎	6:04 am	**3:04 am**
☽♎ □ ♂♋	6:06 am	**3:06 am**
☽♎ ⚻ ♆♓	6:09 am	**3:09 am**
♂♋ △ ♆♓	6:53 am	**3:53 am**
☽♎ ⚻ ⚷♓	12:51 pm	**9:51 am**
☽♎ ☍ ♅♈	1:12 pm	**10:12 am**
☽♎ □ ♇♑	2:53 pm	**11:53 am**
☽♎ ⚹ ♀♌	6:57 pm	**3:57 pm**
☽♎ ⚻ ♃♉	9:18 pm	**6:18 pm**
☽♎ ⚹ ☉♌		**10:05 pm**
☽♎ ☌ ♄♎		**11:53 pm**

4 THU
1st ♎

☽♎ ⚹ ☉♌	1:05 am	
☽♎ ☌ ♄♎	2:53 am	
☿♍ ⚹ ♂♋	7:19 pm	**4:19 pm**
♆ enters ♒	10:54 pm	**7:54 pm**
♀♌ □ ♃♉		**9:34 pm**

♀♌ □ ♃♉	12:34 am		
☉♌ ⚹ ♄♎	6:47 am	**3:47 am**	
☽♎ △ ♆♒	7:56 am	**4:56 am** v/c
☽ enters ♏	7:57 am	**4:57 am**	
☽♏ ⚹ ☿♍	9:33 am	**6:33 am**	
☽♏ △ ♂♋	10:27 am	**7:27 am**	
☽♏ △ ⚷♓	2:44 pm	**11:44 am**	
☽♏ ⚻ ♅♈	3:11 pm	**12:11 pm**	
☽♏ ⚹ ♇♑	4:55 pm	**1:55 pm**	
☽♏ ☍ ♃♉	11:52 pm	**8:52 pm**	
☽♏ □ ♀♌		**10:57 pm**	

Fri 5

1st ♎

☽♏ □ ♀♌	1:57 am		
☽♏ □ ☉♌	7:08 am	**4:08 am**	

Sat 6

1st ♏

◐ 13 ♏ 40

☽♏ □ ♆♒	11:14 am	**8:14 am** v/c
☽ enters ♐	11:21 am	**8:21 am**	
☽♐ □ ☿♍	11:54 am	**8:54 am**	
☽♐ ⚻ ♂♋	4:33 pm	**1:33 pm**	
☽♐ □ ⚷♓	6:12 pm	**3:12 pm**	
☽♐ △ ♅♈	6:45 pm	**3:45 pm**	
♀♌ ⚹ ♄♎	10:19 pm	**7:19 pm**	

Sun 7

2nd ♏

OP: After Moon squares Mercury until Moon enters Capricorn on Tuesday. Do what needs to be done, without expecting everything to work out the way you want.

Eastern Time plain / Pacific Time bold

JULY						
S	M	T	W	T	F	S
					1	2
3	4	5	6	7	8	9
10	11	12	13	14	15	16
17	18	19	20	21	22	23
24	25	26	27	28	29	30
31						

AUGUST						
S	M	T	W	T	F	S
	1	2	3	4	5	6
7	8	9	10	11	12	13
14	15	16	17	18	19	20
21	22	23	24	25	26	27
28	29	30	31			

SEPTEMBER						
S	M	T	W	T	F	S
				1	2	3
4	5	6	7	8	9	10
11	12	13	14	15	16	17
18	19	20	21	22	23	24
25	26	27	28	29	30	

8 MON
2nd ♐

OP: After Moon squares Mercury on Sunday until Moon enters Capricorn on Tuesday. Do what needs to be done, without expecting everything to work out the way you want.

☽ ♐ ⽊ ♃ ♉		4:07 am	**1:07 am**
☿ enters ♌		5:46 am	**2:46 am**
☽ ♐ ✳ ♄ ♎		10:07 am	**7:07 am**
☿ ♌ ☍ ♆ ♒		10:27 am	**7:27 am**
☽ ♐ △ ♀ ♌		11:13 am	**8:13 am**
☽ ♐ △ ☉ ♌		3:22 pm	**12:22 pm**
♂ ♋ △ ⚷ ♓			**9:29 pm**

9 TUE
2nd ♐

♂ ♋ △ ⚷ ♓	12:29 am	
♂ ♋ □ ♅ ♈	12:33 pm	**9:33 am**
☽ ♐ △ ☿ ♌	3:20 pm	**12:20 pm**
☽ ♐ ✳ ♆ ♒	4:24 pm	**1:24 pm** v/c
☽ enters ♑	4:38 pm	**1:38 pm**
☽ ♑ ✳ ⚷ ♓	11:33 pm	**8:33 pm**
☽ ♑ □ ♅ ♈		**9:13 pm**
☽ ♑ ☍ ♂ ♋		**9:51 pm**
☽ ♑ ☌ ♇ ♑		**11:06 pm**

10 WED
2nd ♑

☽ ♑ □ ♅ ♈	12:13 am	
☽ ♑ ☍ ♂ ♋	12:51 am	
☽ ♑ ☌ ♇ ♑	2:06 am	
☽ ♑ △ ♃ ♉	10:17 am	**7:17 am**
☽ ♑ □ ♄ ♎	4:34 pm	**1:34 pm** v/c
☽ ♑ ⽊ ♀ ♌	11:00 pm	**8:00 pm**
♂ ♋ ☍ ♇ ♑		**10:14 pm**
☽ ♑ ⽊ ☉ ♌		**10:58 pm**

11 THU
2nd ♑

♂ ♋ ☍ ♇ ♑	1:14 am	
☽ ♑ ⽊ ☉ ♌	1:58 am	
☽ ♑ ⽊ ☿ ♌	7:50 pm	**4:50 pm**
☽ enters ♒	11:47 pm	**8:47 pm**

☽ ≈ ✶ ♅ ♈ 7:32 am **4:32 am**
☽ ≈ ⊼ ♂ ♋ 11:20 am **8:20 am**
☽ ≈ □ ♃ ♉ 6:20 pm **3:20 pm**
☽ ≈ △ ♄ ♎   **9:57 pm**

FRI 12
2nd ≈

☽ ≈ △ ♄ ♎ 12:57 am
☽ ≈ ☍ ♀ ♌ 1:22 pm **10:22 am**
☽ ≈ ☍ ☉ ♌ 2:58 pm **11:58 am**
☽ ≈ ☍ ☿ ♌   **10:29 pm**

SAT 13
2nd ≈
○ 15 ♎ 47

☽ ≈ ☍ ☿ ♌ 1:29 am
☽ ≈ ☌ ♆ ≈ 8:25 am **5:25 am** v/c
☽ enters ♓ 8:54 am **5:54 am**
☽ ♓ ☌ ♅ ♓ 3:53 pm **12:53 pm**
☽ ♓ ✶ ♇ ♑ 6:55 pm **3:55 pm**
☽ ♓ △ ♂ ♋   **9:07 pm**

SUN 14
3rd ≈

OP: When Moon enters Pisces today until Moon enters Aries on Tuesday. Use this time for helping others, being creative, appreciating the arts, or for meditation.

Eastern Time plain / **Pacific Time bold**

JULY						
S	M	T	W	T	F	S
					1	2
3	4	5	6	7	8	9
10	11	12	13	14	15	16
17	18	19	20	21	22	23
24	25	26	27	28	29	30
31						

AUGUST						
S	M	T	W	T	F	S
	1	2	3	4	5	6
7	8	9	10	11	12	13
14	15	16	17	18	19	20
21	22	23	24	25	26	27
28	29	30	31			

SEPTEMBER						
S	M	T	W	T	F	S
				1	2	3
4	5	6	7	8	9	10
11	12	13	14	15	16	17
18	19	20	21	22	23	24
25	26	27	28	29	30	

Mercury Note: Retrograde Mercury is moving "backwards" at its fastest speed around the time it conjoins the Sun. Things may start to feel almost normal for a while, but that won't last.

15 MON
3rd ♓

OP: When Moon entered Pisces on Sunday until Moon enters Aries on Tuesday. Use this time for helping others, being creative, appreciating the arts, or meditation.

☽	♓	△	♂	♋	12:07 am	
☽	♓	✶	♃	♉	4:21 am	**1:21 am** v/c
☽	♓	⊼	♄	♎	11:24 am	**8:24 am**

16 TUE
3rd ♓

☽	♓	⊼	♀	♌	6:29 am	**3:29 am**
☽	♓	⊼	☉	♌	6:31 am	**3:31 am**
☉	♌	♂	♀	♌	8:08 am	**5:08 am**
☽	♓	⊼	☿	♌	8:33 am	**5:33 am**
☿	♌	♂	♀	♌	7:21 pm	**4:21 pm**
☽ enters ♈					8:01 pm	**5:01 pm**
☉	♌	♂	☿	♌	9:04 pm	**6:04 pm**

17 WED
3rd ♈

OP: After Moon opposes Saturn today until v/c Moon on Friday. Use that Aries energy to catch up now.

☽	♈	♂	♅	♈	4:03 am	**1:03 am**
☽	♈	□	♇	♑	6:17 am	**3:17 am**
☽	♈	□	♂	♋	3:11 pm	**12:11 pm**
☽	♈	☍	♄	♎	11:47 pm	**8:47 pm**

18 THU
3rd ♈

♂	♋	✶	♃	♉	12:49 pm	**9:49 am**
☽	♈	△	☿	♌	5:02 pm	**2:02 pm**
☽	♈	△	☉	♌		**9:13 pm**
☽	♈	△	♀	♌		**10:53 pm**

☽♈△☉♌	12:13 am		
☽♈△♀♌	1:53 am		
☽♈✶♆♒	7:50 am	**4:50 am** v/c
☽ enters ♉	8:36 am	**5:36 am**
☽♉✶⚷♓	3:25 pm	**12:25 pm**
☽♉△♇♑	6:54 pm	**3:54 pm**

Fri 19
3rd ♈

☽♉☌♃♉	5:14 am	**2:14 am**
☽♉✶♂♋	7:27 am	**4:27 am**
☽♉☌♄♎	1:00 pm	**10:00 am**
☽♉□☿♌		**11:13 pm**

Sat 20
3rd ♉

☽♉□☿♌	2:13 am		
♀♌☍♆♒	9:39 am	**6:39 am**	
☽♉□☉♌	5:54 pm	**2:54 pm**	
♀ enters ♍	6:11 pm	**3:11 pm**	
☽♉□♆♒	7:59 pm	**4:59 pm** v/c
☽ enters ♊	8:53 pm	**5:53 pm**	
☽♊□♀♍	9:11 pm	**6:11 pm**	

Sun 21
3rd ♉
◑ 28 ♉ 30

OP: After Moon squares Venus today until v/c Moon on Wednesday. Great for review, editing, and following up on projects which you began before Mercury's Storm and retrograde.

Eastern Time plain / Pacific Time bold

JULY						
S	M	T	W	T	F	S
					1	2
3	4	5	6	7	8	9
10	11	12	13	14	15	16
17	18	19	20	21	22	23
24	25	26	27	28	29	30
31						

AUGUST						
S	M	T	W	T	F	S
	1	2	3	4	5	6
7	8	9	10	11	12	13
14	15	16	17	18	19	20
21	22	23	24	25	26	27
28	29	30	31			

SEPTEMBER						
S	M	T	W	T	F	S
				1	2	3
4	5	6	7	8	9	10
11	12	13	14	15	16	17
18	19	20	21	22	23	24
25	26	27	28	29	30	

22 MON
4th ♊

OP: After Moon squared Venus on Sunday until v/c Moon on Wednesday. Great for review, editing, and following up on projects that you began before Mercury's Storm and retrograde.

☽ ♊ □ ♅ ♓		3:16 am	**12:16 am**
☽ ♊ ✶ ♅ ♈		4:29 am	**1:29 am**
☽ ♊ ⊼ ♇ ♑		6:49 am	**3:49 am**
☉ ♌ ☍ ♆ ≈		7:26 pm	**4:26 pm**
☽ ♊ △ ♄ ♎			**9:46 pm**

23 TUE
4th ♊

☽ ♊ △ ♄ ♎		12:46 am	
☉ enters ♍		7:21 am	**4:21 am**
☽ ♊ ✶ ☿ ♌		10:33 am	**7:33 am**

24 WED
4th ♊

☽ ♊ △ ♆ ≈		5:33 am	**2:33 am** v/c
☽ enters ♋		6:31 am	**3:31 am**
♀ ♍ ☍ ♅ ♓		6:53 am	**3:53 am**
☽ ♋ ✶ ☉ ♍		8:23 am	**5:23 am**
☽ ♋ △ ♅ ♓		12:17 pm	**9:17 am**
☽ ♋ ✶ ♀ ♍		12:53 pm	**9:53 am**
☽ ♋ □ ♅ ♈		1:30 pm	**10:30 am**
☽ ♋ ☍ ♇ ♑		3:47 pm	**12:47 pm**
♀ ♍ ⊼ ♅ ♈		7:22 pm	**4:22 pm**
☽ ♋ ✶ ♃ ♉			**10:25 pm**

25 THU
4th ♋

OP: After Moon conjoins Mars until Moon enters Leo. Do what you need to do, knowing that some things will change drastically very soon.

☽ ♋ ✶ ♃ ♉		1:25 am	
♂ ♋ □ ♄ ♎		6:46 am	**3:46 am**
☽ ♋ □ ♄ ♎		8:59 am	**5:59 am**
☽ ♋ ☌ ♂ ♋		9:04 am	**6:04 am** v/c
♀ ♍ △ ♇ ♑		7:12 pm	**4:12 pm**

Mercury Note: Mercury goes direct on Friday, but remains in its Storm, moving slowly, until August 31. We're not out of the woods yet.

☉♍ ☍ ⚷♓	10:39 am	**7:39 am**
☽♋ ⚻ ♆♒	11:09 am	**8:09 am**
☽ enters ♌	12:09 pm	**9:09 am**
☽♌ ⚻ ⚷♓	5:19 pm	**2:19 pm**
☿ D in ♌	6:03 pm	**3:03 pm**
☽♌ △ ♅♈	6:31 pm	**3:31 pm**
☽♌ ⚻ ♇♑	8:42 pm	**5:42 pm**

Fri 26
4th ♋

☉♍ ⚻ ♅♈	3:24 am	**12:24 am**
☽♌ □ ♃♉	5:44 am	**2:44 am**
☽♌ ✳ ♄♎	1:06 pm	**10:06 am**
☽♌ ♂ ☿♌	7:49 pm	**4:49 pm**

Sat 27
4th ♌

☉♍ △ ♇♑	11:12 am	**8:12 am**
☽♌ ☍ ♆♒	1:11 pm	**10:11 am** v/c
☽ enters ♍	2:13 pm	**11:13 am**
☽♍ ☍ ⚷♓	6:57 pm	**3:57 pm**
☽♍ ⚻ ♅♈	8:08 pm	**5:08 pm**
☽♍ △ ♇♑	10:17 pm	**7:17 pm**
☽♍ ♂ ☉♍	11:04 pm	**8:04 pm**

Sun 28
4th ♌
● 15 ♍ 47

OP: Cazimi Moon is usable ½ hour before and ½ hour after the Sun-Moon conjunction (see page 73–74). Because of the Mercury Storm, use this only to follow through on projects already begun.

Eastern Time plain / **Pacific Time bold**

		JULY				
S	M	T	W	T	F	S
					1	2
3	4	5	6	7	8	9
10	11	12	13	14	15	16
17	18	19	20	21	22	23
24	25	26	27	28	29	30
31						

		AUGUST				
S	M	T	W	T	F	S
	1	2	3	4	5	6
7	8	9	10	11	12	13
14	15	16	17	18	19	20
21	22	23	24	25	26	27
28	29	30	31			

		SEPTEMBER				
S	M	T	W	T	F	S
				1	2	3
4	5	6	7	8	9	10
11	12	13	14	15	16	17
18	19	20	21	22	23	24
25	26	27	28	29	30	

Mercury Note: Mercury leaves its Storm (i.e., speeds up to more than 40 minutes of arc per day) on August 31. Use subsequent OP's to look at your notes. What were your plans before Mercury went retrograde? How do all your newer ideas look in hindsight?

29 Mon
1st ♍

☽ ♍ ☌ ♀ ♍	5:10 am	**2:10 am**
☽ ♍ △ ♃ ♉	6:58 am	**3:58 am**
☽ ♍ ⚹ ♂ ♋	6:15 pm	**3:15 pm** v/c
♀ ♍ △ ♃ ♉		**11:46 pm**

30 Tue
1st ♍
RAMADAN ENDS

♀ ♍ △ ♃ ♉	2:46 am	
♃ ℞	5:17 am	**2:17 am**
☽ ♍ ⚻ ♆ ♒	1:19 pm	**10:19 am**
☽ enters ♎	2:25 pm	**11:25 am**
☽ ♎ ⚻ ⚷ ♓	6:55 pm	**3:55 pm**
☽ ♎ ☍ ♅ ♈	8:08 pm	**5:08 pm**
☽ ♎ □ ♇ ♑	10:21 pm	**7:21 pm**

31 Wed
1st ♎

OP: **After Moon squares Mars until v/c Moon.** Good for helping others, creativity, appreciation of the arts, or meditation.

☽ ♎ ⚻ ♃ ♉	7:00 am	**4:00 am**
☽ ♎ ☌ ♄ ♎	2:43 pm	**11:43 am**
☽ ♎ □ ♂ ♋	8:28 pm	**5:28 pm**
☽ ♎ ⚹ ☿ ♌	11:24 pm	**8:24 pm**

1 Thu
1st ♎

☽ ♎ △ ♆ ♒	1:35 pm	**10:35 am** v/c
☽ enters ♏	2:48 pm	**11:48 am**
☽ ♏ △ ⚷ ♓	7:15 pm	**4:15 pm**
☽ ♏ ⚻ ♅ ♈	8:33 pm	**5:33 pm**
☽ ♏ ⚹ ♇ ♑	10:55 pm	**7:55 pm**

☽ ♏ ⚹ ☉ ♍	6:40 am	**3:40 am**	
☽ ♏ ☍ ♃ ♉	7:51 am	**4:51 am**	
☽ ♏ ⚹ ♀ ♍	3:08 pm	**12:08 pm**	
☉ ♍ △ ♃ ♉	11:59 pm	**8:59 pm**	
☽ ♏ △ ♂ ♋		**9:10 pm**	

Fri 2
1st ♏

☽ ♏ △ ♂ ♋	12:10 am		
☽ ♏ □ ☿ ♌	4:04 am	**1:04 am**	
☽ ♏ □ ♆ ♒	3:41 pm	**12:41 pm** v/c	
☽ enters ♐	5:03 pm	**2:03 pm**	
☽ ♐ □ ⚷ ♓	9:34 pm	**6:34 pm**	
☽ ♐ △ ♅ ♈	10:58 pm	**7:58 pm**	

Sat 3
1st ♏

☽ ♐ ⊼ ♃ ♉	10:57 am	**7:57 am**	
☽ ♐ □ ☉ ♍	1:39 pm	**10:39 am**	
☽ ♐ ⚹ ♄ ♎	8:17 pm	**5:17 pm**	
☽ ♐ □ ♀ ♍	11:54 pm	**8:54 pm**	

Sun 4
1st ♐
☽ 11 ♐ 51

OP: After Moon squares Venus today until Moon enters Capricorn on Monday. Try catching up on things that got backlogged during Mercury's retrograde and slow periods.

Eastern Time plain / **Pacific Time bold**

AUGUST						
S	M	T	W	T	F	S
	1	2	3	4	5	6
7	8	9	10	11	12	13
14	15	16	17	18	19	20
21	22	23	24	25	26	27
28	29	30	31			

SEPTEMBER						
S	M	T	W	T	F	S
				1	2	3
4	5	6	7	8	9	10
11	12	13	14	15	16	17
18	19	20	21	22	23	24
25	26	27	28	29	30	

OCTOBER						
S	M	T	W	T	F	S
						1
2	3	4	5	6	7	8
9	10	11	12	13	14	15
16	17	18	19	20	21	22
23	24	25	26	27	28	29
30	31					

5 MON
2nd ♐
LABOR DAY
OP: After Moon squared Venus on Sunday until Moon enters Capricorn today. Try catching up on things that got backlogged during Mercury's retrograde and slow periods.

☽ ♐	⊼	♂ ♋		6:48 am	**3:48 am**
☽ ♐	△	☿ ♌		1:05 pm	**10:05 am**
☽ ♐	✶	♆ ≈		8:30 pm	**5:30 pm** v/c
☽ enters ♑				10:03 pm	**7:03 pm**
☽ ♑	✶	♅ ♓			**11:37 pm**

6 TUE
2nd ♑

☽ ♑	✶	♅ ♓		2:37 am	
☽ ♑	□	♅ ♈		4:09 am	**1:09 am**
☽ ♑	♂	♇ ♑		7:00 am	**4:00 am**
☽ ♑	△	♃ ♉		4:49 pm	**1:49 pm**
☽ ♑	△	☉ ♍			**9:07 pm**

7 WED
2nd ♑

☽ ♑	△	☉ ♍		12:07 am	
☽ ♑	□	♄ ♎		3:11 am	**12:11 am**
☽ ♑	△	♀ ♍		12:21 pm	**9:21 am**
☽ ♑	♂	♂ ♋		4:35 pm	**1:35 pm** v/c
☽ ♑	⊼	☿ ♌			**11:57 pm**

8 THU
2nd ♑

☽ ♑	⊼	☿ ♌		2:57 am	
☽ enters ≈				5:42 am	**2:42 am**
☿ ♌	♂	♆ ≈		11:25 am	**8:25 am**
☽ ≈	✶	♅ ♈		11:53 am	**8:53 am**
☽ ≈	□	♃ ♉			**10:07 pm**
☿ enters ♍					**10:58 pm**

☽ ♒ □ ♃ ♉	1:07 am	
☿ enters ♍	1:58 am	
☽ ♒ △ ♄ ♎	12:31 pm	**9:31 am**
☽ ♒ ⊼ ☉ ♍	1:37 pm	**10:37 am**

Fri 9
2nd ♒

☽ ♒ ⊼ ♀ ♍	3:52 am	**12:52 am**
☽ ♒ ⊼ ♂ ♋	4:57 am	**1:57 am**
☿ ♍ ☍ ☊ ♓	12:29 pm	**9:29 am**
☽ ♒ ☌ ♆ ♒	1:32 pm	**10:32 am** v/c
☽ enters ♓	3:26 pm	**12:26 pm**
☽ ♓ ☌ ☊ ♓	7:54 pm	**4:54 pm**
☽ ♓ ☍ ☿ ♍	9:06 pm	**6:06 pm**
♀ ♍ ✶ ♂ ♋		**9:22 pm**
☿ ♍ ⊼ ♅ ♈		**10:01 pm**
☽ ♓ ✶ ♇ ♑		**10:02 pm**

Sat 10
2nd ♒

OP: When Moon enters Pisces until Moon enters Aries on **Monday.** Too emotional a period for detail work, but good for empathy, meditation, and creativity.

♀ ♍ ✶ ♂ ♋	12:22 am	
☿ ♍ ⊼ ♅ ♈	1:01 am	
☽ ♓ ✶ ♇ ♑	1:02 am	
☽ ♓ ✶ ♃ ♉	11:17 am	**8:17 am**
☽ ♓ ⊼ ♄ ♎	11:44 pm	**8:44 pm**
☿ ♍ △ ♇ ♑		**10:27 pm**

Sun 11
2rd ♓

Eastern Time plain / **Pacific Time bold**

AUGUST						
S	M	T	W	T	F	S
		1	2	3	4	5	6
7	8	9	10	11	12	13
14	15	16	17	18	19	20
21	22	23	24	25	26	27
28	29	30	31			

SEPTEMBER						
S	M	T	W	T	F	S
				1	2	3
4	5	6	7	8	9	10
11	12	13	14	15	16	17
18	19	20	21	22	23	24
25	26	27	28	29	30	

OCTOBER						
S	M	T	W	T	F	S
						1
2	3	4	5	6	7	8
9	10	11	12	13	14	15
16	17	18	19	20	21	22
23	24	25	26	27	28	29
30	31					

September

12 Mon
2nd ♓
○ 19 ♓ 17

OP: When Moon entered Pisces on Sunday until Moon enters Aries. Too emotional a period for detail work, but good for empathy, meditation, and creativity.

☿ ♍ △ ♇ ♑	1:27 am	
☽ ♓ ☍ ☉ ♍	5:27 am	**2:27 am**
☽ ♓ △ ♂ ♋	7:17 pm	**4:17 pm**
☽ ♓ ☍ ♀ ♍	9:45 pm	**6:45 pm** v/c
☽ enters ♈		**11:49 pm**

13 Tue

☽ enters ♈	2:49 am	
☽ ♈ ☌ ♅ ♈	8:59 am	**5:59 am**
☽ ♈ □ ♇ ♑	12:38 pm	**9:38 am**
☽ ♈ ⊼ ☿ ♍	6:43 pm	**3:43 pm**
♀ ♍ ⊼ ♆ ♒		**11:01 pm**

14 Wed
3rd ♓

♀ ♍ ⊼ ♆ ♒	2:01 am	
☽ ♈ ☍ ♄ ♎	12:26 pm	**9:26 am**
☿ ♍ △ ♃ ♉	9:43 pm	**6:43 pm**
♀ enters ♎	10:40 pm	**7:40 pm**
☽ ♈ ⊼ ☉ ♍	11:04 pm	**8:04 pm**

15 Thu
3rd ♈

☽ ♈ □ ♂ ♋	11:07 am	**8:07 am**
☽ ♈ ✶ ♆ ♒	1:10 pm	**10:10 am** v/c
☽ enters ♉	3:25 pm	**12:25 pm**
☽ ♉ ⊼ ♀ ♎	5:23 pm	**2:23 pm**
☽ ♉ ✶ ♁ ♓	7:35 pm	**4:35 pm**
☽ ♉ △ ♇ ♑		**10:20 pm**

☽ ♉ △ ♇ ♑	1:20 am	
☽ ♉ ♂ ♃ ♉	11:26 am	**8:26 am**
♀ ♎ ⚻ ⚷ ♓	1:44 pm	**10:44 am**
♇ D in ♑	2:24 pm	**11:24 am**
☽ ♉ △ ☿ ♍	6:35 pm	**3:35 pm**
♂ ♋ ⚻ ♆ ♒		**10:14 pm**
☽ ♉ ⚻ ♄ ♎		**10:53 pm**

Fri 16
3rd ♉

♂ ♋ ⚻ ♆ ♒	1:14 am	
☽ ♉ ⚻ ♄ ♎	1:53 am	
♀ ♎ ☍ ⚻ ♈	7:05 am	**4:05 am**
☽ ♉ △ ☉ ♍	5:20 pm	**2:20 pm**
☽ ♉ □ ♆ ♒		**10:46 pm**

Sat 17
3rd ♉

☽ ♉ □ ♆ ♒	1:46 am	
☽ ♉ ✶ ♂ ♋	3:09 am	**12:09 am** v/c
☽ enters ♊	4:06 am	**1:06 am**
☽ ♊ □ ⚷ ♓	8:00 am	**5:00 am**
☽ ♊ ✶ ⚻ ♈	9:51 am	**6:51 am**
☽ ♊ △ ♀ ♎	1:02 pm	**10:02 am**
☽ ♊ ⚻ ♇ ♑	1:52 pm	**10:52 am**
♀ ♎ □ ♇ ♑	9:08 pm	**6:08 pm**
♂ enters ♌	9:51 pm	**6:51 pm**

Sun 18
3rd ♉

Eastern Time plain / **Pacific Time bold**

	AUGUST					
S	M	T	W	T	F	S
	1	2	3	4	5	6
7	8	9	10	11	12	13
14	15	16	17	18	19	20
21	22	23	24	25	26	27
28	29	30	31			

	SEPTEMBER					
S	M	T	W	T	F	S
				1	2	3
4	5	6	7	8	9	10
11	12	13	14	15	16	17
18	19	20	21	22	23	24
25	26	27	28	29	30	

	OCTOBER					
S	M	T	W	T	F	S
						1
2	3	4	5	6	7	8
9	10	11	12	13	14	15
16	17	18	19	20	21	22
23	24	25	26	27	28	29
30	31					

19 Mon
3rd ♊

☽ ♊ △ ♄ ♎			2:20 pm	**11:20 am**	
☽ ♊ □ ☿ ♍			5:30 pm	**2:30 pm**	

20 Tue
3rd ♊
◑ 27 ♊ 15

OP: After Moon squares Sun until v/c Moon. Wait two hours after the Moon squares the Sun, and use the short period remaining for whatever is important to get done right now.

☽ ♊ □ ☉ ♍			9:39 am	**6:39 am**	
☽ ♊ △ ♆ ≈			12:33 pm	**9:33 am** v/c
☽ enters ♋			2:53 pm	**11:53 am**	
☽ ♋ △ ⚷ ♓			6:23 pm	**3:23 pm**	
☽ ♋ □ ♅ ♈			8:10 pm	**5:10 pm**	
☽ ♋ ☍ ♇ ♑				**9:09 pm**	

21 Wed
4th ♋

OP: After Moon squares Saturn until Moon enters Leo. The fourth-quarter Moon says we should be following up rather than innovating. With that understood, good work can get done.

☽ ♋ ☍ ♇ ♑			12:09 am		
☽ ♋ □ ♀ ♎			5:38 am	**2:38 am**	
☽ ♋ ✶ ♃ ♉			8:52 am	**5:52 am**	
♂ ♌ ⊼ ⚷ ♓			8:21 pm	**5:21 pm**	
☉ ♍ ⊼ ♆ ≈			10:17 pm	**7:17 pm**	
☽ ♋ □ ♄ ♎			11:37 pm	**8:37 pm**	

22 Thu
4th ♋

☽ ♋ ✶ ☿ ♍			11:17 am	**8:17 am**	
♀ ♎ ⊼ ♃ ♉			1:23 pm	**10:23 am**	
☽ ♋ ⊼ ♆ ≈			7:40 pm	**4:40 pm**	
☽ ♋ ✶ ☉ ♍			9:22 pm	**6:22 pm** v/c
☽ enters ♌			9:55 pm	**6:55 pm**	
☽ ♌ ⊼ ⚷ ♓				**9:59 pm**	
☽ ♌ ☌ ♂ ♌				**11:24 pm**	
☽ ♌ △ ♅ ♈				**11:38 pm**	

☽♌ ⚻ ♅♓	12:59 am	
☽♌ ☌ ♂♌	2:24 am	
☽♌ △ ♅♈	2:38 am	
☉ enters ♎	5:05 am	**2:05 am**
☽♌ ⚻ ♇♑	6:30 am	**3:30 am**
♂♌ △ ♅♈	7:24 am	**4:24 am**
☽♌ □ ♃♉	2:15 pm	**11:15 am**
☽♌ ✶ ♀♎	4:49 pm	**1:49 pm**

Fri 23
4th ♌
Fall Equinox

☽♌ ✶ ♄♎	4:36 am	**1:36 am**
☉♎ ⚻ ♅♓	9:56 pm	**6:56 pm**
☽♌ ☍ ♆♒	10:39 pm	**7:39 pm** v/c
☿♍ ⚻ ♆♒	11:48 pm	**8:48 pm**
☽ enters ♍		**9:49 pm**

Sat 24
4th ♌

OP: When Moon enters Virgo until v/c Moon. Whatever you're doing early on Sunday can come to a satisfactory conclusion.

☽ enters ♍	12:49 am	
☽♍ ☍ ♅♓	3:32 am	**12:32 am**
☽♍ ⚻ ♅♈	5:05 am	**2:05 am**
☽♍ △ ♇♑	8:49 am	**5:49 am**
☽♍ △ ♃♉	3:47 pm	**12:47 pm** v/c
☿ enters ♎	5:09 pm	**2:09 pm**
☉♎ ☍ ♅♈	8:15 pm	**5:15 pm**

Sun 25
4th ♌

Eastern Time plain / Pacific Time bold

AUGUST						
S	M	T	W	T	F	S
	1	2	3	4	5	6
7	8	9	10	11	12	13
14	15	16	17	18	19	20
21	22	23	24	25	26	27
28	29	30	31			

SEPTEMBER						
S	M	T	W	T	F	S
				1	2	3
4	5	6	7	8	9	10
11	12	13	14	15	16	17
18	19	20	21	22	23	24
25	26	27	28	29	30	

OCTOBER						
S	M	T	W	T	F	S
						1
2	3	4	5	6	7	8
9	10	11	12	13	14	15
16	17	18	19	20	21	22
23	24	25	26	27	28	29
30	31					

September

26 Mon
4th ♍

☿ ♎ ⊼ ♅ ♓	2:13 pm	**11:13 am**
☽ ♍ ⊼ ♆ ♒	10:41 pm	**7:41 pm**
♂ ♌ ⊼ ♇ ♑		**9:20 pm**
☽ enters ♎		**9:51 pm**
☿ ♎ ☍ ♅ ♈		**11:30 pm**

27 Tue
4th ♍
● 4 ♎ 00

♂ ♌ ⊼ ♇ ♑	12:20 am	
☽ enters ♎	12:51 am	
☿ ♎ ☍ ♅ ♈	2:30 am	
☽ ♎ ⊼ ♅ ♓	3:20 am	**12:20 am**
☽ ♎ ☍ ♅ ♈	4:49 am	**1:49 am**
☽ ♎ ☌ ☿ ♎	5:08 am	**2:08 am**
☽ ♎ ☌ ☉ ♎	7:09 am	**4:09 am**
☽ ♎ □ ♇ ♑	8:35 am	**5:35 am**
☽ ♎ ✳ ♂ ♌	8:55 am	**5:55 am**
☽ ♎ ⊼ ♃ ♉	3:03 pm	**12:03 pm**
☽ ♎ ☌ ♀ ♎		**11:33 pm**

28 Wed
1st ♎

☽ ♎ ☌ ♀ ♎	2:33 am	
☉ ♎ □ ♇ ♑	5:37 am	**2:37 am**
☽ ♎ ☌ ♄ ♎	5:37 am	**2:37 am**
☿ ♎ □ ♇ ♑	10:26 am	**7:26 am**
☉ ♎ ☌ ☿ ♎	4:16 pm	**1:16 pm**
☽ ♎ △ ♆ ♒	9:51 pm	**6:51 pm** v/c
☽ enters ♏		**9:05 pm**
☽ ♏ △ ♅ ♓		**11:28 pm**

29 Thu
1st ♎
Rosh Hashanah

☽ enters ♏	12:05 am	
☽ ♏ △ ♅ ♓	2:28 am	
☿ ♎ ✳ ♂ ♌	3:27 am	**12:27 am**
☽ ♏ ⊼ ♅ ♈	3:58 am	**12:58 am**
☽ ♏ ✳ ♇ ♑	7:56 am	**4:56 am**
☽ ♏ □ ♂ ♌	10:12 am	**7:12 am**
☽ ♏ ☍ ♃ ♉	2:12 pm	**11:12 am**
♀ ♎ ☌ ♄ ♎	7:48 pm	**4:48 pm**
☉ ♎ ✳ ♂ ♌		**11:44 pm**

☉⚏⚹ ♂♌	2:44 am	
☿⚏⚻ ♃♉	2:16 pm **11:16 am**	
☽♏□ ♆≈	10:17 pm **7:17 pm** v/c	
☽ enters ♐	**9:42 pm**	

Fri 30
1st ♏

OP: When Moon enters Sagittarius until Moon enters Capricorn on Monday. A lovely weekend for every kind of enjoyment.

☽ enters ♐	12:42 am	
☽♐□ ⚷♓	3:04 am **12:04 am**	
☽♐△ ♅♈	4:38 am **1:38 am**	
☽♐△ ♂♌	1:29 pm **10:29 am**	
☽♐⚹ ☉⚏	2:31 pm **11:31 am**	
☽♐⚻ ♃♉	3:14 pm **12:14 pm**	
☽♐⚹ ☿⚏	6:58 pm **3:58 pm**	
☉⚏⚻ ♃♉	11:57 pm **8:57 pm**	

Sat 1
1st ♏

☽♐⚹ ♄⚏	8:36 am **5:36 am**	
☽♐⚹ ♀⚏	2:03 pm **11:03 am**	
♂♌□ ♃♉	**10:21 pm**	
☽♐⚹ ♆≈	**10:37 pm** v/c	

Sun 2
1st ♐

Eastern Time plain / **Pacific Time bold**

SEPTEMBER						
S	M	T	W	T	F	S
				1	2	3
4	5	6	7	8	9	10
11	12	13	14	15	16	17
18	19	20	21	22	23	24
25	26	27	28	29	30	

OCTOBER						
S	M	T	W	T	F	S
						1
2	3	4	5	6	7	8
9	10	11	12	13	14	15
16	17	18	19	20	21	22
23	24	25	26	27	28	29
30	31					

NOVEMBER						
S	M	T	W	T	F	S
		1	2	3	4	5
6	7	8	9	10	11	12
13	14	15	16	17	18	19
20	21	22	23	24	25	26
27	28	29	30			

3 MON
1st ♐
☽ 10 ♑ 24

♂♌□ ♃♉	1:21 am	
☽♐ ✶ ♆≈	1:37 am	v/c
☽ enters ♑	4:16 am **1:16 am**
☽♑ ✶ ⚷♓	6:40 am **3:40 am**
☽♑ □ ♅♈	8:19 am **5:19 am**
☽♑ ♂ ♇♑	1:08 pm **10:08 am**
☽♑ △ ♃♉	7:24 pm **4:24 pm**
☽♑ ☌ ♂♌	8:23 pm **5:23 pm**
☽♑ □ ☉♎	11:15 pm **8:15 pm**

4 TUE
2nd ♑

☽♑ □ ☿♎	7:47 am **4:47 am**
☽♑ □ ♄♎	2:52 pm **11:52 am**
☽♑ □ ♀♎	**10:58 pm** v/c

5 WED
2nd ♑

☽♑ □ ♀♎	1:58 am	v/c
☽ enters ≈	11:18 am **8:18 am**
☽≈ ✶ ♅♈	3:26 pm **12:26 pm**
☽≈ □ ♃♉	**11:52 pm**

6 THU
2nd ≈

☽≈ □ ♃♉	2:52 am
☽≈ ☍ ♂♌	7:08 am **4:08 am**
☽≈ △ ☉♎	12:14 pm **9:14 am**
☿♎ ☌ ♄♎	6:01 pm **3:01 pm**
☽≈ △ ♄♎	**9:26 pm**
☽≈ △ ☿♎	**10:21 pm**

☽≈ △ ♄♎	12:26 am
☽≈ △ ☿♎	1:21 am
☽≈ △ ♀♎	5:59 pm **2:59 pm**
☽≈ ☌ ♆≈	6:08 pm **3:08 pm** v/c
♀♎ △ ♆≈	7:28 pm **4:28 pm**
☽ enters ♓	9:13 pm **6:13 pm**
☽♓ ☌ ⛢♓	11:34 pm **8:34 pm**

FRI 7
2nd ≈

OP: When Moon enters Pisces today until Moon enters Aries on Monday. Friday evening and Saturday morning are especially fortunate, but the entire weekend is great for helping others, creativity, enjoyment of the arts, and meditation.

☽♓ ✶ ♇♑	7:06 am **4:06 am**
☽♓ ✶ ♃♉	12:51 pm **9:51 am** v/c
☽♓ ⚻ ♂♌	8:47 pm **5:47 pm**
♀ enters ♏	**10:50 pm**

SAT 8
2nd ♓
YOM KIPPUR

♀ enters ♏	1:50 am
☽♓ ⚻ ☉♎	4:19 am **1:19 am**
☽♓ ⚻ ♄♎	12:15 pm **9:15 am**
☽♓ ⚻ ☿♎	10:03 pm **7:03 pm**
♀♏ △ ⛢♓	11:43 pm **8:43 pm**

SUN 9
2nd ♓

Eastern Time plain / **Pacific Time bold**

SEPTEMBER						
S	M	T	W	T	F	S
				1	2	3
4	5	6	7	8	9	10
11	12	13	14	15	16	17
18	19	20	21	22	23	24
25	26	27	28	29	30	

OCTOBER						
S	M	T	W	T	F	S
						1
2	3	4	5	6	7	8
9	10	11	12	13	14	15
16	17	18	19	20	21	22
23	24	25	26	27	28	29
30	31					

NOVEMBER						
S	M	T	W	T	F	S
		1	2	3	4	5
6	7	8	9	10	11	12
13	14	15	16	17	18	19
20	21	22	23	24	25	26
27	28	29	30			

10 Mon
2nd ♓
Columbus Day (observed)

☽ enters ♈	8:57 am	**5:57 am**
☽♈ ⊼ ♀♏	12:34 pm	**9:34 am**
☽♈ ♂ ♅♈	12:58 pm	**9:58 am**
♀♏ ⊼ ♅♈	4:15 pm	**1:15 pm**
☽♈ □ ♇♑	7:06 pm	**4:06 pm**

11 Tue
2nd ♈
○ 18 ♈ 24

☽♈ △ ♂♌	12:03 pm	**9:03 am**
☽♈ ☍ ☉♎	10:06 pm	**7:06 pm**
☽♈ ☍ ♄♎		**10:17 pm**

12 Wed
3rd ♈

☽♈ ☍ ♄♎	1:17 am	
☿♎ △ ♆♒	6:10 am	**3:10 am**
☽♈ ✶ ♆♒	6:14 pm	**3:14 pm**
☽♈ ☍ ☿♎	8:08 pm	**5:08 pm** v/c
☽ enters ♉	9:35 pm	**6:35 pm**
☽♉ ✶ ⚷♓	11:43 pm	**8:43 pm**

13 Thu
3rd ♉

♀♏ ✶ ♇♑	3:43 am	**12:43 am**
☿ enters ♏	6:52 am	**3:52 am**
☽♉ △ ♇♑	7:52 am	**4:52 am**
☽♉ ☍ ♀♏	8:21 am	**5:21 am**
☽♉ ♂ ♃♉	12:25 pm	**9:25 am**
☉♎ ♂ ♄♎	5:13 pm	**2:13 pm**
☿♏ △ ⚷♓	10:19 pm	**7:19 pm**

☽ ♉ □ ♂ ♌	3:54 am **12:54 am**	
☿ ♏ ⊼ ♅ ♈	10:51 am **7:51 am**	
☽ ♉ ⊼ ♄ ♎	2:41 pm **11:41 am**	
☽ ♉ ⊼ ☉ ♎	4:24 pm **1:24 pm**	
♀ ♏ ☍ ♃ ♉	7:53 pm **4:53 pm**	

FRI 14
3rd ♉

☽ ♉ □ ♆ ♒	6:51 am **3:51 am** v/c
☽ enters ♊	10:15 am **7:15 am**
☽ ♊ □ ♅ ♓	12:13 pm **9:13 am**
☽ ♊ ⚹ ♅ ♈	1:53 pm **10:53 am**
☽ ♊ ⊼ ☿ ♏	6:04 pm **3:04 pm**
☽ ♊ ⊼ ♇ ♑	8:30 pm **5:30 pm**

SAT 15
3rd ♉

OP: After Moon squares Neptune today until v/c Moon in Gemini on Monday. Two OP's back to back, the first being a short v/c Moon in Taurus. If you have tasks to accomplish, both Saturday and Sunday are excellent. Monday, in a role reversal, is better for helping others, creativity, the arts, and meditation.

☽ ♊ ⊼ ♀ ♏	3:54 am **12:54 am**
☿ ♏ ⚹ ♇ ♑	12:58 pm **9:58 am**
☽ ♊ ⚹ ♂ ♌	7:06 pm **4:06 pm**

SUN 16
3rd ♊

Eastern Time plain / **Pacific Time bold**

SEPTEMBER						
S	M	T	W	T	F	S
				1	2	3
4	5	6	7	8	9	10
11	12	13	14	15	16	17
18	19	20	21	22	23	24
25	26	27	28	29	30	

OCTOBER						
S	M	T	W	T	F	S
						1
2	3	4	5	6	7	8
9	10	11	12	13	14	15
16	17	18	19	20	21	22
23	24	25	26	27	28	29
30	31					

NOVEMBER						
S	M	T	W	T	F	S
		1	2	3	4	5
6	7	8	9	10	11	12
13	14	15	16	17	18	19
20	21	22	23	24	25	26
27	28	29	30			

17 MON
3rd ♊

OP: **After Moon squared Neptune on Saturday until v/c Moon in Gemini today.** Two OP's back to back, the first being a short v/c Moon in Taurus. If you have tasks to accomplish, both Saturday and Sunday are excellent. Today is better for helping others, creativity, the arts, and meditation.

☽ ♊ △ ♄ ♎	3:16 am	**12:16 am**	
☽ ♊ △ ☉ ♎	9:37 am	**6:37 am**	
☿ ♏ ☍ ♃ ♉	2:55 pm	**11:55 am**	
☽ ♊ △ ♆ ♒	6:18 pm	**3:18 pm**	v/c
☽ enters ♋	9:38 pm	**6:38 pm**	
☽ ♋ △ ⚷ ♓	11:25 pm	**8:25 pm**	
☽ ♋ □ ♅ ♈		**9:57 pm**	

18 TUE
3rd ♋

☽ ♋ □ ♅ ♈	12:57 am	
☽ ♋ ☍ ♇ ♑	7:34 am	**4:34 am**
☽ ♋ ✶ ♃ ♉	10:32 am	**7:32 am**
☽ ♋ △ ☿ ♏	1:30 pm	**10:30 am**
☽ ♋ △ ♀ ♏	9:00 pm	**6:00 pm**

19 WED
3rd ♋
◗ 26 ♋ 24

☽ ♋ □ ♄ ♎	1:21 pm	**10:21 am**	
☽ ♋ □ ☉ ♎	11:30 pm	**8:30 pm**	v/c
☽ ♋ ⊼ ♆ ♒		**11:55 pm**	

20 THU
4th ♋

☽ ♋ ⊼ ♆ ♒	2:55 am	
☽ enters ♌	6:06 am	**3:06 am**
☽ ♌ ⊼ ⚷ ♓	7:41 am	**4:41 am**
☽ ♌ △ ♅ ♈	9:04 am	**6:04 am**
☽ ♌ ⊼ ♇ ♑	3:28 pm	**12:28 pm**
☽ ♌ □ ♃ ♉	5:37 pm	**2:37 pm**

☽♌ □ ☿♏	3:57 am	**12:57 am**
☽♌ □ ♀♏	9:26 am	**6:26 am**
☽♌ ☌ ♂♌	4:11 pm	**1:11 pm**
☽♌ ✶ ♄♎	7:36 pm	**4:36 pm**
☉♎ △ ♆♒	7:57 pm	**4:57 pm**

FRI 21
4th ♌

☽♌ ☍ ♆♒	7:41 am	**4:41 am**
☽♌ ✶ ☉♎	8:34 am	**5:34 am** v/c
☽ enters ♍	10:40 am	**7:40 am**
☽♍ ☍ ⚷♓	12:04 pm	**9:04 am**
☽♍ ⊼ ♅♈	1:18 pm	**10:18 am**
☽♍ △ ♇♑	7:27 pm	**4:27 pm**
☽♍ △ ♃♉	8:55 pm	**5:55 pm**

SAT 22
4th ♌

OP: **When Moon enters Virgo until v/c Moon.** Fourth-quarter Moon tells us to keep our ambitions moderate this weekend. Saturday is best for getting things done and Sunday for more restful pursuits.

☽♍ ✶ ☿♏	12:48 pm	**9:48 am**
☉ enters ♏	2:30 pm	**11:30 am**
☽♍ ✶ ♀♏	4:47 pm	**1:47 pm** v/c

SUN 23
4th ♍

Eastern Time plain / **Pacific Time bold**

SEPTEMBER						
S	M	T	W	T	F	S
				1	2	3
4	5	6	7	8	9	10
11	12	13	14	15	16	17
18	19	20	21	22	23	24
25	26	27	28	29	30	

OCTOBER						
S	M	T	W	T	F	S
						1
2	3	4	5	6	7	8
9	10	11	12	13	14	15
16	17	18	19	20	21	22
23	24	25	26	27	28	29
30	31					

NOVEMBER						
S	M	T	W	T	F	S
		1	2	3	4	5
6	7	8	9	10	11	12
13	14	15	16	17	18	19
20	21	22	23	24	25	26
27	28	29	30			

October

<table>
<tr><td>24 Mon
4th ♍</td><td>

☽♍ ⚻ ♆♒ — 8:57 am **5:57 am**
☉♏ △ ⚷ ♓ — 9:37 am **6:37 am**
☽ enters ♎ — 11:49 am **8:49 am**
☽♎ ⚻ ⚷ ♓ — 1:05 pm **10:05 am**
☽♎ ☍ ♅ ♈ — 2:11 pm **11:11 am**
☽♎ □ ♇ ♑ — 8:12 pm **5:12 pm**
☽♎ ⚻ ♃ ♉ — 9:06 pm **6:06 pm**
☉♏ ⚻ ♅ ♈ — **10:59 pm**

</td></tr>
<tr><td>25 Tue
4th ♎</td><td>

☉♏ ⚻ ♅ ♈ — 1:59 am
☽♎ ✶ ♂♌ — 9:51 pm **6:51 pm**
☽♎ ☌ ♄♎ — 10:04 pm **7:04 pm**

</td></tr>
<tr><td>26 Wed
4th ♎
● 3 ♏ 03</td><td>

♂♌ ✶ ♄♎ — 5:37 am **2:37 am**
☽♎ △ ♆♒ — 8:18 am **5:18 am** v/c
☽ enters ♏ — 11:08 am **8:08 am**
☽♏ △ ⚷ ♓ — 12:20 pm **9:20 am**
☽♏ ⚻ ♅ ♈ — 1:23 pm **10:23 am**
☽♏ ☌ ☉♏ — 3:56 pm **12:56 pm**
♀♏ □ ♂♌ — 6:23 pm **3:23 pm**
☽♏ ✶ ♇ ♑ — 7:28 pm **4:28 pm**
☽♏ ☍ ♃ ♉ — 7:53 pm **4:53 pm**

</td></tr>
<tr><td>27 Thu
1st ♏</td><td>

☽♏ ☌ ☿♏ — 10:08 pm **7:08 pm**
☽♏ □ ♂♌ — 10:56 pm **7:56 pm**
☽♏ ☌ ♀♏ — **9:23 pm**

</td></tr>
</table>

Fri 28
1st ♏

☽♏ ☌ ♀♏	12:23 am	
☽♏ □ ♆≈	7:49 am	**4:49 am** v/c
☽ enters ♐	10:45 am	**7:45 am**
☿♏ □ ♂♌	11:08 am	**8:08 am**
☽♐ □ ♅♓	11:56 am	**8:56 am**
♃♉ △ ♇♑	12:29 pm	**9:29 am**
☽♐ △ ♅♈	12:57 pm	**9:57 am**
☽♐ ⊼ ♃♉	7:21 pm	**4:21 pm**
☉♏ ☍ ♃♉	9:42 pm	**6:42 pm**
☉♏ ✶ ♇♑	11:11 pm	**8:11 pm**

OP: When Moon enters Sagittarius until Moon enters Capricorn. Party on Friday night and take care of business on Saturday.

Sat 29
1st ♐

☽♐ ✶ ♄♎	11:18 pm	**8:18 pm**
☽♐ △ ♂♌		**11:03 pm**

Sun 30
1st ♐

☽♐ △ ♂♌	2:03 am	
☽♐ ✶ ♆≈	9:30 am	**6:30 am** v/c
☽ enters ♑	12:39 pm	**9:39 am**
☽♑ ✶ ♅♓	1:52 pm	**10:52 am**
☽♑ □ ♅♈	2:53 pm	**11:53 am**
☽♑ △ ♃♉	9:19 pm	**6:19 pm**
☽♑ ☌ ♇♑	9:58 pm	**6:58 pm**
☽♑ ✶ ☉♏		**10:34 pm**

Eastern Time plain / **Pacific Time bold**

SEPTEMBER						
S	M	T	W	T	F	S
				1	2	3
4	5	6	7	8	9	10
11	12	13	14	15	16	17
18	19	20	21	22	23	24
25	26	27	28	29	30	

OCTOBER						
S	M	T	W	T	F	S
						1
2	3	4	5	6	7	8
9	10	11	12	13	14	15
16	17	18	19	20	21	22
23	24	25	26	27	28	29
30	31					

NOVEMBER						
S	M	T	W	T	F	S
		1	2	3	4	5
6	7	8	9	10	11	12
13	14	15	16	17	18	19
20	21	22	23	24	25	26
27	28	29	30			

31 MON
1st ♑
HALLOWEEN

☽♑ ⚹ ☉♏	1:34 am	
♀♏ □ ♆♒	5:19 pm	**2:19 pm**

---

1 TUE
1st ♑
OP: After Moon squares Saturn until v/c Moon. Great for sales and customer contact.

☽♑ □ ♄♎	4:15 am	**1:15 am**
☿♏ □ ♆♒	4:37 am	**1:37 am**
☽♑ ⚻ ♂♌	8:58 am	**5:58 am**
☽♑ ⚹ ☿♏	3:55 pm	**12:55 pm**
☽♑ ⚹ ♀♏	5:00 pm	**2:00 pm** v/c
☽ enters ♒	6:08 pm	**3:08 pm**
☽♒ ⚹ ♅♈	8:24 pm	**5:24 pm**
☽♒ □ ♃♉		**11:53 pm**

---

2 WED
1st ♒
◑ 9 ♒ 55

☽ ♒ □ ♃♉	2:53 am	
♀ enters ♐	4:51 am	**1:51 am**
☽♒ □ ☉♏	12:38 pm	**9:38 am**
☿ enters ♐	12:54 pm	**9:54 am**
♀♐ □ ⚷♓	5:53 pm	**2:53 pm**
☿♐ □ ⚷♓		**9:48 pm**

---

3 THU
2nd ♒

☿♐ □ ⚷♓	12:48 am	
♀♐ △ ♅♈	3:54 am	**12:54 am**
☿♐ △ ♅♈	9:58 am	**6:58 am**
☽♒ △ ♄♎	1:06 pm	**10:06 am**
☽♒ ☍ ♂♌	8:06 pm	**5:06 pm**
☽♒ ☌ ♆♒	11:40 pm	**8:40 pm** v/c

☽ enters ♓	3:18 am	**12:18 am**
☽♓ ☌ ⚷♓	4:36 am	**1:36 am**
☽♓ □ ☿♐	8:02 am	**5:02 am**
☽♓ □ ♀♐	8:33 am	**5:33 am**
☽♓ ✶ ♃♉	11:56 am	**8:56 am**
☽♓ ✶ ♇♑	2:06 pm	**11:06 am**

Fri 4
2nd ♒

OP: After Moon squares Venus until Moon enters Aries. Great for helping others, creativity, the arts, and meditation.

☽♓ △ ☉♏	4:05 am	**1:05 am** v/c
♀♐ ⊼ ♃♉	2:52 pm	**11:52 am**
☿♐ ⊼ ♃♉	5:13 pm	**2:13 pm**
☽♓ ⊼ ♄♎		**9:56 pm**

Sat 5
2nd ♓

☽♓ ⊼ ♄♎	12:56 am	
☽♓ ⊼ ♂♌	9:19 am	**6:19 am**
☽ enters ♈	2:02 pm	**11:02 am**
☽♈ ☌ ♅♈	4:15 pm	**1:15 pm**
☽♈ □ ♇♑		**10:15 pm**
☽♈ △ ☿♐		**11:16 pm**
☽♈ △ ♀♐		**11:26 pm**

Sun 6
2nd ♓

Daylight Saving Time ends, 2 am

Eastern Time plain / **Pacific Time bold**

OCTOBER						
S	M	T	W	T	F	S
						1
2	3	4	5	6	7	8
9	10	11	12	13	14	15
16	17	18	19	20	21	22
23	24	25	26	27	28	29
30	31					

NOVEMBER						
S	M	T	W	T	F	S
		1	2	3	4	5
6	7	8	9	10	11	12
13	14	15	16	17	18	19
20	21	22	23	24	25	26
27	28	29	30			

DECEMBER						
S	M	T	W	T	F	S
				1	2	3
4	5	6	7	8	9	10
11	12	13	14	15	16	17
18	19	20	21	22	23	24
25	26	27	28	29	30	31

7 Mon
2nd ♈

☽ ♈ □ ♇ ♑	1:15 am	
☽ ♈ △ ☿ ♐	2:16 am	
☽ ♈ △ ♀ ♐	2:26 am	
♂ ♌ ☍ ♆ ♒	7:34 am	**4:34 am**
☽ ♈ ⊼ ☉ ♏	8:59 pm	**5:59 pm**

8 Tue
2nd ♈
Election Day (general)

☽ ♈ ☍ ♄ ♎	1:10 pm	**10:10 am**
☽ ♈ ✶ ♆ ♒	10:59 pm	**7:59 pm**
☽ ♈ △ ♂ ♌		**9:46 pm** v/c
☽ enters ♉		**11:45 pm**

9 Wed
2nd ♈

☽ ♈ △ ♂ ♌	12:46 am	v/c
☽ enters ♉	2:45 am	
☽ ♉ ✶ ⚷ ♓	4:03 am	**1:03 am**
☽ ♉ ♂ ♃ ♉	10:20 am	**7:20 am**
♆ D in ♒	1:54 pm	**10:54 am**
☽ ♉ △ ♇ ♑	2:08 pm	**11:08 am**
☽ ♉ ⊼ ☿ ♐	10:02 pm	**7:02 pm**
☽ ♉ ⊼ ♀ ♐	10:17 pm	**7:17 pm**

10 Thu
2nd ♉
○ 18 ♎ 05

☽ ♉ ☍ ☉ ♏	3:16 pm	**12:16 pm**
⚷ D in ♓	6:14 pm	**3:14 pm**
♂ enters ♍	11:15 pm	**8:15 pm**
☽ ♉ ⊼ ♄ ♎		**11:19 pm**

Fri 11
3rd ♉
Veterans Day

☽♉⊼♄♎	2:19 am	
☽♉□♆♒	11:27 am	**8:27 am** v/c
☽ enters ♊	3:10 pm	**12:10 pm**
☽♊□♂♍	3:52 pm	**12:52 pm**
☽♊□♀♓	4:27 pm	**1:27 pm**
☽♊✶♅♈	5:07 pm	**2:07 pm**
☽♊⊼♇♑		**11:30 pm**

OP: After Moon squares Neptune until Moon enters Gemini. Wait two hours after the square and then take care of business during the remainder of this period.

OP: After Moon sextiles Uranus until v/c Moon. Late Friday and early Saturday will be great for meeting new people.

Sat 12
3rd ♊

☽♊⊼♇♑	2:30 am	
♂♍☍♀♓	5:57 am	**2:57 am**
☽♊☍☿♐	4:22 pm	**1:22 pm**
☽♊☍♀♐	5:14 pm	**2:14 pm**
♂♍⊼♅♈	8:41 pm	**5:41 pm**

Sun 13
3rd ♊

☽♊⊼☉♏	8:23 am	**5:23 am**
☽♊△♄♎	2:22 pm	**11:22 am**
☽♊△♆♒	10:42 pm	**7:42 pm** v/c
☽ enters ♋		**11:19 pm**

Eastern Time plain / **Pacific Time bold**

| | OCTOBER | | | | | | | NOVEMBER | | | | | | | DECEMBER | | | | | |
S	M	T	W	T	F	S	S	M	T	W	T	F	S	S	M	T	W	T	F	S
						1		1	2	3	4	5						1	2	3
2	3	4	5	6	7	8	6	7	8	9	10	11	12	4	5	6	7	8	9	10
9	10	11	12	13	14	15	13	14	15	16	17	18	19	11	12	13	14	15	16	17
16	17	18	19	20	21	22	20	21	22	23	24	25	26	18	19	20	21	22	23	24
23	24	25	26	27	28	29	27	28	29	30				25	26	27	28	29	30	31
30	31																			

14 MON
3rd ♊

☽ enters ♋	2:19 am	
☽ ♋ △ ⚷ ♓	3:34 am	**12:34 am**
☽ ♋ □ ♅ ♈	4:06 am	**1:06 am**
☽ ♋ ✶ ♂ ♍	5:28 am	**2:28 am**
☽ ♋ ✶ ♃ ♉	8:22 am	**5:22 am**
☽ ♋ ☍ ♇ ♑	1:26 pm	**10:26 am**

15 TUE
3rd ♋

☽ ♋ ⊼ ☿ ♐	7:49 am	**4:49 am**
☽ ♋ ⊼ ♀ ♐	9:54 am	**6:54 am**
☽ ♋ △ ☉ ♏	11:03 pm	**8:03 pm**
☽ ♋ □ ♄ ♎		**9:22 pm** v/c

16 WED
3rd ♋

OP: After Moon squares Saturn until Moon enters Leo. Potentially productive time.

☽ ♋ □ ♄ ♎	12:22 am	v/c
☽ ♋ ⊼ ♆ ♒	7:51 am	**4:51 am**
☽ enters ♌	11:17 am	**8:17 am**
☽ ♌ ⊼ ⚷ ♓	12:30 pm	**9:30 am**
☽ ♌ △ ♅ ♈	12:54 pm	**9:54 am**
☽ ♌ □ ♃ ♉	4:33 pm	**1:33 pm**
♂ ♍ △ ♃ ♉	5:08 pm	**2:08 pm**
☽ ♌ ⊼ ♇ ♑	10:01 pm	**7:01 pm**

17 THU
3rd ♌

☽ ♌ △ ☿ ♐	7:08 pm	**4:08 pm**
☽ ♌ △ ♀ ♐	10:59 pm	**7:59 pm**

Mercury Note: Mercury enters its Storm on November 18, slowing down to less than 40 minutes of arc per day as it approaches next week's retrograde station. The Storm acts like the retrograde. This is not the time to start new projects.

☽♌ ✶ ♄♎	7:28 am	**4:28 am**
☽♌ ☐ ☉♏	10:09 am	**7:09 am**
☽♌ ☍ ♆♒	2:05 pm	**11:05 am** v/c
☽ enters ♍	5:19 pm	**2:19 pm**
☽♍ ☍ ⚷♓	6:29 pm	**3:29 pm**
☽♍ ⊼ ♅♈	6:46 pm	**3:46 pm**
☽♍ △ ♃♉	9:50 pm	**6:50 pm**
☽♍ ☌ ♂♍		**9:12 pm**

Fri 18
3rd ♌
◑ 25 ♌ 55

☽♍ ☌ ♂♍	12:12 am	
☽♍ △ ♇♑	3:32 am	**12:32 am**
☽♍ ☐ ☿♐		**10:51 pm**

Sat 19
4th ♍

☽♍ ☐ ☿♐	1:51 am	
☽♍ ☐ ♀♐	7:54 am	**4:54 am**
☉♏ ☐ ♆♒	3:42 pm	**12:42 pm**
☽♍ ⊼ ♆♒	5:15 pm	**2:15 pm**
☽♍ ✶ ☉♏	5:21 pm	**2:21 pm** v/c
☽ enters ♎	8:16 pm	**5:16 pm**
☽♎ ⊼ ⚷♓	9:25 pm	**6:25 pm**
☽♎ ☍ ♅♈	9:35 pm	**6:35 pm**
☽♎ ⊼ ♃♉		**9:10 pm**

Sun 20
4th ♍

OP: After Moon squares Venus until v/c Moon. Fourth-quarter Moon indicates that this will be a pleasant Sunday, and to take it easy.

Eastern Time plain / **Pacific Time bold**

OCTOBER						
S	M	T	W	T	F	S
						1
2	3	4	5	6	7	8
9	10	11	12	13	14	15
16	17	18	19	20	21	22
23	24	25	26	27	28	29
30	31					

NOVEMBER						
S	M	T	W	T	F	S
		1	2	3	4	5
6	7	8	9	10	11	12
13	14	15	16	17	18	19
20	21	22	23	24	25	26
27	28	29	30			

DECEMBER						
S	M	T	W	T	F	S
				1	2	3
4	5	6	7	8	9	10
11	12	13	14	15	16	17
18	19	20	21	22	23	24
25	26	27	28	29	30	31

November

Mercury Note: Mercury goes retrograde on November 23 or 24, depending on your time zone, and remains so until December 13. It is more appropriate to review and revise than to begin new projects now. Buying Christmas gifts too early may lead to regrets about poor judgment.

21 Mon
4th ♎

☽ ♎ ⊼ ♃ ♉	12:10 am	
☽ ♎ □ ♇ ♑	6:04 am	**3:04 am**

22 Tue
4th ♎

OP: After Moon conjoins Saturn until v/c Moon. As the Moon approaches its trine to Neptune, the vibes get more compassionate, contemplative, and artistic.

♀ ♐ ✶ ♄ ♎	3:19 am	**12:19 am**
☽ ♎ ✶ ☿ ♐	4:39 am	**1:39 am**
☉ enters ♐	11:08 am	**8:08 am**
☽ ♎ ♂ ♄ ♎	12:43 pm	**9:43 am**
☽ ♎ ✶ ♀ ♐	1:30 pm	**10:30 am**
☽ ♎ △ ♆ ♒	6:04 pm	**3:04 pm** v/c
☽ enters ♏	8:58 pm	**5:58 pm**
☽ ♏ △ ⚷ ♓	10:07 pm	**7:07 pm**
☽ ♏ ⊼ ♅ ♈	10:12 pm	**7:12 pm**
☽ ♏ ☍ ♃ ♉		**9:25 pm**

23 Wed
4th ♏

☽ ♏ ☍ ♃ ♉	12:25 am	
☉ ♐ □ ⚷ ♓	4:13 am	**1:13 am**
☉ ♐ △ ♅ ♈	5:14 am	**2:14 am**
☽ ♏ ✶ ♂ ♍	6:30 am	**3:30 am**
☽ ♏ ✶ ♇ ♑	6:35 am	**3:35 am**
♂ ♍ △ ♇ ♑	9:07 am	**6:07 am**
☿ ℞ in ♐		**11:19 pm**

24 Thu
4th ♏

● 2 ♐ 37 (Pacific)

Thanksgiving Day

☿ ℞ in ♐	2:19 am	
☉ ♐ ⊼ ♃ ♉	10:43 am	**7:43 am**
☽ ♏ □ ♆ ♒	6:04 pm	**3:04 pm** v/c
♀ ♐ ✶ ♆ ♒	8:52 pm	**5:52 pm**
☽ enters ♐	8:57 pm	**5:57 pm**
☽ ♐ △ ♅ ♈	10:09 pm	**7:09 pm**
☽ ♐ □ ⚷ ♓	10:09 pm	**7:09 pm**
☽ ♐ ⊼ ♃ ♉		**9:06 pm**
☽ ♐ ♂ ☉ ♐		**10:10 pm**

☽♐ ⊼ ♃♉	12:06 am	
☽♐ ♂ ☉♐	1:10 am	
☽♐ □ ♂♍	8:06 am	**5:06 am**

FRI 25
4th ♐
(Eastern) ● 2 ♐ 37
Solar Eclipse (partial)

OP: After Moon squares Mars until Moon enters Capricorn. The Moon is combust and under Sun's beams at the start of this period. By Saturday afternoon, more possibilities present themselves.

☽♐ ♂ ☿♐	5:03 am	**2:03 am**
♀ enters ♑	7:36 am	**4:36 am**
☽♐ ✶ ♄♎	2:12 pm	**11:12 am**
☽♐ ✶ ♆♒	7:06 pm	**4:06 pm** v/c
♀♑ □ ♅♈	9:27 pm	**6:27 pm**
☽ enters ♑	10:05 pm	**7:05 pm**
♀♑ ✶ ⚷♓	10:35 pm	**7:35 pm**
☽♑ □ ♅♈	11:17 pm	**8:17 pm**
☽♑ ✶ ⚷♓	11:23 pm	**8:23 pm**
☽♑ ♂ ♀♑	11:27 pm	**8:27 pm**
☽♑ △ ♃♉		**10:01 pm**

SAT 26
1st ♐

☽♑ △ ♃♉	1:01 am	
☽♑ ♂ ♇♑	8:26 am	**5:26 am**
☽♑ △ ♂♍	11:23 am	**8:23 am**
♀♑ △ ♃♉	4:23 pm	**1:23 pm**

SUN 27
1st ♑

Eastern Time plain / **Pacific Time bold**

OCTOBER						
S	M	T	W	T	F	S
						1
2	3	4	5	6	7	8
9	10	11	12	13	14	15
16	17	18	19	20	21	22
23	24	25	26	27	28	29
30	31					

NOVEMBER						
S	M	T	W	T	F	S
		1	2	3	4	5
6	7	8	9	10	11	12
13	14	15	16	17	18	19
20	21	22	23	24	25	26
27	28	29	30			

DECEMBER						
S	M	T	W	T	F	S
				1	2	3
4	5	6	7	8	9	10
11	12	13	14	15	16	17
18	19	20	21	22	23	24
25	26	27	28	29	30	31

28 Mon
1st ♑

☽ ♑ □ ♄ ♎	6:01 pm	**3:01 pm** v/c
☽ enters ♒		**11:02 pm**

29 Tue
1st ♑

☽ enters ♒	2:02 am	
☽ ♒ ✳ ♅ ♈	3:16 am	**12:16 am**
☽ ♒ □ ♃ ♉	4:50 am	**1:50 am**
☽ ♒ ✳ ☉ ♐	3:09 pm	**12:09 pm**
☽ ♒ ⚻ ♂ ♍	6:07 pm	**3:07 pm**

30 Wed
1st ♒

☽ ♒ ✳ ☿ ♐	8:36 am	**5:36 am**
☽ ♒ △ ♄ ♎		**10:37 pm**

1 Thu
1st ♒

☽ ♒ △ ♄ ♎	1:37 am	
☽ ♒ ☌ ♆ ♒	6:27 am	**3:27 am** v/c
♀ ♑ ☌ ♇ ♑	8:51 am	**5:51 am**
☽ enters ♓	9:45 am	**6:45 am**
☽ ♓ ☌ ⚷ ♓	11:24 am	**8:24 am**
☽ ♓ ✳ ♃ ♉	12:23 pm	**9:23 am**
☽ ♓ ✳ ♇ ♑	9:54 pm	**6:54 pm**
☽ ♓ ✳ ♀ ♑	11:19 pm	**8:19 pm**

☽♓ □ ☉♐   4:52 am   **1:52 am**
☽♓ ☍ ♂♍   5:02 am   **2:02 am**
☉♐ □ ♂♍   8:08 am   **5:08 am**
☽♓ □ ☿♐   1:06 pm **10:06 am** v/c

Fri 2
1st ♓
☽ 9 ♓ 52

OP: After Moon squares Mercury until Moon enters Aries. Helping others, creativity, the arts, and meditation are all in order now.

☽♓ ⚻ ♄♎   12:48 pm   **9:48 am**
☽ enters ♈   8:51 pm   **5:51 pm**
☽♈ ☌ ♅♈   10:11 pm   **7:11 pm**

Sat 3
2nd ♓

☉♐ ☌ ☿♐   3:52 am **12:52 am**
☽♈ □ ♇♑   9:40 am   **6:40 am**
☽♈ □ ♀♑   5:56 pm   **2:56 pm**
☿♐ □ ♂♍   6:19 pm   **3:19 pm**
☽♈ △ ☿♐   7:00 pm   **4:00 pm**
☽♈ ⚻ ♂♍   7:06 pm   **4:06 pm**
☽♈ △ ☉♐   10:20 pm   **7:20 pm**

Sun 4
2nd ♈

Eastern Time plain / **Pacific Time bold**

NOVEMBER						
S	M	T	W	T	F	S
		1	2	3	4	5
6	7	8	9	10	11	12
13	14	15	16	17	18	19
20	21	22	23	24	25	26
27	28	29	30			

DECEMBER						
S	M	T	W	T	F	S
				1	2	3
4	5	6	7	8	9	10
11	12	13	14	15	16	17
18	19	20	21	22	23	24
25	26	27	28	29	30	31

JANUARY 2012						
S	M	T	W	T	F	S
1	2	3	4	5	6	7
8	9	10	11	12	13	14
15	16	17	18	19	20	21
22	23	24	25	26	27	28
29	30	31				

5 MON
2nd ♈

♀♈ △ ♂♍	10:07 am	**7:07 am**
☽♈ ☍ ♄♎		**10:56 pm**

6 TUE
2nd ♈

☽♈ ☍ ♄♎	1:56 am	
☽♈ ⚹ ♆♒	6:13 am	**3:13 am** v/c
☽ enters ♉	9:34 am	**6:34 am**
☽♉ ⚹ ⚷♓	11:33 am	**8:33 am**
☽♉ ☌ ♃♉	11:36 am	**8:36 am**
♃♉ ⚹ ⚷♓	7:03 pm	**4:03 pm**
☽♉ △ ♇♑	10:38 pm	**7:38 pm**
☽♉ ⚻ ☿♐		**10:48 pm**

7 WED
2nd ♉

☽♉ ⚻ ☿♐	1:48 am	
☽♉ △ ♂♍	10:02 am	**7:02 am**
☽♉ △ ♀♑	1:46 pm	**10:46 am**
☽♉ ⚻ ☉♐	4:45 pm	**1:45 pm**

8 THU
2nd ♉

☽♉ ⚻ ♄♎	2:51 pm	**11:51 am**
☽♉ □ ♆♒	6:39 pm	**3:39 pm** v/c

OP: After Moon squares Neptune until Moon enters Gemini. Wait two hours after the square before tackling anything important. You'll still have over an hour to deal with it.

☽ enters ♊	9:52 pm	**6:52 pm**
☽♊ ⚹ ♅♈	11:09 pm	**8:09 pm**
☽♊ □ ⚷♓	11:56 pm	**8:56 pm**

☽ ♊ ☍ ☿ ♐	9:07 am	**6:07 am**
☽ ♊ ⊼ ♇ ♑	10:48 am	**7:48 am**
☽ ♊ □ ♂ ♍	11:44 pm	**8:44 pm**
♅ D in ♈		**11:04 pm**

Fri 9
2nd ♊

♅ D in ♈	2:04 am	
☽ ♊ ⊼ ♀ ♑	8:02 am	**5:02 am**
☽ ♊ ☍ ☉ ♐	9:36 am	**6:36 am**
☽ ♊ △ ♄ ♎		**11:05 pm**

Sat 10
2nd ♊
○ 18 ♊ 11
Lunar Eclipse (Total)

☽ ♊ △ ♄ ♎	2:05 am	
☽ ♊ △ ♆ ♒	5:24 am	**2:24 am** v/c
☽ enters ♋	8:26 am	**5:26 am**
☽ ♋ □ ♅ ♈	9:40 am	**6:40 am**
☽ ♋ ✶ ♃ ♉	9:49 am	**6:49 am**
☽ ♋ △ ⚷ ♓	10:34 am	**7:34 am**
☽ ♋ ⊼ ☿ ♐	4:36 pm	**1:36 pm**
☽ ♋ ☍ ♇ ♑	9:04 pm	**6:04 pm**

Sun 11
3rd ♊

Eastern Time plain / **Pacific Time bold**

NOVEMBER						
S	M	T	W	T	F	S
		1	2	3	4	5
6	7	8	9	10	11	12
13	14	15	16	17	18	19
20	21	22	23	24	25	26
27	28	29	30			

DECEMBER						
S	M	T	W	T	F	S
				1	2	3
4	5	6	7	8	9	10
11	12	13	14	15	16	17
18	19	20	21	22	23	24
25	26	27	28	29	30	31

JANUARY 2012						
S	M	T	W	T	F	S
1	2	3	4	5	6	7
8	9	10	11	12	13	14
15	16	17	18	19	20	21
22	23	24	25	26	27	28
29	30	31				

December

Mercury Note: Mercury goes direct on December 13, but remains in its Storm until December 18. Continue to review and revise rather than beginning anything new, for now.

12 Mon
3rd ♋

☽♋	✶	♂♍	11:08 am	**8:08 am**
☽♋	☍	♀♑	11:27 pm	**8:27 pm**
☽♋	⚻	☉♐	11:46 pm	**8:46 pm**

13 Tue
3rd ♋

OP: After Moon squares Saturn until Moon enters Leo. Wait two hours after the square, then do what needs to be done.

☽♋	□	♄♎	11:05 am	**8:05 am** v/c
☽♋	⚻	♆♒	1:58 pm	**10:58 am**
☽ enters ♌			4:48 pm	**1:48 pm**
☽♌	□	♃♉	5:56 pm	**2:56 pm**
☽♌	△	♅♈	6:00 pm	**3:00 pm**
☽♌	⚻	⚷♓	6:59 pm	**3:59 pm**
☿ D in ♐			8:43 pm	**5:43 pm**
☽♌	△	☿♐	11:53 pm	**8:53 pm**

14 Wed
3rd ♌

☽♌	⚻	♇♑	5:05 am	**2:05 am**

15 Thu
3rd ♌

☽♌	△	☉♐	11:06 am	**8:06 am**
☽♌	⚻	♀♑	11:52 am	**8:52 am**
☽♌	✶	♄♎	5:50 pm	**2:50 pm**
☽♌	☍	♆♒	8:20 pm	**5:20 pm** v/c
☽ enters ♍			10:58 pm	**7:58 pm**
☽♍	△	♃♉	11:55 pm	**8:55 pm**
☽♍	⚻	♅♈		**9:08 pm**
☽♍	☍	⚷♓		**10:12 pm**

Mercury Note: Mercury leaves its Storm on December 18, moving more than 40 minutes of arc per day as it revs up toward its maximum speed.

☽ ♍ ⊼ ♅ ♈	12:08 am	
☽ ♍ ☍ ⚷ ♓	1:12 am	
☽ ♍ ▢ ☿ ♐	6:36 am	**3:36 am**
☽ ♍ △ ♇ ♑	10:55 am	**7:55 am**
☽ ♍ ☌ ♂ ♍		**11:34 pm**

Fri 16
3rd ♍

☽ ♍ ☌ ♂ ♍	2:34 am	
☽ ♍ ▢ ☉ ♐	7:48 pm	**4:48 pm**
☽ ♍ △ ♀ ♑	9:29 pm	**6:29 pm** v/c
☽ ♍ ⊼ ♆ ♒		**9:38 pm**

Sat 17
3rd ♍
◑ 25 ♍ 44

☽ ♍ ⊼ ♆ ♒	12:38 am	
☽ enters ♎	3:06 am	**12:06 am**
☽ ♎ ⊼ ♃ ♉	3:54 am	**12:54 am**
☽ ♎ ☍ ♅ ♈	4:15 am	**1:15 am**
☽ ♎ ⊼ ⚷ ♓	5:23 am	**2:23 am**
♀ ♑ ▢ ♄ ♎	9:18 am	**6:18 am**
☽ ♎ ✶ ☿ ♐	12:24 pm	**9:24 am**
☽ ♎ ▢ ♇ ♑	2:45 pm	**11:45 am**

Sun 18
4th ♍

Eastern Time plain / **Pacific Time bold**

NOVEMBER						
S	M	T	W	T	F	S
		1	2	3	4	5
6	7	8	9	10	11	12
13	14	15	16	17	18	19
20	21	22	23	24	25	26
27	28	29	30			

DECEMBER						
S	M	T	W	T	F	S
				1	2	3
4	5	6	7	8	9	10
11	12	13	14	15	16	17
18	19	20	21	22	23	24
25	26	27	28	29	30	31

JANUARY 2012						
S	M	T	W	T	F	S
1	2	3	4	5	6	7
8	9	10	11	12	13	14
15	16	17	18	19	20	21
22	23	24	25	26	27	28
29	30	31				

December

19 Mon
4th ♎

☉♐ ⚹ ♄♎	11:24 am	**8:24 am**
☽♎ ☌ ♄♎		**10:19 pm**
☽♎ ⚹ ☉♐		**11:17 pm**

20 Tue
4th ♎

☽♎ ☌ ♄♎	1:19 am	
☽♎ ⚹ ☉♐	2:17 am	
☽♎ △ ♆♒	3:13 am	**12:13 am**
☽♎ □ ♀♑	4:49 am	**1:49 am** v/c
☽ enters ♏	5:33 am	**2:33 am**
☽♏ ☍ ♃♉	6:14 am	**3:14 am**
☽♏ ⚻ ♅♈	6:41 am	**3:41 am**
☽♏ △ ⚷♓	7:54 am	**4:54 am**
♀ enters ♒	1:26 pm	**10:26 am**
☉♐ ⚹ ♆♒	3:46 pm	**12:46 pm**
☽♏ ⚹ ♇♑	5:01 pm	**2:01 pm**
♀♒ □ ♃♉	9:19 pm	**6:19 pm**
♀♒ ⚹ ♅♈		**11:56 pm**

21 Wed
4th ♏
Hannukah begins
Winter Solstice (Pacific)

♀♒ ⚹ ♅♈	2:56 am	
☽♏ ⚹ ♂♍	9:57 am	**6:57 am**
☉ enters ♑		**9:30 pm**

22 Thu
4th ♏
Winter Solstice (Eastern)

☉ enters ♑	12:30 am	
☽♏ □ ♆♒	4:49 am	**1:49 am** v/c
☽ enters ♐	7:03 am	**4:03 am**
☽♐ ⚻ ♃♉	7:41 am	**4:41 am**
☽♐ △ ♅♈	8:12 am	**5:12 am**
☽♐ □ ⚷♓	9:30 am	**6:30 am**
☉♑ △ ♃♉	9:33 am	**6:33 am**
☽♐ ⚹ ♀♒	10:53 am	**7:53 am**
☉♑ □ ♅♈	5:14 pm	**2:14 pm**
☽♐ ☌ ☿♐	10:10 pm	**7:10 pm**

☽ ♐ □ ♂ ♍	12:30 pm	**9:30 am**
☉ ♑ ⚹ ⚷ ♓	12:48 pm	**9:48 am**

FRI 23
4th ♐

☽ ♐ ⚹ ♄ ♎	5:03 am	**2:03 am**
☽ ♐ ⚹ ♆ ♒	6:36 am	**3:36 am** v/c
☽ enters ♑	8:47 am	**5:47 am**
☽ ♑ △ ♃ ♉	9:24 am	**6:24 am**
☽ ♑ □ ♅ ♈	10:00 am	**7:00 am**
☽ ♑ ⚹ ⚷ ♓	11:26 am	**8:26 am**
☽ ♑ ♂ ☉ ♑	1:06 pm	**10:06 am**
☽ ♑ ♂ ♇ ♑	8:42 pm	**5:42 pm**

SAT 24
4th ♐
● 2 ♑ 34
CHRISTMAS EVE

☽ ♑ △ ♂ ♍	4:11 pm	**1:11 pm**
♃ D in ♉	5:08 pm	**2:08 pm**

SUN 25
1st ♑
CHRISTMAS DAY

Eastern Time plain / **Pacific Time bold**

NOVEMBER						
S	M	T	W	T	F	S
		1	2	3	4	5
6	7	8	9	10	11	12
13	14	15	16	17	18	19
20	21	22	23	24	25	26
27	28	29	30			

DECEMBER						
S	M	T	W	T	F	S
				1	2	3
4	5	6	7	8	9	10
11	12	13	14	15	16	17
18	19	20	21	22	23	24
25	26	27	28	29	30	31

JANUARY 2012						
S	M	T	W	T	F	S
1	2	3	4	5	6	7
8	9	10	11	12	13	14
15	16	17	18	19	20	21
22	23	24	25	26	27	28
29	30	31				

26 Mon
1st ♑
Kwanzaa begins

☽ ♑ □ ♄ ♎	8:36 am	**5:36 am** v/c
☽ enters ♒	12:14 pm	**9:14 am**
☽ ♒ □ ♃ ♉	12:53 pm	**9:53 am**
☽ ♒ ✶ ♅ ♈	1:34 pm	**10:34 am**
☽ ♒ ♂ ♀ ♒		**11:33 pm**

27 Tue
1st ♒
Hannukah ends

☽ ♒ ♂ ♀ ♒	2:33 am	
☽ ♒ ✶ ☿ ♐	2:01 pm	**11:01 am**
☽ ♒ ⊼ ♂ ♍	10:34 pm	**7:34 pm**

28 Wed
1st ♒

☽ ♒ △ ♄ ♎	3:10 pm	**12:10 pm**
☽ ♒ ♂ ♆ ♒	4:31 pm	**1:31 pm** v/c
☽ enters ♓	6:45 pm	**3:45 pm**
☽ ♓ ✶ ♃ ♉	7:28 pm	**4:28 pm**
☽ ♓ ♂ ⚷ ♓	10:05 pm	**7:05 pm**
☉ ♑ ♂ ♇ ♑		**11:43 pm**

29 Thu
1st ♓

☉ ♑ ♂ ♇ ♑	2:43 am	
☽ ♓ ✶ ♇ ♑	8:27 am	**5:27 am**
☽ ♓ ✶ ☉ ♑	8:56 am	**5:56 am**

☽ ♓ □ ☿ ♐	4:40 am **1:40 am**	
☽ ♓ ☍ ♂ ♍	8:37 am **5:37 am** v/c	
☽ ♓ ⊼ ♄ ♎	**10:19 pm**	

Fri 30
1st ♓

OP: After Moon opposes Mars until Moon enters Aries. Favorable for helping others, creativity, the arts, and meditation.

☽ ♓ ⊼ ♄ ♎	1:19 am
☽ enters ♈	4:48 am **1:48 am**
☽ ♈ ♂ ♅ ♈	6:28 am **3:28 am**
☽ ♈ □ ♇ ♑	7:25 pm **4:25 pm**
☿ ♐ □ ♂ ♍	**10:06 pm**
☽ ♈ □ ☉ ♑	**10:15 pm**

Sat 31
1st ♓
◐ 10 ♈ 13 (Pacific
New Year's Eve

☿ ♈ □ ♂ ♍	1:06 am
☽ ♈ □ ☉ ♑	1:15 am
☽ ♈ ⚹ ♀ ♒	10:03 am **7:03 am**
☽ ♈ ⊼ ♂ ♍	9:45 pm **6:45 pm**
☽ ♈ △ ☿ ♐	11:56 pm **8:56 pm**

Sun 1
1st ♈
◐ 10 ♈ 13 (Eastern)
New Year's Day

Eastern Time plain / **Pacific Time bold**

NOVEMBER						
S	M	T	W	T	F	S
		1	2	3	4	5
6	7	8	9	10	11	12
13	14	15	16	17	18	19
20	21	22	23	24	25	26
27	28	29	30			

DECEMBER						
S	M	T	W	T	F	S
				1	2	3
4	5	6	7	8	9	10
11	12	13	14	15	16	17
18	19	20	21	22	23	24
25	26	27	28	29	30	31

JANUARY 2012						
S	M	T	W	T	F	S
1	2	3	4	5	6	7
8	9	10	11	12	13	14
15	16	17	18	19	20	21
22	23	24	25	26	27	28
29	30	31				

Blank Horoscope Chart

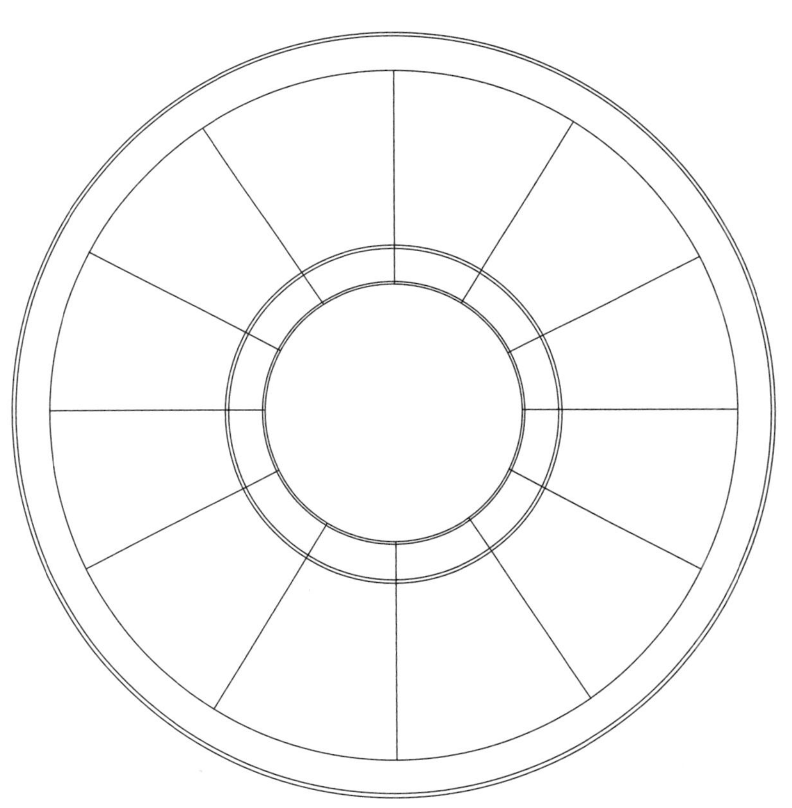

World Time Zones
Compared to Eastern Standard Time

(R)	EST (used in *Guide*)	(D) Add 9 hours
(S)	CST/Subtract 1 hour	(D*) Add 9.5 hours
(Q)	Add 1 hour	(E) Add 10 hours
(P)	Add 2 hours	(E*) Add 10.5 hours
(O)	Add 3 hours	(F) Add 11 hours
(Z)	Add 5 hours	(F*) Add 11.5 hours
(T)	MST/Subtract 2 hours	(G) Add 12 hours
(U)	PST/Subtract 3 hours	(H) Add 13 hours
(U*)	Subtract 3.5 hours	(I) Add 14 hours
(V)	Subtract 4 hours	(I*) Add 14.5 hours
(V*)	Subtract 4.5 hours	(K) Add 15 hours
(W)	Subtract 5 hours	(K*) Add 15.5 hours
(X)	Subtract 6 hours	(L) Add 16 hours
(Y)	Subtract 7 hours	(L*) Add 16.5 hours
(A)	Add 6 hours	(M) Add 17 hours
(B)	Add 7 hours	(M*) Add 18 hours
(C)	Add 8 hours	(P*) Add 2.5 hours
(C*)	Add 8.5 hours	

Eastern Standard Time = Universal Time (Greenwich Mean Time) + or - the value from the table.

World Map of Time Zones

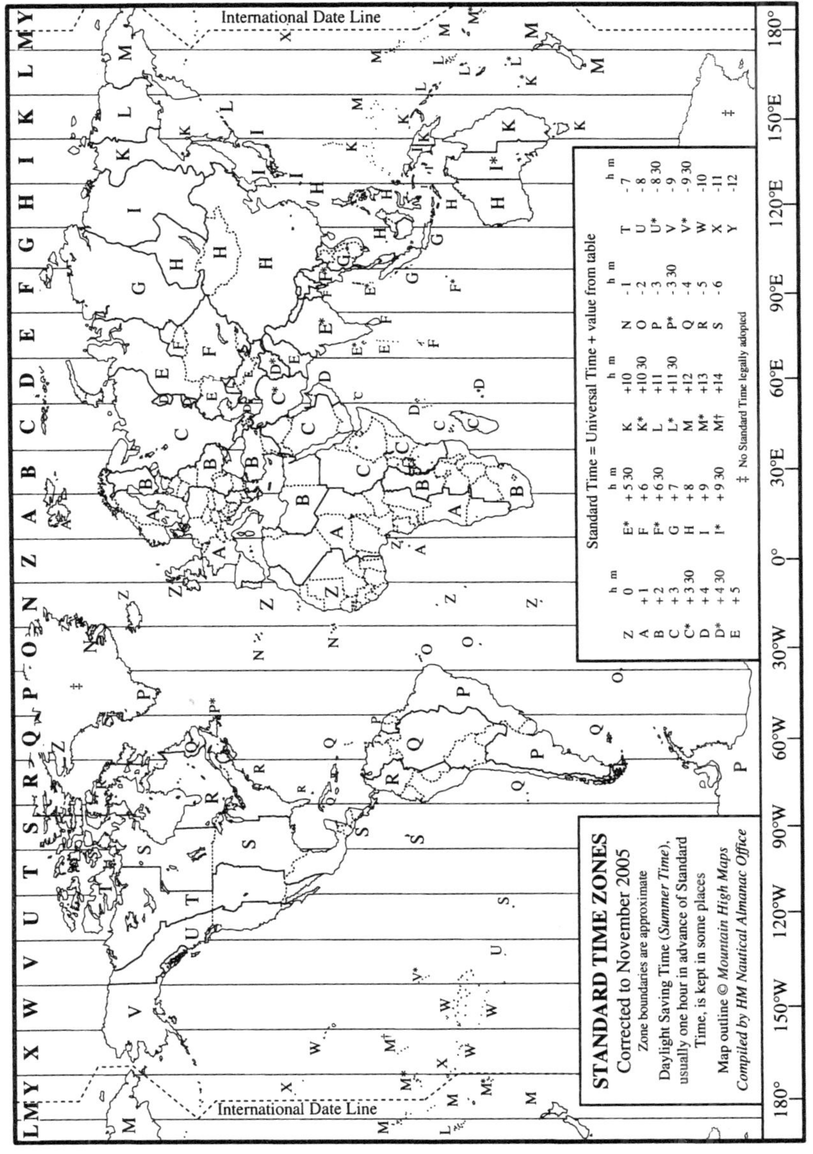

DATE	SID.TIME	SUN	MOON	N.NODE	MERCURY	VENUS	MARS	JUPITER	SATURN	URANUS	NEPTUNE	PLUTO	CERES	PALLAS	JUNO	VESTA	CHIRON
1 Sa	6:41:13	10 ♑ 12 11	29 ♏ 14	2 ♑ 46	19 ♐ 50	23 ♏ 34	18 ♑ 22	26 ♓ 33	16 ♎ 40	26 ♓ 58	26 ♒ 44	5 ♑ 20	28 ♑ 59	4 ♑ 30	28 ♍ 28	15 ♐ 22	27 ♒ 37
2 Su	6:45:09	11 13 21	12 ♐ 39	2 47	20 09	24 32	19 09	26 41	16 42	26 59	26 46	5 22	29 22	4 54	28 36	15 53	27 40
3 M	6:49:06	12 14 32	25 51	2 47 Rx	20 35	25 30	19 55	26 49	16 45	27 00	26 48	5 24	29 46	5 19	28 43	16 25	27 43
4 T	6:53:02	13 15 43	8 ♑ 49	2 47	21 08	26 29	20 42	26 58	16 47	27 02	26 49	5 26	0 ♒ 09	5 43	28 49	16 57	27 47
5 W	6:56:59	14 16 54	21 34	2 47	21 46	27 28	21 28	27 06	16 49	27 03	26 51	5 28	0 33	6 07	28 56	17 29	27 50
6 Th	7:00:56	15 18 04	4 ♒ 05	2 45	22 30	28 28	22 15	27 15	16 52	27 05	26 53	5 31	0 56	6 31	29 02	18 01	27 53
7 F	7:04:52	16 19 15	16 24	2 43	23 19	29 28	23 02	27 24	16 54	27 06	26 55	5 33	1 19	6 55	29 07	18 32	27 56
8 Sa	7:08:49	17 20 25	28 31	2 41	24 12	0 ♐ 29	23 48	27 33	16 56	27 08	26 57	5 35	1 43	7 19	29 12	19 04	28 00
9 Su	7:12:45	18 21 35	10 ♓ 30	2 39	25 09	1 30	24 35	27 42	16 58	27 10	26 58	5 37	2 06	7 43	29 17	19 36	28 03
10 M	7:16:42	19 22 44	22 24	2 37	26 09	2 32	25 22	27 51	16 59	27 11	27 00	5 39	2 30	8 07	29 21	20 07	28 07
11 T	7:20:38	20 23 53	4 ♈ 15	2 35	27 12	3 33	26 08	28 01	17 01	27 13	27 02	5 41	2 54	8 31	29 25	20 39	28 10
12 W	7:24:35	21 25 01	16 09	2 34 D	28 18	4 36	26 55	28 10	17 03	27 15	27 04	5 43	3 17	8 55	29 29	21 10	28 13
13 Th	7:28:31	22 26 09	28 10	2 34	29 27	5 38	27 42	28 20	17 04	27 17	27 06	5 45	3 41	9 19	29 32	21 42	28 17
14 F	7:32:28	23 27 16	10 ♉ 24	2 35	0 ♑ 37	6 41	28 29	28 30	17 06	27 19	27 08	5 48	4 04	9 43	29 34	22 13	28 20
15 Sa	7:36:25	24 28 23	22 53	2 36	1 50	7 44	29 16	28 40	17 07	27 20	27 10	5 50	4 28	10 07	29 37	22 45	28 24
16 Su	7:40:21	25 29 29	5 ♊ 44	2 38	3 04	8 48	0 ♒ 03	28 50	17 08	27 22	27 12	5 52	4 51	10 31	29 39	23 16	28 28
17 M	7:44:18	26 30 34	18 57	2 39	4 20	9 52	0 49	29 00	17 09	27 24	27 14	5 54	5 15	10 54	29 40	23 48	28 31
18 T	7:48:14	27 31 39	2 ♋ 36	2 40 Rx	5 37	10 56	1 36	29 10	17 10	27 27	27 16	5 56	5 39	11 18	29 41	24 19	28 35
19 W	7:52:11	28 32 43	16 39	2 39	6 56	12 00	2 23	29 20	17 11	27 29	27 18	5 58	6 02	11 41	29 42 Rx	24 50	28 39
20 Th	7:56:07	29 33 47	1 ♌ 03	2 37	8 16	13 05	3 10	29 31	17 11	27 31	27 20	6 00	6 26	12 05	29 42	25 22	28 42
21 F	8:00:04	0 ♒ 34 49	15 43	2 34	9 37	14 10	3 57	29 42	17 12	27 33	27 22	6 02	6 50	12 29	29 41	25 53	28 46
22 Sa	8:04:00	1 35 52	0 ♍ 31	2 30	10 59	15 15	4 44	29 52	17 13	27 35	27 24	6 04	7 13	12 52	29 41	26 24	28 50
23 Su	8:07:57	2 36 53	15 19	2 25	12 22	16 20	5 31	0 ♈ 03	17 13	27 37	27 26	6 06	7 37	13 15	29 40	26 55	28 54
24 M	8:11:54	3 37 54	0 ♎ 01	2 21	13 47	17 26	6 19	0 14	17 13	27 40	27 29	6 08	8 01	13 39	29 38	27 26	28 57
25 T	8:15:50	4 38 55	14 29	2 18	15 12	18 32	7 06	0 25	17 14	27 42	27 31	6 10	8 24	14 02	29 36	27 57	29 01
26 W	8:19:47	5 39 55	28 41	2 17 D	16 38	19 38	7 53	0 36	17 14 Rx	27 44	27 33	6 12	8 48	14 25	29 34	28 28	29 05
27 Th	8:23:43	6 40 55	12 ♏ 34	2 17	18 04	20 45	8 40	0 47	17 14	27 47	27 35	6 14	9 12	14 48	29 31	28 59	29 09
28 F	8:27:40	7 41 54	26 09	2 18	19 32	21 51	9 27	0 59	17 13	27 49	27 37	6 16	9 35	15 12	29 27	29 30	29 13
29 Sa	8:31:36	8 42 53	9 ♐ 26	2 19	21 00	22 58	10 14	1 10	17 13	27 52	27 39	6 17	9 59	15 35	29 24	0 ♑ 01	29 17
30 Su	8:35:33	9 43 51	22 28	2 21 Rx	22 30	24 05	11 02	1 22	17 13	27 54	27 41	6 19	10 23	15 58	29 20	0 32	29 21
31 M	8:39:29	10 44 48	5 ♑ 17	2 21	24 00	25 12	11 49	1 33	17 12	27 57	27 44	6 21	10 47	16 21	29 15	1 03	29 25

Tables are for midnight Greenwich Mean Time

DATE	SID.TIME	SUN	MOON	N.NODE	MERCURY	VENUS	MARS	JUPITER	SATURN	URANUS	NEPTUNE	PLUTO	CERES	PALLAS	JUNO	VESTA	CHIRON
1 T	8:43:26	11 ♒45 44	17 ♑ 53	2 ♑ 20	25 ♑ 30	26 ♐ 20	12 ♒ 36	1 ♈ 45	17 ♎ 12	27 ♓ 59	27 ♒ 46	6 ♑ 23	11 ♒ 10	16 ♑ 44	29 ♍ 10	1 ♑ 33	29 ♒ 29
2 W	8:47:23	12 46 40	0 ♒ 20	2 16 ℞	27 02	27 27	13 23	1 57	17 11 ℞	28 02	27 48	6 25	11 34	17 06	29 04 ℞	2 04	29 33
3 Th	8:51:19	13 47 34	12 37	2 11	28 34	28 35	14 11	2 09	17 10	28 05	27 50	6 27	11 58	17 29	28 58	2 34	29 37
4 F	8:55:16	14 48 28	24 46	2 04	0 ♒ 07	29 43	14 58	2 21	17 09	28 07	27 53	6 29	12 21	17 52	28 52	3 05	29 41
5 Sa	8:59:12	15 49 20	6 ♓ 48	1 55	1 40	0 ♑ 51	15 45	2 33	17 08	28 10	27 55	6 30	12 45	18 14	28 45	3 35	29 45
6 Su	9:03:09	16 50 11	18 45	1 46	3 14	1 59	16 33	2 45	17 07	28 13	27 57	6 32	13 09	18 37	28 38	4 06	29 49
7 M	9:07:05	17 51 00	0 ♈ 37	1 37	4 50	3 08	17 20	2 58	17 06	28 16	27 59	6 34	13 32	18 59	28 31	4 36	29 53
8 T	9:11:02	18 51 49	12 28	1 30	6 25	4 16	18 07	3 10	17 05	28 18	28 02	6 35	13 56	19 22	28 23	5 06	29 57
9 W	9:14:58	19 52 35	24 20	1 24	8 02	5 25	18 55	3 22	17 03	28 21	28 04	6 37	14 19	19 44	28 14	5 37	0 ♓ 01
10 Th	9:18:55	20 53 21	6 ♉ 19	1 21	9 39	6 34	19 42	3 35	17 02	28 24	28 06	6 39	14 43	20 06	28 06	6 07	0 05
11 F	9:22:52	21 54 04	18 28	1 19 D	11 18	7 43	20 29	3 47	17 00	28 27	28 08	6 41	15 07	20 29	27 56	6 37	0 09
12 Sa	9:26:48	22 54 47	0 ♊ 52	1 20	12 57	8 52	21 17	4 00	16 59	28 30	28 11	6 42	15 30	20 51	27 47	7 07	0 13
13 Su	9:30:45	23 55 27	13 36	1 21	14 36	10 01	22 04	4 13	16 57	28 33	28 13	6 44	15 54	21 13	27 37	7 37	0 17
14 M	9:34:41	24 56 06	26 45	1 22 ℞	16 17	11 10	22 51	4 26	16 55	28 36	28 15	6 45	16 17	21 35	27 27	8 07	0 21
15 T	9:38:38	25 56 44	10 ♋ 22	1 21	17 59	12 19	23 39	4 39	16 53	28 39	28 17	6 47	16 41	21 57	27 16	8 37	0 25
16 W	9:42:34	26 57 19	24 27	1 19	19 41	13 29	24 26	4 51	16 51	28 42	28 20	6 48	17 04	22 18	27 05	9 06	0 29
17 Th	9:46:31	27 57 53	9 ♌ 00	1 14	21 24	14 38	25 13	5 04	16 49	28 45	28 22	6 50	17 28	22 40	26 54	9 36	0 33
18 F	9:50:27	28 58 25	23 56	1 07	23 08	15 48	26 01	5 18	16 46	28 48	28 24	6 52	17 51	23 02	26 42	10 06	0 37
19 Sa	9:54:24	29 58 56	9 ♍ 05	0 59	24 53	16 58	26 48	5 31	16 44	28 51	28 27	6 53	18 15	23 23	26 31	10 35	0 42
20 Su	9:58:21	0 ♓ 59 25	24 18	0 49	26 39	18 08	27 36	5 44	16 42	28 54	28 29	6 54	18 38	23 44	26 18	11 05	0 46
21 M	10:02:17	1 59 53	9 ♎ 25	0 40	28 26	19 18	28 23	5 57	16 39	28 57	28 31	6 56	19 02	24 06	26 06	11 34	0 50
22 T	10:06:14	3 00 20	24 15	0 33	0 ♓ 14	20 28	29 10	6 10	16 36	29 01	28 33	6 57	19 25	24 27	25 53	12 03	0 54
23 W	10:10:10	4 00 45	8 ♏ 42	0 28	2 03	21 38	29 58	6 24	16 34	29 04	28 36	6 59	19 48	24 48	25 40	12 32	0 58
24 Th	10:14:07	5 01 09	22 43	0 25 D	3 52	22 49	0 ♓ 45	6 37	16 31	29 07	28 38	7 00	20 12	25 09	25 27	13 02	1 02
25 F	10:18:03	6 01 31	6 ♐ 19	0 25	5 43	23 59	1 33	6 51	16 28	29 10	28 40	7 01	20 35	25 30	25 14	13 31	1 06
26 Sa	10:22:00	7 01 52	19 31	0 25 ℞	7 34	25 09	2 20	7 04	16 25	29 13	28 42	7 03	20 58	25 51	25 00	14 00	1 10
27 Su	10:25:56	8 02 12	2 ♑ 22	0 25	9 27	26 20	3 07	7 18	16 22	29 17	28 45	7 04	21 22	26 12	24 46	14 29	1 14
28 M	10:29:53	9 02 30	14 57	0 24	11 20	27 31	3 55	7 32	16 19	29 20	28 47	7 05	21 45	26 33	24 32	14 57	1 18

March

DATE	SID.TIME	SUN	MOON	N.NODE	MERCURY	VENUS	MARS	JUPITER	SATURN	URANUS	NEPTUNE	PLUTO	CERES	PALLAS	JUNO	VESTA	CHIRON
1 T	10:33:50	10 ♓ 02 47	27 ♑ 19	0 ♑ 21	13 ♓ 13	28 ♑ 41	4 ♓ 42	7 ♈ 45	16 ♎ 15	29 ♓ 23	28 ≈ 49	7 ♑ 06	22 ≈ 08	26 ♑ 53	24 ♍ 18	15 ♑ 26	1 ♓ 22
2 W	10:37:46	11 03 02	9 ≈ 32	0 15 ℞	15 08	29 52	5 30	7 59	16 12 ℞	29 26	28 51	7 08	22 31	27 14	24 03 ℞	15 55	1 26
3 Th	10:41:43	12 03 16	21 37	0 06	17 03	1 ≈ 03	6 17	8 13	16 09	29 30	28 54	7 09	22 54	27 34	23 49	16 23	1 31
4 F	10:45:39	13 03 27	3 ♓ 36	29 ♐ 54	18 58	2 14	7 04	8 27	16 05	29 33	28 56	7 10	23 18	27 54	23 34	16 52	1 35
5 Sa	10:49:36	14 03 37	15 32	29 41	20 54	3 25	7 52	8 40	16 02	29 36	28 58	7 11	23 41	28 14	23 19	17 20	1 39
6 Su	10:53:32	15 03 46	27 25	29 26	22 50	4 36	8 39	8 54	15 58	29 40	29 00	7 12	24 04	28 34	23 05	17 48	1 43
7 M	10:57:29	16 03 52	9 ♈ 17	29 12	24 45	5 47	9 26	9 08	15 54	29 43	29 03	7 13	24 27	28 54	22 50	18 16	1 47
8 T	11:01:25	17 03 56	21 09	29 00	26 41	6 58	10 14	9 22	15 51	29 46	29 05	7 14	24 50	29 14	22 35	18 44	1 51
9 W	11:05:22	18 03 58	3 ♉ 03	28 50	28 36	8 09	11 01	9 36	15 47	29 50	29 07	7 15	25 13	29 34	22 20	19 12	1 55
10 Th	11:09:18	19 03 59	15 03	28 43	0 ♈ 29	9 21	11 48	9 50	15 43	29 53	29 09	7 16	25 36	29 53	22 05	19 40	1 59
11 F	11:13:15	20 03 57	27 11	28 38	2 22	10 32	12 35	10 04	15 39	29 56	29 11	7 17	25 58	0 ≈ 13	21 50	20 08	2 02
12 Sa	11:17:12	21 03 53	9 ♊ 32	28 37 D	4 13	11 43	13 23	10 19	15 35	0 ♈ 00	29 13	7 18	26 21	0 32	21 35	20 35	2 06
13 Su	11:21:08	22 03 47	22 11	28 36 ℞	6 01	12 55	14 10	10 33	15 31	0 03	29 16	7 19	26 44	0 51	21 20	21 03	2 10
14 M	11:25:05	23 03 38	5 ♋ 13	28 36	7 48	14 06	14 57	10 47	15 27	0 07	29 18	7 20	27 07	1 10	21 05	21 30	2 14
15 T	11:29:01	24 03 28	18 40	28 35	9 31	15 18	15 44	11 01	15 23	0 10	29 20	7 20	27 29	1 29	20 50	21 58	2 18
16 W	11:32:58	25 03 15	2 ♌ 38	28 32	11 10	16 29	16 32	11 15	15 19	0 14	29 22	7 21	27 52	1 48	20 35	22 25	2 22
17 Th	11:36:54	26 03 00	17 04	28 27	12 46	17 41	17 19	11 30	15 14	0 17	29 24	7 22	28 15	2 06	20 20	22 52	2 26
18 F	11:40:51	27 02 42	1 ♍ 57	28 18	14 17	18 53	18 06	11 44	15 10	0 20	29 26	7 23	28 37	2 25	20 06	23 19	2 30
19 Sa	11:44:47	28 02 23	17 10	28 08	15 43	20 04	18 53	11 58	15 06	0 24	29 28	7 23	29 00	2 43	19 51	23 46	2 33
20 Su	11:48:44	29 02 01	2 ♎ 32	27 56	17 04	21 16	19 40	12 13	15 01	0 27	29 30	7 24	29 22	3 01	19 37	24 12	2 37
21 M	11:52:41	0 ♈ 01 38	17 51	27 46	18 19	22 28	20 27	12 27	14 57	0 31	29 32	7 25	29 44	3 19	19 23	24 39	2 41
22 T	11:56:37	1 01 12	2 ♏ 57	27 36	19 27	23 40	21 14	12 41	14 53	0 34	29 34	7 25	0 ♓ 07	3 37	19 09	25 05	2 45
23 W	12:00:34	2 00 45	17 39	27 29	20 29	24 52	22 01	12 56	14 48	0 37	29 36	7 26	0 29	3 55	18 55	25 32	2 48
24 Th	12:04:30	3 00 16	1 ♐ 54	27 25	21 24	26 03	22 48	13 10	14 44	0 41	29 38	7 26	0 51	4 13	18 42	25 58	2 52
25 F	12:08:27	3 59 45	15 39	27 24 D	22 12	27 15	23 35	13 25	14 39	0 44	29 40	7 27	1 14	4 30	18 28	26 24	2 56
26 Sa	12:12:23	4 59 13	28 56	27 23 ℞	22 52	28 27	24 22	13 39	14 35	0 48	29 42	7 27	1 36	4 48	18 15	26 50	2 59
27 Su	12:16:20	5 58 39	11 ♑ 49	27 23	23 25	29 39	25 09	13 53	14 30	0 51	29 44	7 28	1 58	5 05	18 02	27 16	3 03
28 M	12:20:16	6 58 03	24 21	27 22	23 51	0 ♓ 51	25 56	14 08	14 25	0 55	29 46	7 28	2 20	5 22	17 50	27 41	3 06
29 T	12:24:13	7 57 25	6 ≈ 37	27 19	24 08	2 03	26 43	14 22	14 21	0 58	29 48	7 28	2 42	5 39	17 37	28 07	3 10
30 W	12:28:10	8 56 45	18 43	27 13	24 19 ℞	3 16	27 30	14 37	14 16	1 01	29 50	7 29	3 04	5 56	17 25	28 32	3 13
31 Th	12:32:06	9 56 04	0 ♓ 41	27 05	24 21	4 28	28 17	14 51	14 11	1 05	29 52	7 29	3 25	6 12	17 13	28 57	3 17

Tables are for midnight Greenwich Mean Time

192

April

DATE	SID.TIME	SUN	MOON	N.NODE	MERCURY	VENUS	MARS	JUPITER	SATURN	URANUS	NEPTUNE	PLUTO	CERES	PALLAS	JUNO	VESTA	CHIRON
1 F	12:36:03	10 ♈ 55 20	12 ♓ 34	26 ♐ 54	24 ♈ 17	5 ♓ 40	29 ♓ 04	15 ♈ 06	14 ♎ 07	1 ♈ 08	29 ≈ 54	7 ♑ 29	3 ♓ 47	6 ≈ 29	17 ♍ 02	29 ♑ 22	3 ♓ 20
2 Sa	12:39:59	11 54 35	24 26	26 41 ℞	24 05 ℞	6 52	29 51	15 20	14 02 ℞	1 12	29 55	7 30	4 09	6 45	16 51 ℞	29 47	3 24
3 Su	12:43:56	12 53 48	6 ♈ 18	26 27	23 47	8 04	0 ♈ 37	15 35	13 57	1 15	29 57	7 30	4 31	7 01	16 40	0 ≈ 12	3 27
4 M	12:47:52	13 52 58	18 11	26 13	23 23	9 17	1 24	15 49	13 53	1 18	29 59	7 30	4 52	7 17	16 29	0 37	3 30
5 T	12:51:49	14 52 07	0 ♉ 07	26 01	22 53	10 29	2 11	16 04	13 48	1 22	0 ♓ 01	7 30	5 14	7 32	16 19	1 01	3 34
6 W	12:55:45	15 51 14	12 07	25 51	22 19	11 41	2 57	16 18	13 43	1 25	0 02	7 30	5 35	7 48	16 09	1 26	3 37
7 Th	12:59:42	16 50 18	24 14	25 44	21 40	12 53	3 44	16 33	13 39	1 28	0 04	7 30	5 56	8 03	15 59	1 50	3 40
8 F	13:03:39	17 49 21	6 ♊ 28	25 40	20 58	14 06	4 31	16 48	13 34	1 32	0 06	7 30	6 18	8 18	15 50	2 14	3 44
9 Sa	13:07:35	18 48 21	18 54	25 38 D	20 14	15 18	5 17	17 02	13 30	1 35	0 08	7 30 ℞	6 39	8 33	15 41	2 37	3 47
10 Su	13:11:32	19 47 19	1 ♋ 35	25 38	19 28	16 30	6 04	17 17	13 25	1 38	0 09	7 30	7 00	8 48	15 33	3 01	3 50
11 M	13:15:28	20 46 14	14 35	25 39 ℞	18 42	17 43	6 50	17 31	13 20	1 42	0 11	7 30	7 21	9 03	15 24	3 24	3 53
12 T	13:19:25	21 45 07	27 57	25 39	17 56	18 55	7 37	17 46	13 16	1 45	0 12	7 30	7 42	9 17	15 17	3 48	3 56
13 W	13:23:21	22 43 58	11 ♌ 44	25 37	17 11	20 08	8 23	18 00	13 11	1 48	0 14	7 30	8 03	9 31	15 09	4 11	3 59
14 Th	13:27:18	23 42 47	25 58	25 33	16 27	21 20	9 10	18 14	13 07	1 51	0 16	7 30	8 24	9 45	15 02	4 34	4 02
15 F	13:31:14	24 41 33	10 ♍ 37	25 27	15 47	22 33	9 56	18 29	13 02	1 55	0 17	7 30	8 45	9 59	14 56	4 56	4 05
16 Sa	13:35:11	25 40 17	25 36	25 19	15 10	23 45	10 42	18 43	12 58	1 58	0 19	7 30	9 05	10 12	14 49	5 19	4 08
17 Su	13:39:08	26 38 59	10 ♎ 47	25 11	14 36	24 57	11 29	18 58	12 53	2 01	0 20	7 30	9 26	10 26	14 43	5 41	4 11
18 M	13:43:04	27 37 39	26 01	25 02	14 07	26 10	12 15	19 12	12 49	2 04	0 21	7 29	9 46	10 39	14 38	6 03	4 13
19 T	13:47:01	28 36 17	11 ♏ 05	24 55	13 43	27 22	13 01	19 27	12 44	2 07	0 23	7 29	10 07	10 52	14 33	6 25	4 16
20 W	13:50:57	29 34 53	25 52	24 49	13 23	28 35	13 47	19 41	12 40	2 11	0 24	7 29	10 27	11 04	14 28	6 47	4 19
21 Th	13:54:54	0 ♉ 33 27	10 ♐ 14	24 46	13 08	29 48	14 33	19 55	12 35	2 14	0 26	7 28	10 47	11 17	14 23	7 09	4 22
22 F	13:58:50	1 32 00	24 08	24 45 D	12 58	1 ♈ 00	15 19	20 10	12 31	2 17	0 27	7 28	11 08	11 29	14 19	7 30	4 24
23 Sa	14:02:47	2 30 31	7 ♑ 33	24 46	12 54 D	2 13	16 05	20 24	12 27	2 20	0 28	7 28	11 28	11 41	14 16	7 51	4 27
24 Su	14:06:43	3 29 01	20 32	24 47	12 54	3 25	16 51	20 38	12 23	2 23	0 30	7 27	11 48	11 53	14 13	8 12	4 29
25 M	14:10:40	4 27 28	3 ≈ 08	24 48 ℞	12 59	4 38	17 37	20 53	12 19	2 26	0 31	7 27	12 07	12 04	14 10	8 33	4 32
26 T	14:14:37	5 25 54	15 26	24 47	13 10	5 51	18 23	21 07	12 14	2 29	0 32	7 26	12 27	12 15	14 07	8 53	4 34
27 W	14:18:33	6 24 19	27 31	24 45	13 25	7 03	19 09	21 21	12 10	2 32	0 33	7 26	12 47	12 27	14 05	9 13	4 37
28 Th	14:22:30	7 22 42	9 ♓ 28	24 40	13 45	8 16	19 55	21 36	12 06	2 35	0 34	7 25	13 06	12 37	14 03	9 33	4 39
29 F	14:26:26	8 21 03	21 20	24 34	14 09	9 29	20 41	21 50	12 02	2 38	0 36	7 25	13 26	12 48	14 02	9 53	4 41
30 Sa	14:30:23	9 19 23	3 ♈ 11	24 26	14 37	10 41	21 27	22 04	11 59	2 41	0 37	7 24	13 45	12 58	14 01	10 12	4 43

May

DATE	SID.TIME	SUN	MOON	N.NODE	MERCURY	VENUS	MARS	JUPITER	SATURN	URANUS	NEPTUNE	PLUTO	CERES	PALLAS	JUNO	VESTA	CHIRON
1 Su	14:34:19	10♉17 40	15♈04	24♐18	15♈10	11♈54	22♈12	22♈18	11♎55	2♈44	0♓38	7♑23	14♓05	13♒08	14♍00℞	10♒32	4♓46
2 M	14:38:16	11 15 57	27 01	24 09℞	15 47	13 07	22 58	22 32	11 51℞	2 47	0 39	7 23℞	14 24	13 18	14 00 D	10 51	4 48
3 T	14:42:12	12 14 11	9♉03	24 02	16 27	14 19	23 44	22 46	11 47	2 49	0 40	7 22	14 43	13 27	14 00	11 09	4 50
4 W	14:46:09	13 12 24	21 13	23 56	17 11	15 32	24 29	23 00	11 44	2 52	0 41	7 21	15 02	13 37	14 01	11 28	4 52
5 Th	14:50:05	14 10 36	3♊32	23 52	17 59	16 45	25 15	23 14	11 40	2 55	0 42	7 21	15 20	13 45	14 01	11 46	4 54
6 F	14:54:02	15 08 45	16 00	23 50 D	18 50	17 58	26 00	23 28	11 37	2 58	0 43	7 20	15 39	13 54	14 03	12 04	4 56
7 Sa	14:57:59	16 06 53	28 39	23 50	19 44	19 10	26 46	23 42	11 33	3 01	0 44	7 19	15 58	14 02	14 04	12 22	4 58
8 Su	15:01:55	17 04 59	11♋32	23 51	20 42	20 23	27 31	23 56	11 30	3 03	0 44	7 18	16 16	14 11	14 06	12 39	5 00
9 M	15:05:52	18 03 03	24 40	23 53	21 42	21 36	28 16	24 10	11 26	3 06	0 45	7 17	16 35	14 18	14 08	12 56	5 01
10 T	15:09:48	19 01 05	8♌06	23 54℞	22 46	22 49	29 01	24 24	11 23	3 09	0 46	7 16	16 53	14 26	14 11	13 13	5 03
11 W	15:13:45	19 59 05	21 51	23 54	23 52	24 01	29 47	24 38	11 20	3 11	0 47	7 16	17 11	14 33	14 14	13 30	5 05
12 Th	15:17:41	20 57 03	5♍55	23 54	25 01	25 14	0♉32	24 51	11 17	3 14	0 48	7 15	17 29	14 40	14 17	13 46	5 07
13 F	15:21:38	21 54 59	20 18	23 51	26 12	26 27	1 17	25 05	11 14	3 16	0 48	7 14	17 47	14 47	14 20	14 02	5 08
14 Sa	15:25:34	22 52 53	4♎57	23 48	27 27	27 40	2 02	25 19	11 11	3 19	0 49	7 13	18 04	14 53	14 24	14 18	5 10
15 Su	15:29:31	23 50 46	19 46	23 44	28 43	28 53	2 47	25 32	11 08	3 21	0 50	7 12	18 22	14 59	14 29	14 33	5 11
16 M	15:33:28	24 48 37	4♏38	23 40	0♉02	0♉05	3 32	25 46	11 06	3 24	0 50	7 11	18 39	15 05	14 33	14 48	5 12
17 T	15:37:24	25 46 26	19 25	23 36	1 24	1 18	4 17	25 59	11 03	3 26	0 51	7 10	18 57	15 10	14 38	15 03	5 14
18 W	15:41:21	26 44 14	4♐00	23 34	2 48	2 31	5 02	26 13	11 00	3 28	0 51	7 09	19 14	15 15	14 43	15 17	5 15
19 Th	15:45:17	27 42 01	18 16	23 33 D	4 14	3 44	5 47	26 26	10 58	3 31	0 52	7 08	19 31	15 20	14 49	15 32	5 16
20 F	15:49:14	28 39 46	2♑08	23 33	5 43	4 57	6 31	26 40	10 56	3 33	0 52	7 06	19 48	15 24	14 54	15 45	5 18
21 Sa	15:53:10	29 37 30	15 36	23 34	7 14	6 10	7 16	26 53	10 53	3 35	0 53	7 05	20 04	15 28	15 00	15 59	5 19
22 Su	15:57:07	0♊35 13	28 39	23 35	8 47	7 23	8 01	27 06	10 51	3 38	0 53	7 04	20 21	15 32	15 07	16 12	5 20
23 M	16:01:04	1 32 55	11♒20	23 37	10 22	8 35	8 45	27 19	10 49	3 40	0 54	7 03	20 37	15 35	15 13	16 25	5 21
24 T	16:05:00	2 30 36	23 42	23 38℞	12 00	9 48	9 30	27 32	10 47	3 42	0 54	7 02	20 54	15 38	15 20	16 37	5 22
25 W	16:08:57	3 28 15	5♓51	23 38	13 40	11 01	10 14	27 46	10 45	3 44	0 54	7 01	21 10	15 41	15 27	16 49	5 23
26 Th	16:12:53	4 25 54	17 49	23 37	15 22	12 14	10 59	27 59	10 43	3 46	0 55	7 00	21 26	15 43	15 35	17 01	5 23
27 F	16:16:50	5 23 32	29 42	23 36	17 07	13 27	11 43	28 12	10 41	3 48	0 55	6 58	21 42	15 45	15 42	17 12	5 24
28 Sa	16:20:46	6 21 08	11♈34	23 34	18 53	14 40	12 28	28 24	10 40	3 50	0 55	6 57	21 57	15 47	15 50	17 23	5 25
29 Su	16:24:43	7 18 44	23 29	23 32	20 42	15 53	13 12	28 37	10 38	3 52	0 55	6 56	22 13	15 48	15 59	17 34	5 26
30 M	16:28:39	8 16 19	5♉31	23 29	22 33	17 06	13 56	28 50	10 37	3 54	0 55	6 54	22 28	15 49	16 07	17 44	5 26
31 T	16:32:36	9 13 53	17 41	23 27	24 27	18 19	14 40	29 03	10 35	3 56	0 55	6 53	22 43	15 50℞	16 16	17 54	5 27

Tables are for midnight Greenwich Mean Time

June

DATE	SID.TIME	SUN	MOON	N.NODE	MERCURY	VENUS	MARS	JUPITER	SATURN	URANUS	NEPTUNE	PLUTO	CERES	PALLAS	JUNO	VESTA	CHIRON
1 W	16:36:33	10 ♊ 11 26	0 ♊ 02	23 ♐ 26 ℞	26 ♉ 22	19 ♉ 32	15 ♉ 25	29 ♈ 15	10 ♎ 34	3 ♈ 58	0 ♓ 56	6 ♑ 52	22 ♓ 58	15 ♒ 50	16 ♍ 25	18 ♒ 03	5 ♓ 27
2 Th	16:40:29	11 08 58	12 35	23 25 D	28 20	20 45	16 09	29 28	10 33 ℞	3 59	0 56	6 51 ℞	23 13	15 50 ℞	16 34	18 12	5 28
3 F	16:44:26	12 06 29	25 22	23 24	0 ♊ 20	21 58	16 53	29 40	10 32	4 01	0 56 ℞	6 49	23 27	15 49	16 44	18 21	5 28
4 Sa	16:48:22	13 03 58	8 ♋ 22	23 25	2 22	23 11	17 37	29 53	10 31	4 03	0 56	6 48	23 42	15 48	16 53	18 29	5 28
5 Su	16:52:19	14 01 27	21 35	23 25	4 25	24 24	18 20	0 ♉ 05	10 30	4 05	0 56	6 46	23 56	15 47	17 03	18 37	5 29
6 M	16:56:15	14 58 55	5 ♌ 02	23 26	6 31	25 37	19 04	0 17	10 29	4 06	0 56	6 45	24 10	15 45	17 14	18 44	5 29
7 T	17:00:12	15 56 21	18 43	23 27	8 38	26 50	19 48	0 30	10 29	4 08	0 55	6 44	24 24	15 43	17 24	18 51	5 29
8 W	17:04:08	16 53 46	2 ♍ 35	23 27	10 46	28 03	20 32	0 42	10 28	4 09	0 55	6 42	24 38	15 40	17 35	18 57	5 29 ℞
9 Th	17:08:05	17 51 10	16 39	23 28 ℞	12 56	29 16	21 16	0 54	10 28	4 11	0 55	6 41	24 51	15 38	17 46	19 03	5 29
10 F	17:12:02	18 48 33	0 ♎ 53	23 28	15 06	0 ♊ 29	21 59	1 06	10 27	4 12	0 55	6 39	25 04	15 34	17 57	19 09	5 29
11 Sa	17:15:58	19 45 54	15 15	23 27	17 18	1 42	22 43	1 18	10 27	4 14	0 55	6 38	25 17	15 31	18 08	19 14	5 29
12 Su	17:19:55	20 43 15	29 40	23 27	19 29	2 55	23 26	1 29	10 27	4 15	0 54	6 37	25 30	15 27	18 19	19 19	5 29
13 M	17:23:51	21 40 35	14 ♏ 05	23 27	21 41	4 09	24 10	1 41	10 27 D	4 16	0 54	6 35	25 43	15 22	18 31	19 23	5 29
14 T	17:27:48	22 37 53	28 26	23 27 D	23 53	5 22	24 53	1 53	10 27	4 18	0 54	6 34	25 55	15 18	18 43	19 27	5 28
15 W	17:31:44	23 35 11	12 ♐ 37	23 27 ℞	26 05	6 35	25 36	2 04	10 27	4 19	0 53	6 32	26 07	15 12	18 55	19 30	5 28
16 Th	17:35:41	24 32 29	26 34	23 27	28 16	7 48	26 20	2 16	10 27	4 20	0 53	6 31	26 19	15 07	19 07	19 33	5 28
17 F	17:39:37	25 29 46	10 ♑ 14	23 27	0 ♋ 26	9 01	27 03	2 27	10 27	4 21	0 53	6 29	26 31	15 01	19 20	19 35	5 27
18 Sa	17:43:34	26 27 02	23 34	23 26	2 35	10 14	27 46	2 38	10 28	4 22	0 52	6 28	26 43	14 55	19 33	19 37	5 27
19 Su	17:47:31	27 24 17	6 ♒ 35	23 26	4 43	11 27	28 29	2 49	10 28	4 23	0 52	6 26	26 54	14 48	19 45	19 39	5 26
20 M	17:51:27	28 21 33	19 16	23 25	6 50	12 41	29 12	3 00	10 29	4 24	0 51	6 25	27 05	14 41	19 58	19 40	5 25
21 T	17:55:24	29 18 48	1 ♓ 40	23 25	8 54	13 54	29 55	3 11	10 30	4 25	0 51	6 23	27 16	14 34	20 12	19 40 ℞	5 25
22 W	17:59:20	0 ♋ 16 02	13 50	23 24	10 57	15 07	0 ♊ 38	3 22	10 31	4 26	0 50	6 22	27 27	14 26	20 25	19 40	5 24
23 Th	18:03:17	1 13 17	25 50	23 24 D	12 59	16 20	1 21	3 33	10 31	4 27	0 49	6 20	27 37	14 18	20 39	19 40	5 23
24 F	18:07:13	2 10 31	7 ♈ 44	23 24	14 58	17 33	2 03	3 44	10 33	4 28	0 49	6 19	27 47	14 09	20 52	19 39	5 22
25 Sa	18:11:10	3 07 46	19 37	23 24	16 55	18 47	2 46	3 54	10 34	4 28	0 48	6 17	27 57	14 00	21 06	19 37	5 22
26 Su	18:15:06	4 05 00	1 ♉ 34	23 25	18 50	20 00	3 29	4 05	10 35	4 29	0 47	6 16	28 07	13 51	21 20	19 36	5 21
27 M	18:19:03	5 02 14	13 38	23 26	20 43	21 13	4 12	4 15	10 36	4 30	0 47	6 14	28 16	13 41	21 34	19 33	5 20
28 T	18:23:00	5 59 28	25 54	23 27	22 34	22 27	4 54	4 25	10 38	4 30	0 46	6 13	28 25	13 31	21 49	19 30	5 18
29 W	18:26:56	6 56 42	8 ♊ 24	23 28	24 23	23 40	5 37	4 36	10 39	4 31	0 45	6 11	28 34	13 21	22 03	19 27	5 17
30 Th	18:30:53	7 53 56	21 12	23 29 ℞	26 10	24 53	6 19	4 46	10 41	4 31	0 44	6 09	28 42	13 10	22 18	19 23	5 16

July

DATE	SID.TIME	SUN	MOON	N.NODE	MERCURY	VENUS	MARS	JUPITER	SATURN	URANUS	NEPTUNE	PLUTO	CERES	PALLAS	JUNO	VESTA	CHIRON
1 F	18:34:49	8 ♋ 51 10	4 ♋ 17	23 ♐ 28	27 ♋ 54	26 ♊ 07	7 ♊ 01	4 ♉ 56	10 ♎ 43	4 ♈ 32	0 ♓ 44	6 ♑ 08	28 ♓ 51	12 ♒ 59	22 ♍ 33	19 ♒ 19	5 ♓ 15
2 Sa	18:38:46	9 48 24	17 40	23 27 ℞	29 36	27 20	7 44	5 05	10 44	4 32	0 43 ℞	6 06 ℞	28 59	12 48 ℞	22 48	19 14 ℞	5 14 ℞
3 Su	18:42:42	10 45 38	1 ♌ 19	23 26	1 ♌ 16	28 33	8 26	5 15	10 46	4 33	0 42	6 05	29 07	12 36	23 03	19 08	5 12
4 M	18:46:39	11 42 51	15 12	23 23	2 54	29 47	9 08	5 25	10 48	4 33	0 41	6 03	29 14	12 24	23 18	19 03	5 11
5 T	18:50:35	12 40 04	29 16	23 21	4 30	1 ♋ 00	9 50	5 34	10 50	4 33	0 40	6 02	29 21	12 12	23 34	18 56	5 10
6 W	18:54:32	13 37 17	13 ♍ 27	23 19	6 04	2 14	10 32	5 43	10 53	4 33	0 39	6 00	29 28	12 00	23 49	18 50	5 08
7 Th	18:58:29	14 34 30	27 41	23 17	7 35	3 27	11 14	5 53	10 55	4 34	0 38	5 59	29 35	11 47	24 05	18 43	5 07
8 F	19:02:25	15 31 42	11 ♎ 56	23 16 D	9 04	4 41	11 56	6 02	10 57	4 34	0 37	5 57	29 41	11 34	24 21	18 35	5 05
9 Sa	19:06:22	16 28 54	26 09	23 16	10 31	5 54	12 38	6 11	11 00	4 34	0 36	5 56	29 47	11 20	24 37	18 27	5 03
10 Su	19:10:18	17 26 06	10 ♏ 17	23 17	11 56	7 08	13 20	6 19	11 02	4 34 ℞	0 35	5 54	29 52	11 07	24 53	18 18	5 02
11 M	19:14:15	18 23 18	24 19	23 19	13 18	8 21	14 02	6 28	11 05	4 34	0 34	5 53	29 58	10 53	25 09	18 09	5 00
12 T	19:18:11	19 20 30	8 ♐ 13	23 20	14 38	9 35	14 43	6 37	11 08	4 34	0 33	5 51	0 ♈ 03	10 39	25 25	18 00	4 58
13 W	19:22:08	20 17 42	21 57	23 21 ℞	15 56	10 48	15 25	6 45	11 11	4 34	0 32	5 50	0 08	10 24	25 41	17 50	4 56
14 Th	19:26:04	21 14 54	5 ♑ 29	23 20	17 11	12 02	16 06	6 53	11 14	4 33	0 30	5 48	0 12	10 10	25 58	17 40	4 54
15 F	19:30:01	22 12 06	18 49	23 18	18 23	13 15	16 48	7 02	11 17	4 33	0 29	5 47	0 16	9 55	26 15	17 30	4 53
16 Sa	19:33:58	23 09 18	1 ♒ 54	23 15	19 33	14 29	17 29	7 10	11 20	4 33	0 28	5 46	0 20	9 40	26 31	17 19	4 51
17 Su	19:37:54	24 06 31	14 43	23 11	20 41	15 43	18 11	7 17	11 23	4 33	0 27	5 44	0 23	9 25	26 48	17 08	4 49
18 M	19:41:51	25 03 44	27 18	23 05	21 46	16 56	18 52	7 25	11 26	4 32	0 26	5 43	0 27	9 10	27 05	16 56	4 47
19 T	19:45:47	26 00 58	9 ♓ 39	23 00	22 48	18 10	19 33	7 33	11 30	4 32	0 24	5 41	0 29	8 55	27 22	16 44	4 44
20 W	19:49:44	26 58 12	21 47	22 55	23 47	19 24	20 14	7 40	11 33	4 31	0 23	5 40	0 32	8 39	27 39	16 32	4 42
21 Th	19:53:40	27 55 27	3 ♈ 46	22 51	24 43	20 37	20 56	7 48	11 37	4 31	0 22	5 38	0 34	8 24	27 57	16 19	4 40
22 F	19:57:37	28 52 43	15 40	22 49	25 35	21 51	21 37	7 55	11 40	4 30	0 20	5 37	0 36	8 08	28 14	16 07	4 38
23 Sa	20:01:33	29 49 59	27 32	22 48 D	26 25	23 05	22 18	8 02	11 44	4 30	0 19	5 36	0 37	7 52	28 32	15 54	4 36
24 Su	20:05:30	0 ♌ 47 16	9 ♉ 28	22 48	27 11	24 19	22 59	8 09	11 48	4 29	0 18	5 34	0 38	7 36	28 49	15 40	4 33
25 M	20:09:27	1 44 34	21 32	22 49	27 54	25 32	23 39	8 15	11 52	4 29	0 16	5 33	0 39	7 20	29 07	15 27	4 31
26 T	20:13:23	2 41 54	3 ♊ 50	22 51	28 33	26 46	24 20	8 22	11 56	4 28	0 15	5 32	0 39 ℞	7 04	29 25	15 13	4 29
27 W	20:17:20	3 39 14	16 25	22 52 ℞	29 08	28 00	25 01	8 28	12 00	4 27	0 14	5 30	0 40	6 48	29 42	14 59	4 26
28 Th	20:21:16	4 36 34	29 21	22 52	29 39	29 14	25 42	8 35	12 04	4 26	0 12	5 29	0 39	6 32	0 ♎ 00	14 45	4 24
29 F	20:25:13	5 33 56	12 ♋ 40	22 50	0 ♍ 06	0 ♌ 28	26 22	8 41	12 08	4 25	0 11	5 28	0 39	6 16	0 18	14 30	4 21
30 Sa	20:29:09	6 31 19	26 22	22 47	0 29	1 42	27 03	8 47	12 12	4 24	0 09	5 27	0 38	6 00	0 36	14 16	4 19
31 Su	20:33:06	7 28 42	10 ♌ 25	22 41	0 47	2 56	27 43	8 52	12 17	4 23	0 08	5 25	0 36	5 44	0 55	14 01	4 16

Tables are for midnight Greenwich Mean Time

August

DATE	SID.TIME	SUN	MOON	N.NODE	MERCURY	VENUS	MARS	JUPITER
1 M	20:37:03	8 ♌ 26 07	24 ♌ 45	22 ♐ 35	1 ♍ 00	4 ♌ 10	28 ♊ 24	8 ♉ 58
2 T	20:40:59	9 23 31	9 ♍ 17	22 27 Rx	1 09	5 23	29 04	9 03
3 W	20:44:56	10 20 57	23 53	22 21	1 12 Rx	6 37	29 44	9 09
4 Th	20:48:52	11 18 23	8 ♎ 27	22 15	1 10	7 51	0 ♋ 25	9 14
5 F	20:52:49	12 15 50	22 53	22 12	1 03	9 05	1 05	9 19
6 Sa	20:56:45	13 13 18	7 ♏ 08	22 10 D	0 51	10 19	1 45	9 23
7 Su	21:00:42	14 10 46	21 09	22 10	0 33	11 33	2 25	9 28
8 M	21:04:38	15 08 15	4 ♐ 57	22 11	0 11	12 47	3 05	9 32
9 T	21:08:35	16 05 45	18 31	22 12 Rx	29 ♌ 43	14 01	3 45	9 36
10 W	21:12:32	17 03 15	1 ♑ 52	22 11	29 10	15 16	4 24	9 40
11 Th	21:16:28	18 00 47	15 01	22 09	28 33	16 30	5 04	9 44
12 F	21:20:25	18 58 19	27 58	22 04	27 52	17 44	5 44	9 48
13 Sa	21:24:21	19 55 53	10 ♒ 44	21 57	27 08	18 58	6 23	9 51
14 Su	21:28:18	20 53 27	23 19	21 48	26 21	20 12	7 03	9 55
15 M	21:32:14	21 51 03	5 ♓ 43	21 37	25 32	21 26	7 42	9 58
16 T	21:36:11	22 48 40	17 56	21 26	24 42	22 40	8 22	10 01
17 W	21:40:07	23 46 18	29 59	21 16	23 51	23 54	9 01	10 03
18 Th	21:44:04	24 43 58	11 ♈ 55	21 07	23 01	25 09	9 40	10 06
19 F	21:48:00	25 41 39	23 47	21 00	22 14	26 23	10 19	10 08
20 Sa	21:51:57	26 39 22	5 ♉ 37	20 55	21 29	27 37	10 59	10 11
21 Su	21:55:54	27 37 06	17 31	20 53 D	20 47	28 51	11 38	10 12
22 M	21:59:50	28 34 52	29 33	20 53	20 11	0 ♍ 06	12 17	10 14
23 T	22:03:47	29 32 40	11 ♊ 49	20 53 Rx	19 39	1 20	12 55	10 16
24 W	22:07:43	0 ♍ 30 30	24 23	20 53	19 14	2 34	13 34	10 17
25 Th	22:11:40	1 28 21	7 ♋ 20	20 52	18 56	3 49	14 13	10 18
26 F	22:15:36	2 26 14	20 44	20 49	18 45 D	5 03	14 52	10 19
27 Sa	22:19:33	3 24 09	4 ♌ 35	20 43	18 42	6 17	15 30	10 20
28 Su	22:23:29	4 22 05	18 53	20 35	18 46	7 32	16 09	10 21
29 M	22:27:26	5 20 03	3 ♍ 34	20 25	18 59	8 46	16 47	10 21
30 T	22:31:23	6 18 02	18 29	20 14	19 20	10 00	17 26	10 21 Rx

DATE	SATURN	URANUS	NEPTUNE	PLUTO	CERES	PALLAS	JUNO	VESTA	CHIRON
1 M	12 ♎ 21	4 ♈ 22	0 ♓ 06	5 ♑ 24	0 ♈ 34	5 ♒ 28	1 ♎ 13	13 ♒ 46	4 ♓ 14
2 T	12 26	4 21 Rx	0 05 Rx	5 23 Rx	0 32 Rx	5 12 Rx	1 31	13 32 Rx	4 11 Rx
3 W	12 30	4 20	0 03	5 22	0 30	4 57	1 50	13 17	4 09
4 Th	12 35	4 19	0 02	5 21	0 27	4 41	2 08	13 02	4 06
5 F	12 40	4 18	0 00	5 19	0 24	4 25	2 27	12 47	4 03
6 Sa	12 44	4 17	29 ♒ 59	5 18	0 20	4 10	2 46	12 32	4 01
7 Su	12 49	4 16	29 57	5 17	0 16	3 55	3 04	12 18	3 58
8 M	12 54	4 14	29 56	5 16	0 12	3 39	3 23	12 03	3 55
9 T	12 59	4 13	29 54	5 15	0 07	3 24	3 42	11 48	3 52
10 W	13 04	4 12	29 52	5 14	0 02	3 09	4 01	11 34	3 50
11 Th	13 09	4 10	29 51	5 13	29 ♓ 57	2 55	4 20	11 19	3 47
12 F	13 15	4 09	29 49	5 12	29 51	2 40	4 39	11 05	3 44
13 Sa	13 20	4 07	29 48	5 11	29 45	2 26	4 58	10 51	3 41
14 Su	13 25	4 06	29 46	5 10	29 39	2 12	5 18	10 37	3 38
15 M	13 31	4 04	29 44	5 09	29 32	1 58	5 37	10 23	3 36
16 T	13 36	4 02	29 43	5 08	29 25	1 45	5 56	10 10	3 33
17 W	13 41	4 01	29 41	5 07	29 18	1 31	6 16	9 56	3 30
18 Th	13 47	3 59	29 39	5 06	29 10	1 18	6 35	9 43	3 27
19 F	13 53	3 57	29 38	5 06	29 02	1 06	6 55	9 30	3 24
20 Sa	13 58	3 56	29 36	5 05	28 54	0 53	7 14	9 18	3 21
21 Su	14 04	3 54	29 35	5 04	28 45	0 41	7 34	9 06	3 18
22 M	14 10	3 52	29 33	5 03	28 36	0 29	7 54	8 54	3 15
23 T	14 16	3 50	29 31	5 02	28 27	0 17	8 13	8 42	3 12
24 W	14 22	3 48	29 30	5 02	28 17	0 06	8 33	8 31	3 09
25 Th	14 28	3 47	29 28	5 01	28 07	29 ♑ 55	8 53	8 20	3 06
26 F	14 34	3 45	29 26	5 00	27 57	29 45	9 13	8 10	3 03
27 Sa	14 40	3 43	29 25	5 00	27 46	29 34	9 33	7 59	3 00
28 Su	14 46	3 41	29 23	4 59	27 36	29 24	9 53	7 50	2 57
29 M	14 52	3 39	29 21	4 59	27 25	29 15	10 13	7 40	2 55
30 T	14 58	3 37	29 20	4 58	27 14	29 05	10 33	7 31	2 52

September

DATE	SID.TIME	SUN	MOON	N.NODE	MERCURY	VENUS	MARS	JUPITER	SATURN	URANUS	NEPTUNE	PLUTO	CERES	PALLAS	JUNO	VESTA	CHIRON
1 Th	22:39:16	8 ♍14 06	18 ♎26	19 ♐55	20 ♌26	12 ♍29	18 ♋42	10 ♉21	15 ♎11	3 ♈32	29 ♒17	4 ♑57	26 ♓50	28 ♑48	11 ♎13	7 ♒15	2 ♓46
2 F	22:43:12	9 12 10	3 ♏10	19 49Rx	21 11	13 44	19 21	10 21Rx	15 17	3 30Rx	29 15Rx	4 57Rx	26 39Rx	28 40Rx	11 33	7 07Rx	2 43Rx
3 Sa	22:47:09	10 10 15	17 37	19 45	22 04	14 58	19 59	10 20	15 24	3 28	29 13	4 56	26 26	28 32	11 54	7 00	2 40
4 Su	22:51:05	11 08 22	1 ♐43	19 44 D	23 04	16 12	20 37	10 19	15 30	3 26	29 12	4 56	26 14	28 24	12 14	6 53	2 37
5 M	22:55:02	12 06 30	15 27	19 44Rx	24 10	17 27	21 15	10 18	15 37	3 24	29 10	4 55	26 02	28 17	12 34	6 47	2 34
6 T	22:58:58	13 04 39	28 52	19 44	25 24	18 41	21 52	10 17	15 43	3 22	29 09	4 55	25 49	28 10	12 55	6 41	2 31
7 W	23:02:55	14 02 50	11 ♑59	19 42	26 43	19 56	22 30	10 16	15 50	3 19	29 07	4 55	25 37	28 04	13 15	6 36	2 28
8 Th	23:06:52	15 01 03	24 51	19 39	28 07	21 10	23 08	10 14	15 56	3 17	29 05	4 54	25 24	27 58	13 36	6 31	2 25
9 F	23:10:48	15 59 16	7 ♒31	19 32	29 37	22 25	23 45	10 12	16 03	3 15	29 04	4 54	25 11	27 52	13 56	6 27	2 23
10 Sa	23:14:45	16 57 32	20 00	19 23	1 ♍11	23 39	24 23	10 10	16 10	3 13	29 02	4 54	24 58	27 47	14 17	6 23	2 20
11 Su	23:18:41	17 55 49	2 ♓20	19 11	2 49	24 54	25 00	10 08	16 16	3 10	29 01	4 54	24 44	27 42	14 37	6 19	2 17
12 M	23:22:38	18 54 08	14 31	18 58	4 30	26 08	25 38	10 05	16 23	3 08	28 59	4 54	24 31	27 37	14 58	6 16	2 14
13 T	23:26:34	19 52 29	26 35	18 44	6 14	27 23	26 15	10 03	16 30	3 06	28 58	4 54	24 18	27 33	15 18	6 14	2 11
14 W	23:30:31	20 50 51	8 ♈33	18 30	8 01	28 37	26 52	10 00	16 37	3 03	28 56	4 53	24 04	27 29	15 39	6 12	2 09
15 Th	23:34:27	21 49 15	20 26	18 18	9 49	29 52	27 29	9 57	16 44	3 01	28 55	4 53	23 51	27 26	16 00	6 10	2 06
16 F	23:38:24	22 47 42	2 ♉16	18 09	11 39	1 ♎06	28 07	9 54	16 51	2 59	28 53	4 53 D	23 38	27 23	16 20	6 09	2 03
17 Sa	23:42:21	23 46 10	14 05	18 02	13 30	2 21	28 43	9 50	16 58	2 56	28 52	4 53	23 24	27 20	16 41	6 08 D	2 01
18 Su	23:46:17	24 44 41	25 58	17 58	15 21	3 35	29 20	9 47	17 04	2 54	28 50	4 53	23 11	27 18	17 02	6 08	1 58
19 M	23:50:14	25 43 14	7 ♊58	17 57 D	17 13	4 50	29 57	9 43	17 11	2 52	28 49	4 53	22 57	27 16	17 22	6 08	1 55
20 T	23:54:10	26 41 49	20 11	17 57Rx	19 05	6 04	0 ♌34	9 39	17 18	2 49	28 48	4 53	22 44	27 14	17 43	6 09	1 53
21 W	23:58:07	27 40 26	2 ♋41	17 57	20 58	7 19	1 11	9 35	17 25	2 47	28 46	4 54	22 30	27 13	18 04	6 10	1 50
22 Th	0:02:03	28 39 06	15 35	17 56	22 50	8 34	1 47	9 31	17 33	2 44	28 45	4 54	22 17	27 12	18 25	6 12	1 48
23 F	0:06:00	29 37 47	28 55	17 53	24 41	9 48	2 24	9 26	17 40	2 42	28 43	4 54	22 04	27 11	18 46	6 14	1 45
24 Sa	0:09:56	0 ♎36 31	12 ♌44	17 48	26 33	11 03	3 00	9 22	17 47	2 40	28 42	4 54	21 51	27 11 D	19 07	6 17	1 43
25 Su	0:13:53	1 35 17	27 04	17 40	28 23	12 17	3 36	9 17	17 54	2 37	28 41	4 54	21 38	27 11	19 27	6 20	1 40
26 M	0:17:50	2 34 06	11 ♍50	17 30	0 ♎13	13 32	4 12	9 12	18 01	2 35	28 39	4 55	21 25	27 12	19 48	6 23	1 38
27 T	0:21:46	3 32 56	26 56	17 19	2 02	14 47	4 48	9 07	18 08	2 32	28 38	4 55	21 12	27 13	20 09	6 27	1 35
28 W	0:25:43	4 31 48	12 ♎11	17 09	3 51	16 01	5 24	9 01	18 15	2 30	28 37	4 55	20 59	27 14	20 30	6 31	1 33
29 Th	0:29:39	5 30 43	27 25	17 00	5 38	17 16	6 00	8 56	18 23	2 27	28 36	4 56	20 47	27 15	20 51	6 36	1 31
30 F	0:33:36	6 29 39	12 ♏28	16 54	7 25	18 30	6 36	8 50	18 30	2 25	28 34	4 56	20 34	27 17	21 12	6 41	1 29

Tables are for midnight Greenwich Mean Time

198

October

DATE	SID.TIME	SUN	MOON	N.NODE	MERCURY	VENUS	MARS	JUPITER	SATURN	URANUS	NEPTUNE	PLUTO	CERES	PALLAS	JUNO	VESTA	CHIRON
1 Sa	0:37:32	7♎28 37	27♏10	16♐50℞	9♎11	19♎45	7♌12	8♉44	18♎37	2♈23	28♒33	4♑56	20♓22	27♑19	21♎33	6♒47	1♓26
2 Su	0:41:29	8 27 37	11♐28	16 49 D	10 56	21 00	7 47	8 38℞	18 44	2 20℞	28 32℞	4 57	20 10℞	27 22	21 54	6 53	1 24℞
3 M	0:45:25	9 26 39	25 20	16 49	12 40	22 14	8 23	8 32	18 52	2 18	28 31	4 57	19 59	27 25	22 15	6 59	1 22
4 T	0:49:22	10 25 42	8♑46	16 49℞	14 23	23 29	8 58	8 26	18 59	2 16	28 30	4 58	19 47	27 28	22 36	7 06	1 20
5 W	0:53:18	11 24 47	21 50	16 48	16 06	24 43	9 34	8 20	19 06	2 13	28 29	4 58	19 36	27 31	22 57	7 14	1 18
6 Th	0:57:15	12 23 54	4♒35	16 46	17 48	25 58	10 09	8 13	19 13	2 11	28 28	4 59	19 25	27 35	23 18	7 21	1 16
7 F	1:01:12	13 23 03	17 05	16 41	19 28	27 13	10 44	8 06	19 21	2 08	28 27	5 00	19 14	27 39	23 39	7 29	1 14
8 Sa	1:05:08	14 22 13	29 23	16 34	21 08	28 27	11 19	8 00	19 28	2 06	28 26	5 00	19 04	27 43	24 00	7 38	1 12
9 Su	1:09:05	15 21 25	11♓31	16 24	22 48	29 42	11 54	7 53	19 35	2 04	28 25	5 01	18 54	27 48	24 21	7 47	1 10
10 M	1:13:01	16 20 39	23 33	16 13	24 26	0♏56	12 29	7 46	19 43	2 01	28 24	5 02	18 44	27 53	24 42	7 56	1 08
11 T	1:16:58	17 19 55	5♈29	16 02	26 04	2 11	13 03	7 39	19 50	1 59	28 23	5 02	18 34	27 58	25 03	8 05	1 07
12 W	1:20:54	18 19 13	17 22	15 51	27 41	3 26	13 38	7 31	19 57	1 57	28 22	5 03	18 25	28 04	25 25	8 15	1 05
13 Th	1:24:51	19 18 34	29 13	15 41	29 17	4 40	14 12	7 24	20 05	1 55	28 21	5 04	18 16	28 09	25 46	8 26	1 03
14 F	1:28:47	20 17 56	11♉04	15 33	0♏52	5 55	14 47	7 17	20 12	1 52	28 20	5 05	18 07	28 16	26 07	8 36	1 02
15 Sa	1:32:44	21 17 20	22 56	15 28	2 27	7 10	15 21	7 09	20 19	1 50	28 19	5 06	17 59	28 22	26 28	8 47	1 00
16 Su	1:36:41	22 16 47	4♊52	15 25 D	4 01	8 24	15 55	7 02	20 27	1 48	28 18	5 07	17 51	28 29	26 49	8 59	0 58
17 M	1:40:37	23 16 16	16 55	15 25	5 35	9 39	16 29	6 54	20 34	1 46	28 18	5 07	17 43	28 35	27 10	9 10	0 57
18 T	1:44:34	24 15 47	29 10	15 25	7 07	10 53	17 03	6 46	20 41	1 43	28 17	5 08	17 35	28 43	27 31	9 22	0 56
19 W	1:48:30	25 15 20	11♋39	15 27	8 40	12 08	17 37	6 38	20 49	1 41	28 16	5 09	17 28	28 50	27 52	9 35	0 54
20 Th	1:52:27	26 14 56	24 29	15 27℞	10 11	13 23	18 10	6 30	20 56	1 39	28 15	5 10	17 22	28 58	28 13	9 47	0 53
21 F	1:56:23	27 14 34	7♌43	15 27	11 42	14 37	18 44	6 23	21 03	1 37	28 15	5 11	17 15	29 06	28 34	10 00	0 52
22 Sa	2:00:20	28 14 14	21 24	15 24	13 12	15 52	19 17	6 15	21 10	1 35	28 14	5 13	17 09	29 14	28 55	10 13	0 50
23 Su	2:04:16	29 13 56	5♍33	15 20	14 42	17 06	19 50	6 06	21 18	1 33	28 14	5 14	17 04	29 22	29 16	10 27	0 49
24 M	2:08:13	0♏13 41	20 10	15 14	16 11	18 21	20 23	5 58	21 25	1 31	28 13	5 15	16 58	29 31	29 37	10 41	0 48
25 T	2:12:10	1 13 28	5♎08	15 07	17 39	19 36	20 56	5 50	21 32	1 29	28 12	5 16	16 54	29 40	29 58	10 55	0 47
26 W	2:16:06	2 13 17	20 21	15 01	19 07	20 50	21 29	5 42	21 40	1 27	28 12	5 17	16 49	29 49	0♏19	11 09	0 46
27 Th	2:20:03	3 13 08	5♏38	14 55	20 34	22 05	22 02	5 34	21 47	1 25	28 11	5 18	16 45	29 59	0 40	11 24	0 45
28 F	2:23:59	4 13 01	20 48	14 51	22 01	23 19	22 35	5 26	21 54	1 23	28 11	5 19	16 41	0♒08	1 01	11 39	0 44
29 Sa	2:27:56	5 12 56	5♐42	14 49 D	23 27	24 34	23 07	5 18	22 01	1 21	28 11	5 21	16 38	0 18	1 22	11 55	0 44
30 Su	2:31:52	6 12 53	20 12	14 49	24 52	25 49	23 39	5 10	22 08	1 19	28 10	5 22	16 35	0 28	1 43	12 10	0 43
31 M	2:35:49	7 12 51	4♑15	14 50	26 16	27 03	24 11	5 01	22 16	1 17	28 10	5 23	16 32	0 38	2 04	12 26	0 42

November

DATE	SID.TIME	SUN	MOON	N.NODE	MERCURY	VENUS	MARS	JUPITER	SATURN	URANUS	NEPTUNE	PLUTO	CERES	PALLAS	JUNO	VESTA	CHIRON
1 T	2:39:45	8 ♏ 12 51	17 ♑ 51	14 ♐ 51	27 ♏ 40	28 ♏ 18	24 ♌ 43	4 ♉ 53	22 ♎ 23	1 ♈ 16	28 ♒ 10	5 ♑ 25	16 ♓ 30	0 ♒ 49	2 ♏ 25	12 ♒ 42	0 ♓ 42
2 W	2:43:42	9 12 53	1 ♒ 01	14 53 Rx	29 02	29 32	25 15	4 45 Rx	22 30	1 14 Rx	28 09 Rx	5 26	16 28 Rx	1 00	2 46	12 59	0 41 Rx
3 Th	2:47:39	10 12 56	13 48	14 53	0 ♐ 24	0 ♐ 47	25 47	4 37	22 37	1 12	28 09	5 27	16 26	1 11	3 07	13 15	0 40
4 F	2:51:35	11 13 01	26 16	14 52	1 45	2 02	26 19	4 29	22 44	1 10	28 09	5 29	16 25	1 22	3 28	13 32	0 40
5 Sa	2:55:32	12 13 07	8 ♓ 29	14 49	3 05	3 16	26 50	4 21	22 51	1 09	28 09	5 30	16 25	1 33	3 49	13 49	0 40
6 Su	2:59:28	13 13 15	20 32	14 45	4 23	4 31	27 21	4 13	22 58	1 07	28 08	5 32	16 24 D	1 45	4 10	14 07	0 39
7 M	3:03:25	14 13 24	2 ♈ 28	14 40	5 40	5 45	27 52	4 05	23 05	1 06	28 08	5 33	16 24	1 56	4 30	14 24	0 39
8 T	3:07:21	15 13 35	14 20	14 34	6 56	7 00	28 23	3 57	23 12	1 04	28 08	5 35	16 25	2 08	4 51	14 42	0 39
9 W	3:11:18	16 13 48	26 10	14 29	8 10	8 14	28 54	3 50	23 19	1 03	28 08 D	5 36	16 25	2 20	5 12	15 00	0 39
10 Th	3:15:14	17 14 03	8 ♉ 02	14 24	9 23	9 29	29 24	3 42	23 26	1 01	28 08	5 38	16 25	2 33	5 33	15 18	0 39 D
11 F	3:19:11	18 14 19	19 56	14 21	10 34	10 44	29 55	3 34	23 33	1 00	28 08	5 39	16 26	2 45	5 53	15 37	0 38
12 Sa	3:23:08	19 14 37	1 ♊ 55	14 19	11 42	11 58	0 ♍ 25	3 27	23 40	0 58	28 08	5 41	16 30	2 58	6 14	15 56	0 39
13 Su	3:27:04	20 14 56	14 01	14 18 D	12 48	13 13	0 55	3 19	23 47	0 57	28 08	5 42	16 32	3 11	6 35	16 15	0 39
14 M	3:31:01	21 15 18	26 14	14 19	13 51	14 27	1 25	3 12	23 54	0 56	28 09	5 44	16 34	3 24	6 55	16 34	0 39
15 T	3:34:57	22 15 41	8 ♋ 39	14 20	14 51	15 42	1 54	3 05	24 00	0 55	28 09	5 46	16 37	3 37	7 16	16 53	0 39
16 W	3:38:54	23 16 06	21 17	14 22	15 47	16 56	2 24	2 57	24 07	0 53	28 09	5 47	16 41	3 50	7 36	17 13	0 39
17 Th	3:42:50	24 16 33	4 ♌ 11	14 23	16 40	18 11	2 53	2 50	24 14	0 52	28 09	5 49	16 44	4 04	7 57	17 32	0 40
18 F	3:46:47	25 17 02	17 24	14 24 Rx	17 28	19 25	3 22	2 43	24 20	0 51	28 09	5 51	16 48	4 17	8 18	17 52	0 40
19 Sa	3:50:43	26 17 33	0 ♍ 58	14 24	18 11	20 40	3 51	2 36	24 27	0 50	28 10	5 53	16 53	4 31	8 38	18 12	0 40
20 Su	3:54:40	27 18 05	14 55	14 23	18 48	21 54	4 20	2 30	24 34	0 49	28 10	5 54	16 57	4 45	8 58	18 33	0 41
21 M	3:58:37	28 18 39	29 14	14 22	19 19	23 09	4 48	2 23	24 40	0 48	28 10	5 56	17 02	4 59	9 19	18 53	0 42
22 T	4:02:33	29 19 15	13 ♎ 53	14 20	19 43	24 23	5 16	2 17	24 47	0 47	28 11	5 58	17 08	5 14	9 39	19 14	0 42
23 W	4:06:30	0 ♐ 19 53	28 46	14 18	19 59	25 38	5 44	2 10	24 53	0 46	28 11	6 00	17 13	5 28	10 00	19 35	0 43
24 Th	4:10:26	1 20 32	13 ♏ 47	14 17	20 07 Rx	26 52	6 12	2 04	24 59	0 45	28 12	6 02	17 19	5 43	10 20	19 56	0 44
25 F	4:14:23	2 21 13	28 47	14 16	20 05	28 06	6 40	1 58	25 06	0 44	28 12	6 03	17 26	5 57	10 40	20 17	0 44
26 Sa	4:18:19	3 21 56	13 ♐ 37	14 15 D	19 53	29 21	7 07	1 52	25 12	0 44	28 13	6 05	17 32	6 12	11 00	20 38	0 45
27 Su	4:22:16	4 22 40	28 10	14 16	19 30	0 ♑ 35	7 34	1 47	25 18	0 43	28 13	6 07	17 39	6 27	11 20	21 00	0 46
28 M	4:26:12	5 23 25	12 ♑ 20	14 16	18 57	1 50	8 01	1 41	25 25	0 42	28 14	6 09	17 46	6 42	11 40	21 21	0 47
29 T	4:30:09	6 24 11	26 04	14 17	18 13	3 04	8 28	1 36	25 31	0 42	28 15	6 11	17 54	6 58	12 01	21 43	0 48
30 W	4:34:06	7 24 58	9 ♒ 22	14 18	17 18	4 19	8 54	1 30	25 37	0 41	28 15	6 13	18 02	7 13	12 21	22 05	0 49

Tables are for midnight Greenwich Mean Time

December

DATE	SID.TIME	SUN	MOON	N.NODE	MERCURY	VENUS	MARS	JUPITER	SATURN	URANUS	NEPTUNE	PLUTO	CERES	PALLAS	JUNO	VESTA	CHIRON
1 Th	4:38:02	8 ♐ 25 46	22 ♒ 15	14 ♐ 18	16 ♐ 14	5 ♑ 33	9 ♍ 20	1 ♉ 25	25 ♎ 43	0 ♈ 41	28 ♒ 16	6 ♑ 15	18 ♓ 10	7 ♒ 29	12 ♏ 40	22 ♒ 27	0 ♓ 51
2 F	4:41:59	9 26 34	4 ♓ 47	14 18 Rx	15 02 Rx	6 47	9 46	1 21 Rx	25 49	0 40 Rx	28 17	6 17	18 19	7 44	13 00	22 49	0 52
3 Sa	4:45:55	10 27 24	17 02	14 18	13 43	8 02	10 11	1 16	25 55	0 40	28 17	6 19	18 27	8 00	13 20	23 12	0 53
4 Su	4:49:52	11 28 15	29 05	14 18	12 21	9 16	10 37	1 11	26 01	0 40	28 18	6 21	18 37	8 16	13 40	23 34	0 55
5 M	4:53:48	12 29 06	10 ♈ 59	14 18	10 59	10 30	11 02	1 07	26 06	0 39	28 19	6 23	18 46	8 32	14 00	23 57	0 56
6 T	4:57:45	13 29 59	22 49	14 18 D	9 38	11 45	11 26	1 03	26 12	0 39	28 20	6 25	18 56	8 48	14 19	24 20	0 57
7 W	5:01:41	14 30 52	4 ♉ 39	14 18	8 21	12 59	11 51	0 59	26 18	0 39	28 21	6 27	19 06	9 04	14 39	24 43	0 59
8 Th	5:05:38	15 31 46	16 33	14 18	7 12	14 13	12 15	0 55	26 24	0 39	28 22	6 29	19 16	9 21	14 59	25 06	1 01
9 F	5:09:35	16 32 41	28 33	14 18	6 12	15 28	12 39	0 52	26 29	0 39	28 23	6 31	19 26	9 37	15 18	25 29	1 02
10 Sa	5:13:31	17 33 37	10 ♊ 42	14 18 Rx	5 21	16 42	13 02	0 48	26 35	0 39 D	28 24	6 33	19 37	9 54	15 37	25 52	1 04
11 Su	5:17:28	18 34 34	23 01	14 18	4 42	17 56	13 26	0 45	26 40	0 39	28 25	6 35	19 48	10 10	15 57	26 16	1 06
12 M	5:21:24	19 35 31	5 ♋ 32	14 18	4 14	19 10	13 48	0 42	26 45	0 39	28 26	6 37	19 59	10 27	16 16	26 39	1 07
13 T	5:25:21	20 36 30	18 15	14 17	3 57	20 24	14 11	0 39	26 51	0 39	28 27	6 39	20 11	10 44	16 35	27 03	1 09
14 W	5:29:17	21 37 29	1 ♌ 12	14 16	3 51 D	21 39	14 33	0 37	26 56	0 39	28 28	6 41	20 23	11 01	16 55	27 27	1 11
15 Th	5:33:14	22 38 30	14 22	14 15	3 56	22 53	14 55	0 34	27 01	0 39	28 29	6 43	20 35	11 18	17 14	27 51	1 13
16 F	5:37:10	23 39 31	27 46	14 14	4 09	24 07	15 17	0 32	27 06	0 39	28 30	6 45	20 47	11 35	17 33	28 15	1 15
17 Sa	5:41:07	24 40 34	11 ♍ 24	14 14	4 32	25 21	15 38	0 30	27 11	0 40	28 32	6 47	20 59	11 52	17 52	28 39	1 17
18 Su	5:45:04	25 41 37	25 16	14 13 D	5 02	26 35	15 59	0 28	27 16	0 40	28 33	6 49	21 12	12 10	18 11	29 03	1 19
19 M	5:49:00	26 42 41	9 ♎ 22	14 13	5 39	27 49	16 19	0 27	27 21	0 40	28 34	6 52	21 25	12 27	18 29	29 28	1 22
20 T	5:52:57	27 43 46	23 40	14 14	6 22	29 03	16 39	0 26	27 26	0 41	28 35	6 54	21 38	12 45	18 48	29 52	1 24
21 W	5:56:53	28 44 53	8 ♏ 07	14 15	7 11	0 ♒ 17	16 59	0 24	27 31	0 41	28 37	6 56	21 52	13 02	19 07	0 ♓ 17	1 26
22 Th	6:00:50	29 45 59	22 41	14 17	8 05	1 31	17 18	0 23	27 35	0 42	28 38	6 58	22 05	13 20	19 25	0 41	1 28
23 F	6:04:46	0 ♑ 47 07	7 ♐ 15	14 17 Rx	9 03	2 45	17 37	0 23	27 40	0 43	28 40	7 00	22 19	13 38	19 44	1 06	1 31
24 Sa	6:08:43	1 48 16	21 45	14 17	10 04	3 59	17 56	0 22	27 44	0 43	28 41	7 02	22 33	13 55	20 02	1 31	1 33
25 Su	6:12:40	2 49 24	6 ♑ 04	14 16	11 09	5 13	18 14	0 22 D	27 49	0 44	28 42	7 04	22 48	14 13	20 20	1 56	1 36
26 M	6:16:36	3 50 33	20 07	14 14	12 17	6 27	18 31	0 22	27 53	0 45	28 44	7 07	23 02	14 31	20 39	2 21	1 38
27 T	6:20:33	4 51 43	3 ♒ 50	14 11	13 28	7 41	18 48	0 22	27 57	0 46	28 45	7 09	23 17	14 50	20 57	2 46	1 41
28 W	6:24:29	5 52 52	17 10	14 08	14 41	8 54	19 05	0 22	28 02	0 47	28 47	7 11	23 32	15 08	21 15	3 11	1 43
29 Th	6:28:26	6 54 02	0 ♓ 08	14 05	15 56	10 08	19 21	0 23	28 06	0 48	28 49	7 13	23 47	15 26	21 33	3 37	1 46
30 F	6:32:22	7 55 11	12 44	14 02	17 12	11 22	19 37	0 24	28 10	0 49	28 50	7 15	24 02	15 44	21 51	4 02	1 49
31 Sa	6:36:19	8 56 21	25 03	14 00	18 30	12 36	19 52	0 25	28 14	0 50	28 52	7 17	24 18	16 03	22 08	4 27	1 51

The Planetary Hours

The selection of an auspicious time for starting any activity is an important matter. Its existence tends to take on a nature corresponding to the conditions under which it was begun. Each hour is ruled by a planet, and the nature of any hour corresponds to the nature of the planet ruling it. The nature of the planetary hours is the same as the description of each of the planets. Uranus, Neptune, and Pluto are considered here as higher octaves of Mercury, Venus, and Mars.

Sunrise Hour	Sun	Mon	Tue	Wed	Thu	Fri	Sat
1	☉	☽	♂	☿	♃	♀	♄
2	♀	♄	☉	☽	♂	☿	♃
3	☿	♃	♀	♄	☉	☽	♂
4	☽	♂	☿	♃	♀	♄	☉
5	♄	☉	☽	♂	☿	♃	♀
6	♃	♀	♄	☉	☽	♂	☿
7	♂	☿	♃	♀	♄	☉	☽
8	☉	☽	♂	☿	♃	♀	♄
9	♀	♄	☉	☽	♂	☿	♃
10	☿	♃	♀	♄	☉	☽	♂
11	☽	♂	☿	♃	♀	♄	☉
12	♄	☉	☽	♂	☿	♃	♀

Sunset Hour	Sun	Mon	Tue	Wed	Thu	Fri	Sat
1	♃	♀	♄	☉	☽	♂	☿
2	♂	☿	♃	♀	♄	☉	☽
3	☉	☽	♂	☿	♃	♀	♄
4	♀	♄	☉	☽	♂	☿	♃
5	☿	♃	♀	♄	☉	☽	♂
6	☽	♂	☿	♃	♀	♄	☉
7	♄	☉	☽	♂	☿	♃	♀
8	♃	♀	♄	☉	☽	♂	☿
9	♂	☿	♃	♀	♄	☉	☽
10	☉	☽	♂	☿	♃	♀	♄
11	♀	♄	☉	☽	♂	☿	♃
12	☿	♃	♀	♄	☉	☽	♂

Table of Rising and Setting Signs

Sun Sign	6–8 am	8–10 am	10 am–12 pm	12–2 pm	2–4 pm	4–6 pm
Aries	Taurus	Gemini	Cancer	Leo	Virgo	Libra
Taurus	Gemini	Cancer	Leo	Virgo	Libra	Scorpio
Gemini	Cancer	Leo	Virgo	Libra	Scorpio	Sagittarius
Cancer	Leo	Virgo	Libra	Scorpio	Sagittarius	Capricorn
Leo	Virgo	Libra	Scorpio	Sagittarius	Capricorn	Aquarius
Virgo	Libra	Scorpio	Sagittarius	Capricorn	Aquarius	Pisces
Libra	Scorpio	Sagittarius	Capricorn	Aquarius	Pisces	Aries
Scorpio	Sagittarius	Capricorn	Aquarius	Pisces	Aries	Taurus
Sagittarius	Capricorn	Aquarius	Pisces	Aries	Taurus	Gemini
Capricorn	Aquarius	Pisces	Aries	Taurus	Gemini	Cancer
Aquarius	Pisces	Aries	Taurus	Gemini	Cancer	Leo
Pisces	Aries	Taurus	Gemini	Cancer	Leo	Virgo

Sun Sign	6–8 pm	8–10 pm	10 pm–12 am	12–2 am	2–4 am	4–6 am
Aries	Scorpio	Sagittarius	Capricorn	Aquarius	Pisces	Aries
Taurus	Sagittarius	Capricorn	Aquarius	Pisces	Aries	Taurus
Gemini	Capricorn	Aquarius	Pisces	Aries	Taurus	Gemini
Cancer	Aquarius	Pisces	Aries	Taurus	Gemini	Cancer
Leo	Pisces	Aries	Taurus	Gemini	Cancer	Leo
Virgo	Aries	Taurus	Gemini	Cancer	Leo	Virgo
Libra	Taurus	Gemini	Cancer	Leo	Virgo	Libra
Scorpio	Gemini	Cancer	Leo	Virgo	Libra	Scorpio
Sagittarius	Cancer	Leo	Virgo	Libra	Scorpio	Sagittarius
Capricorn	Leo	Virgo	Libra	Scorpio	Sagittarius	Capricorn
Aquarius	Virgo	Libra	Scorpio	Sagittarius	Capricorn	Aquarius
Pisces	Libra	Scorpio	Sagittarius	Capricorn	Aquarius	Pisces

To find your approximate Ascendant, locate your Sun sign in the left column and determine the approximate time of your birth. Line up your Sun sign with birth time to find Ascendant. Note: This table will give you the approximate Ascendant only. To obtain your exact Ascendant you must consult your natal chart.

Address Book

Name

Address

City, State, Zip

Phone   Phone

E-mail

Name

Address

City, State, Zip

Phone   Phone

E-mail

Name

Address

City, State, Zip

Phone   Phone

E-mail

Name

Address

City, State, Zip

Phone   Phone

E-mail

Name

Address

City, State, Zip

Phone   Phone

E-mail

Name
____

Address
____

City, State, Zip
____

Phone   Phone
____

E-mail
____

Name
____

Address
____

City, State, Zip
____

Phone   Phone
____

E-mail
____

Name
____

Address
____

City, State, Zip
____

Phone   Phone
____

E-mail
____

Name
____

Address
____

City, State, Zip
____

Phone   Phone
____

E-mail
____

Name
____

Address
____

City, State, Zip
____

Phone   Phone
____

E-mail
____

Name
____

Address
____

City, State, Zip
____

Phone   Phone
____

E-mail
____

Name
____

Address
____

City, State, Zip
____

Phone   Phone
____

E-mail
____

Name
____

Address
____

City, State, Zip
____

Phone   Phone
____

E-mail
____

Name
____

Address
____

City, State, Zip
____

Phone   Phone
____

E-mail
____

Name
____

Address
____

City, State, Zip
____

Phone   Phone
____

E-mail
____

~ Notes ~

~ Notes ~